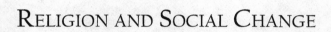

RELIGION AND SOCIAL CHANGE

RELIGION AND SOCIAL CHANGE

THE INFLUENCE OF RELIGION ON AMERICAN CULTURE

GERHARD FALK

Algora Publishing
New York

Library of Congress Cataloging-in-Publication Data —

Names: Falk, Gerhard, 1924- author.
Title: Religion and social change: the influence of religion on American
    culture. / Gerhard Falk.
Description: New York: Algora Publishing, 2018. | Includes bibliographical
    references and index.
Identifiers: LCCN 2018035201 (print) | LCCN 2018036188 (ebook) | ISBN
    9781628943474 (pdf) | ISBN 9781628943450 (soft cover: alk. paper) | ISBN
    9781628943467 (hard cover: alk. paper)
Subjects: LCSH: United States—Religion. | Religions. | Social influence. |
    Religion and culture—United States.
Classification: LCC BL2525 (ebook) | LCC BL2525 .F355 2018 (print) | DDC
    201/.70973—dc23
LC record available at https://lccn.loc.gov/2018035201

Printed in the United States

I am indebted to my son, Clifford Falk, for helping me with the endless vagaries of the computer.

Table of Contents

Chapter 1: The Condition of American Christianity in the Early 21st Century

The American religious landscape is undergoing major changes in the early 21st century. Some of these changes are quite dramatic. For example, between 2007 and 2014, the Christian share of the population of the United States fell from 78.4% to 70.6%. This decrease was mainly due to a decline among mainline Protestants and Catholics. At the same time, the percentage of Americans who are religiously unaffiliated and who are either atheists or agnostics or "nothing in particular" has risen by more than 6%, from 16.1% to 22.8%.

The First Amendment to the United States Constitution does not allow the United States government, including the United States Census, to ask questions of citizens concerning religion. Therefore students of religion have to rely on other sources to provide such information. Of these, the Pew Charitable Trust is most reliable. It was founded by the wife and two sons and two daughters of the Sun Oil Company founder Joseph Newton Pew. Included in that trust is the Pew Research Center, devoted to research on Religion and Public Life, that publishes "The Religious Landscape Study." The following is taken entirely from that study.

According to that research organization, the greatest change among American Catholics has been the increase in Hispanics among them. There are now more Hispanic Catholics than ever before in the United States; they now constitute 41% of total Catholics, up from 35% in 2007. Among evangelicals, 24% are Hispanics, up from 19% in 2007.[1]

The American Christian Population

In 2007, there were 227 million adults in the United States, of whom a little more than 78%, or about 178 million, viewed themselves as Christians. By 2014, the American adult population reached nearly 254 million. Then the share of adults identified as Christians fell to a little less than 71%.

It appears that the greatest drop in absolute numbers among American Christians has occurred among the mainline Protestants, that is the United Methodists, the American Baptist Church, and the Episcopal Church. As of 2014, they were roughly 36 million, or a decline of 5 million over seven years.

Meanwhile, it is possible that the number of evangelicals has risen by 5 million since 2007. Protestants and Catholics appear to be declining both as a percentage of the population and in absolute numbers. The new survey by Pew Research indicates there are about 51 million Catholic adults in the United States today, or about 3 million fewer than in 2007. At the same time, the number of religiously unaffiliated adults has increased by roughly 19 million since 2007, so that there are now approximately 56 million religiously unaffiliated adults in the United States. This group is larger than either Catholics or mainline Protestants.[2]

Christians represent a declining share in America largely due to the lack of generational replacement. For example, 36% of young people who are between the ages of 18 and 24 are religiously unaffiliated, as are those between the ages of 25 and 33. Even people of the older generation are increasingly disavowing association with organized religion. About a third of adults in their late 20s and early 30s say they have no religion, which is up 9% among this cohort since 2007.[3]

Whites are less likely to adhere to religion than is true of blacks or Hispanics. 24% of whites say they have no religion, compared to 20% of Hispanics and 18% of blacks, and all three of these groups have grown as a share of the population. This is particularly true of the percentage of college graduates who are religiously affiliated, which declined from 73% to 64% between 2007 and 2017. The share of Americans associated with religions other than Christianity has grown from 4.0% to 5.8%.

This Landscape Study is most significant because it indicates that the United States has moved radically from being the most Christian nation on earth in the 19th and 20th centuries to become principally secularized, as the unaffiliated sector has grown in size and many people have become less religious over time. This goes so far that one third of religiously unaffiliated adults say they do not believe in God, up 11 points since 2007.[4] Meanwhile,

Europe has experienced an even greater abandonment of Christianity than the U.S.A. in favor of a secular view of the world.

It is therefore necessary to explore the reasons why Europe and America have become more secularized.

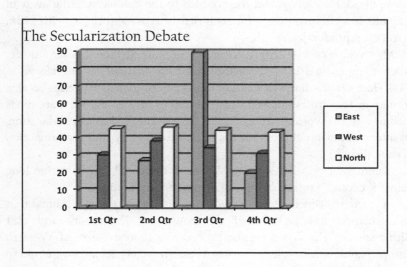

Secularization became the subject of philosophical discussion in France upon the publication of the work of Auguste Comte (1798–1857), who coined the word "sociology" for the new science he had developed. Between 1830 and 1842, Comte issued a series of essays, later translated into English, called "The Course of Positive Philosophy." Here he describes what he calls The Law of Three Stages. According to Comte, human thought progresses from the theological to the metaphysical and the positive. The positive is also called the scientific stage, which depends on observation and classification of phenomena.[5]

Karl Marx (1818–1883) was undoubtedly the most influential philosopher of the 19th century. Marx was a materialist who rejected religion entirely. His most famous phrase concerning religion was included in the introduction of his book *A Contribution to the Critique of Hegel's Philosophy of Right*. In English translation, Marx wrote: "Religion is the sigh of the oppressed creature, the heart of a heartless world, and the soul of soulless conditions. It is the opium of the people."[6]

Emile Durkheim (1858–1917), one of the fathers of sociology, published *The Elementary Forms of Religious Life* in 1915. In this work Durkheim argued that industrialized societies are characterized by functional differentiation.

He meant that in such societies, healthcare, education, social control, politics, and welfare replaced most of the tasks once carried out exclusively in Western Europe by religion in the forms of monasteries, priests, and parish churches. State funded schools and welfare safety nets for the unemployed, the elderly, and the poor led to the gradual wasting away of religious institutions, except for such rituals as are associated with birth, maturity, reproduction and death.[7]

Max Weber (1863–1920) wrote one of the most cited books ever written, when he published *Die Protestantische Ethik und der Geist des Kapitalismus* in 1904. Here Weber shows that asceticism as practiced in monasteries became secular in the Protestant version. Protestants viewed all occupations as "callings" in the worldly, secular realm. This in turn led to more education, an interest in material progress, the rejection of luxury, and the promotion of capitalism.[8]

Comte, Marx, Durkheim, and Weber all discussed secularization long before it became a principal topic of dispute among scholars.

In modern times, Peter Berger, in his *Sacred Canopy*, claims that secularization has undermined the power of Christianity and that Christianity itself caused secularization. The Protestantism of Western Europe played a main role in shaping Western society, as men were told to read the Bible instead of recognizing that the clergy had special privilege. Berger argued that the biblical values are also the sources of secular values. Thus, secular people see each person as contributing to the growth of reason and progress without the intermediary role of priests. Therefore, rationality becomes the highest value in the Western world. Since religion is not rational, life becomes entirely secular in European and American society. Berger also wrote that the success of the secular life is measured by wealth, depending on freedom to work, to make money, and to invest money for further wealth.

Berger holds that in secular societies, people give allegiance to the nation-state, so that secular concerns become more important that religious concerns. This in turn leads to the concept of progress, which is a means of ever increasing efficiency and controlling the world.[9]

It is significant that Berger revised his views later, and rejected the argument that religion would soon disappear altogether.

Rodney Stark, undoubtedly the leading sociologist of religion at this time, showed in a lengthy article published in *Sociology of Religion* in 1999 that the secularization thesis is untenable because the so-called Age of Faith is a myth, and because religious participation was lacking in the past as in the present. He further shows that scientists themselves are often associated with religious institutions, and that religious believers far outnumber skeptics, agnostics, and atheists. Stark calls the secularization doctrine a myth and the product of wishful thinking.[10]

The belief that Christianity, Judaism, Islam, Buddhism, and a host of other religions would simply disappear because of advances in science cannot be sustained. Nevertheless, there is a great deal of evidence that numerous aspects of organized, institutionalized religion receive less support from the American public in the early 21st century than was true in the second half of the 20th century.

It is further evident that the power of the clergy has been greatly curtailed when compared to 17th-century New England or to the power of the papacy in Europe for numerous centuries.

Such changes do not mean that there is a total rejection of religion in favor of a purely rational secular community. This is so not only because science has not answered and cannot answer all questions, but also because we humans want to live in a world which includes such religious dogma as the existence of God, rewards and punishments in the afterlife, celebration of the lifecycle, celebration of the cycle of nature, the enjoyment of religious ceremonies, and numerous other functions available within the institution of religion.

An excellent example of an attack on religion is the book *The End of Faith* by Sam Harris. Harris has degrees in philosophy and neuroscience. His book seeks to show that religion is irrational and divisive. According to Harris, the Bible is "life-destroying gibberish." Harris blames the Jews for their persecution and seeks the destruction of Israel (Harris' mother is Jewish).[11]

If Harris is right, then the admonition to "love your neighbor as yourself" is gibberish, as are lifecycle ceremonies, charitable donations to religious organizations, the admonition to help the poor, efforts to promote peace, communion with other human beings, and the promotion of respect for the rights of individuals and the support of a moral society. All of these functions of religion and more are, according to Harris, nonsense.

Harris' book remained on the New York Times bestseller list for many months. This indicates that, at least among the pseudo-intellectuals who believe they are super minds because they read the *New York Times*, religion is about to expire.

There also some scientists who believe or want to believe that physics explains the universe. For example, Alex Filipenko at the University of California at Berkeley rejects religion on the grounds that it is not trustworthy. He believes that one ought to trust the laws of physics rather than the laws found in religious texts. Are there laws of physics which prohibit murder, adultery, theft, lies and envy?[12]

A reasonable analysis leads to the conclusion that religion is a permanent aspect of human existence and that the institution of religion will not come to an end now or in the future. Nevertheless, secularization in the United States and in Western Europe is also a fact. This means that during the half-century ending in 2017 there has been a considerable decline in church membership, in attendance at religious services and ceremonies, and in the authority attributed to the clergy.

It was during those years that disputes erupted concerning the ordination of women as priests. In 1974, 11 women were ordained as Episcopal priests, causing a great deal of conflict. Meanwhile, Roman Catholic parishioners began to favor the appointment of women deacons in their church, although this was vehemently opposed by the Pope and the all-male clergy. Partly as a consequence of this, Protestants were six times more likely to show confidence in religious authorities than was true of Catholics.[13]

It is also reasonable to assume that the Nixon-Watergate scandals contributed to the lack of confidence in government and all institutions after President Nixon's resignation in 1974.

Between 1987 and 1988, a number of accusations began to surface concerning sexual misconduct on the part of both Protestant and Catholic clergy. Among Protestants, these accusations dealt with the televangelists Jim Bakker and Jimmy Swaggart, both of whom had a large following. It was then that Catholics began to suspect that they too were faced with sexual problems on the part of their clergy. After the year 2000, the Roman Catholic clergy became the target of a major sexual abuse scandal. At that time, *The Boston Globe* published a series of stories outlining abuses committed by at least 70 priests as well as the manner in which the archdiocese of Boston covered up these abuses. This led to the resignation of Cardinal Bernard Law, as his authority was gravely compromised and weakened.[14]

Since the year 2000, a number of institutions other than religion have also been weakened by a loss of confidence in their authority. This is most certainly true of the family, of education, and of government. Therefore, the decline of religious authority during the past 25 years may well be associated with the decline of all authority in the United States during that time. The decline of the authority of the clergy may not necessarily be a function of secularization but will more likely be recognized as related to the overall challenge of authority in all American institutions in the early 21st century.[15]

Beginning in the 1970s, a good number of scholars and others believed that college education necessarily leads to irreligion and that religious beliefs and behavior have decreased significantly from previous historical periods.

According to this view, religion has lost much of its influence and is therefore less important than in earlier years in the lives of people.[16]

Numerous writers since the '70s claimed that science and industrialization all contributed to secularization and the rejection of religion, so that more and more individuals lead their lives without the benefit of a religious interpretation.[17]

Yet, even in the '70s, at least one half of all Americans attended a religious service once a week, so that it is evident that even then America was truly not a secularized nation.

Today, in the 21st century, it has become evident that scientific and religious commitment are mutually exclusive, so that those engaged in scientific work are seldom but not exclusively willing to associate with religion, even as a large number of Americans continue to support religion, particularly because they are barely acquainted with science and its demands.

Indeed, those who are engaged in intellectual work show higher levels of apostasy from religion than the vast majority, although there are scientists such as Einstein Albert who would not subscribe to atheism.

Max Jammer has published a book, *Einstein and Religion*, which contains Einstein's dictum, "Science without religion is lame; religion without science is blind." Evidently Einstein subscribed to the God of Spinoza, which has specific theologically significant implications.[18]

Baruch Spinoza (1632–1672), a Dutch philosopher, was excommunicated by the Jewish community because he wrote *A Treatise on Theology and Politics*, in which he stated that he could not see much difference between the lifestyles of Jews, Christians, and agnostics. He viewed religion as nonsense promoted by those who hold reason in contempt and are seeking to hang on to their authority at any cost. Spinoza considered "Holy Writ" as a human invention and denied the authority of the Pope. Spinoza also denied prophecy and viewed prophecy as nonsense. He also denied the divinity of Jesus, but asserted that God is nature in the sense that the laws of nature are the laws of God, who has no interest in human affairs.[19]

This, then, was Einstein's view of the divide between religion and science when he referred to quantum mechanics and wrote that "God does not play dice with the universe."

There are numerous Americans who reject religion on the grounds that physics, and particularly astronomy, has finally settled the questions as to the origin of the universe. This attitude is supported by promoting the "big bang" theory, making religion obsolete.

Yet the fact is that there are numerous unsolved problems in physics because existing theories cannot explain many observed phenomena.[20]

A list of such problems in physics is easily available to anyone who seeks to become acquainted with them. These problems involve cosmology and general relativity, quantum gravity, high energy physics, astrophysics, nuclear physics, molecular physics, condensed matter physics, and biophysics. Each of these areas provides students of physics with many unanswered questions, so that physics is far from explaining all there is to know about the universe and our position in it.

Therefore physics cannot be used as a reason for rejecting religion. Such a rejection needs to be based on personal preference but not on science. Furthermore, the Hubble telescope has demonstrated that the universe is far larger and more complex than heretofore assumed. Therefore, astronomy cannot now explain the origin of everything, so that this very failure of science to be all-knowing has given religion a boost.

Religion has a number of functions other than belief in the supernatural. Therefore it is entirely possible for someone who believes that there is no God to nevertheless participate in a religious community. Several studies have shown that atheists and agnostics are nevertheless affiliated with religious organizations. The principal reasons for these affiliations are that many atheists and agnostics want their children to have a moral compass by gaining association with a moral community, as Durkheim called religious groups over a century ago. Another reason is that many an atheist is married to a spouse who practices a religion. Social support is another reason for membership in a religious community on the part of atheists and agnostics who want and need friends. Other atheists want their children to make their own choices concerning religion and seek to avoid indoctrinating them with atheism. These findings contradict the assumption that people who are associating with religious communities are therefore believers in the supernatural, including the belief in a god.[21]

In the first place, religion gives some folks emotional support in face of all the pains and problems common to human existence.

Religion also promotes social solidarity, as explained by Durkheim and others. Religion integrates people into a group and into human society, which strengthen unity and solidarity.

Thirdly, religion tends to suppress aggression and other qualities which threaten the ability of humans to live with one another. Religion preserves expected behavior, also known as social norms, and strengthens social control. Therefore religion becomes an agent of socialization allowing the individual to become a member of the society to which he is born.[22]

Religion also promotes welfare. It induces people to feed the poor and the needy and it develops philanthropy (love of man.) Mutual help cooperation is supported by religion as is organized welfare.[23]

Religion also influences the political system. For centuries, the Roman Catholic Popes had enormous power in Europe and were in fact the reigning monarchs on the entire continent. Even in today's democracies, religion plays a role, as demonstrated by the fact that politicians swear on the Bible to perform their duties honestly.[24]

Yet another function of religion is that it can preserve and increase self-confidence. Many religious groups whose beliefs and customs are different from those of the mainstream society find dignity, if not pride, in their distinction; this can be seen in the Orthodox Jewish community, the Amish, and other more modern alternative spiritual groups.

Chapter 2: The Influence of Religion on the Family

All social institutions influence one another. As expected, religion has a profound impact on the family. This becomes evident in several ways. For example, divorce occurs less frequently among the members of religious bodies than among the many nonmembers. Some researchers say they have found that participation in religious activities may be instrumental in supporting a happy marriage and reduce premarital sexual activity. Religious involvement is also credited with reducing the number of religiously mixed marriages.

Despite these positive influences of religion in the family, it is also known that religion can be responsible for breaking up marriages and families.

Of course, religion is not the only institution influencing family life. Education, socioeconomic status, social class, and subcultural conduct such as speaking a foreign language also influence the lives of family members. Whether one lives in a city or in a rural area appears to make a difference in religious affiliation. One of the outcomes of these influences on the family is seen in variations in fertility rates. Thus, Jewish fertility in America is a good deal lower than Christian fertility, and Catholic fertility is generally higher than Protestant fertility.[25]

However, Muslim fertility makes it possible, although not certain, that in fact Muslims will change the world with more births than Christians or any other religion now and in the future. Presently, Christians still outnumber Muslims worldwide, and particularly in the United States. Yet the Pew Research Center predicts that by 2060, Christians and Muslims will achieve parity, with each tradition accounting for about one in three people on earth. Over the next 45 years, it is predicted that the Christian population of the world will be about 31%, and the Muslim population will rise from the present 24% to the same level. Muslims are experiencing a baby boom, while the Christian fertility rate is declining. In the United States, it is expected that the 3,300,000 Muslims who are now 1% of the American population will become 2.1% by 2050; and 63% of Muslims in the United States are immigrants.[26]

Still, despite these predictions, any speculation concerning a long period of time cannot be considered reliable, because human history has always involved unexpected events which defeated earlier assumptions.[27]

Judaism

The foundation and the root of Judaism may be found in the Bible. Nevertheless, modern Judaism is largely based on the Talmud, a Hebrew word meaning instruction or learning. Someone has described the Talmud, which is a vast collection of laws, stories, explanations, and descriptions, as similar to the publication of all the lecture notes ever lectured at Harvard University since its founding in 1636. Although the Talmud is studied only by a few fundamentalists on a full time basis, it is the guide for the Responsa, or answers, annually decided by the various rabbinical assemblies in an ever continuing effort to adjust Judaism to the contemporary world. Moreover, there are Talmud classes in every synagogue, led by the rabbi.

The Talmud includes a number of exhortations concerning marriage and the family. It requires that the husband honors his wife more than himself, and that before the children, father and mother are equals and both are to be respected.[28]

The Talmud also teaches that the children are the fulfillment of married life. The Talmud holds that it is man's elemental duty to the continuity of life to bring children into the world and to raise them properly. The Talmud gives detailed advice how to bring up children. Parents must treat all children equally and avoid any favoritism between them. The Talmud recommends that parents not overindulge children because that leads to depravity.[29]

The Catholic Cathechism (Teaching)

The word catechism means teaching. The Catholic Church includes in its teachings a consideration of the family. The first teaching concerning the family refers to the Ten Commandments revealed by God to Moses on Mount Sinai. In addition, Catholicism teaches that the greatest and first commandment is found in Leviticus 19:18, which commands that "you shall love your neighbor as yourself." As we have already seen, the 10

Commandments and Leviticus 19:18 are found in the Hebrew Bible, which is the foundation of Judaism. It is in no sense surprising that Christians would rely on the Jewish Bible, which is in turn the foundation of Christianity. The Catholic catechism explains that those who would adhere to the 10 Commandments, which demand that we not kill, nor commit adultery, nor steal, nor lie, nor envy, will, by observing these rules, fulfill the commandment to love one's neighbor as oneself.

Protestant Christianity

The majority of American Protestants are evangelical Christians, who believe in affectionate children rearing practices. Evangelical child raising manuals emphasize the involvement of fathers with their children, while child rearing manuals admonish fathers not to become so engrossed in their careers that they neglect their children. There is evidence that evangelicals are more likely than "progressives" to avoid yelling at children, and to be more openly emotional in their encounters with children than is true of "progressives."[30]

Interfaith Marriage

Interfaith marriage has become more frequent than ever since the beginning of the 21st century. Since then, one in five American children have been raised in a mixed religious background. Of these, 6% had one Protestant and one Catholic parent, and 3% had one Christian and one non-Christian parent. In addition, 12% of children had one religiously affiliated parent and one who was not affiliated.[31]

The Pew Religious Landscape study in 2015 shows that 62% of Catholics raised solely by Catholics remain Catholics for life. This is also true of adults raised by two unaffiliated parents. However, only 29% of US adults from a mixed Protestant-Catholic background identify as Catholics, while 38% are Protestants and 26% are unaffiliated. Protestants retain 80% of those raised exclusively within Protestantism and even 56% of those raised by a Protestant parent and one unaffiliated parent identify as Protestants.[32]

It is significant that the overwhelming number of adults raised in mixed faith families say that they found very little discord or disputes between parents of different religious affiliations. Where only one parent was religiously affiliated, 85% of children found few signs of religious disputes between their parents. Among those in which both parents were affiliated or one parent unaffiliated, 73% say they found little dispute between parents regarding religion. This indicates that religion was not given very much attention by those surveyed. It is likely that this attitude of inattention to religion is very common in the United States in the 21st century.[33]

A more recent trend concerning interfaith marriages is an effort on the part of the 40% involved to "be both." In an effort to achieve an interfaith marriage in which both religions are practiced, there is an Interfaith Family School in Chicago which seeks to teach both Catholicism and Judaism to people involved in both religions. This recent development negates the commonly held view that in the event of an interfaith engagement, one person should convert to the religion of the other so as to make the family unified.

Yet, since the 1960s religious intermarriage has become much more frequent than ever before. At the beginning of the 20th century, only one in 10 marriages were interfaith, because at that time the vast majority of Americans did not approve of interfaith marriages. However, since 2008, 80% of adults aged 18 to 23 approve of intermarriage.

This approval has led to the Interfaith Families Project in Washington DC. This is led by the Rev. Julia Jarvis, a Protestant minister, and Rabbi Harold White, the chaplain at Georgetown University. At their meetings the group recites interfaith responsive reading written by members of the Palo Alto, California interfaith community. These responsive readings include such recitations as: "some of us gather as the children of Israel, some of us gather in the name of Jesus of Nazareth." The group also recites: "Hear O Israel the Lord our God is One," which is the core prayer of Jews. They then recite the Lord's Prayer, which is the core prayer of Christians. The group also holds discussions and conducts a Sunday school for children of interfaith marriages. Those who participate in these ceremonies say that they feel a lot more accepted among such interfaith groups than in most common religious organizations.

One of the problems that some interfaith couples face is that they feel comfortable with one another until children are born, and the issue of raising children in one religion or another becomes paramount. This leads such couples to either pick a new religion together, or drop all religions altogether, or have one spouse convert to the religion of the other.

A Pew Research Center study found that since the year 2015, 60% of American Jews had a non-Jewish spouse. Of these, only 20% said they were raising the children Jewish, so that Jewish Americans are assimilating themselves out of existence.

In 2008, a Pew Religious Landscape Survey found that 28% of Americans had left the religion of their childhood and had switched to a new religion or no religion. Of these, 44% switch between Protestant faiths. A good number of young Americans have left religion for a time but returned to it at an older age, particularly after they had children. Then the issue of religion involves not only the married couple but also their families and the grandparents of the children. In addition, the issue of burial in either a Jewish or Christian cemetery must be considered.[34]

Children

In 2015, *The Los Angeles Times* published a study by the Pew Research Center concerning child raising among the offspring of our ever growing secular population. Secular people are those who view themselves as believing in nothing in particular and who therefore are not affiliated with any religious organization. Thus the number of American children raised with in a nonreligious household has grown since the 1950s, when fewer than 4% of Americans had no connection to religion. Among those born after 1970, somewhat more than 11% are now raised in a nonreligious household. Furthermore, a considerable number of people affiliated in one form or another with a religious organization hardly pay attention to religion other than to make occasional financial contributions.

The advocates of religion claim that they are needed as instructors in ethics and morality. Yet, those raised without religion have succeeded in instilling in their children the so-called Golden Rule to the effect that one must treat other people as one would like to be treated. Evidently, it requires no supernatural beliefs to understand the need to be supportive of others. Research has shown that the so-called godless adults exhibit less racism than their religious counterparts, according to a 2010 Duke University study. Secular people also are more likely to support women's equality than is true of religious people.

It is also of interest that atheists are almost absent from the American prison population. Criminologists have known for some time that the unaffiliated and the nonreligious engage in far fewer crimes than the religious. Furthermore, countries with the lowest levels of religious faith, such as Sweden, Denmark, Japan, Belgium, and New Zealand have the lowest violent crime rates in the world.[35]

Divorce

Because the burden of staying together in an interfaith marriage is considerably greater than in an intra-faith marriage, the divorce rate among interfaith marriages is higher than the average. According to the Barna

Research Group as well as Americans for Divorce Reform, about 50% of all American marriages end in divorce.[36]

In 2014 there were 31.0 marriages per 1,000 women in the United States. In that same year, divorces amounted to 17.6 per thousand women. In 2015, divorce constituted 16.9 per one thousand women. In that same year, 41% of first marriages ended in divorce, 50% of second marriages ended in divorce, and 71% of third marriages ended in divorce.

The total number of divorces in one year amount to about 876,000. The average length of marriage in the U.S. is eight years and the average age at divorce is thirty.

The Catholic Church prohibits divorce on the grounds that lifelong marriage is sanctioned by God and that the state cannot dissolve what is divinely endorsed. The Catholic catechism includes this teaching and relies on the Jewish Bible, with particular reference to Genesis 1:27; 2:21; and 2:23.[37]

Although annulment of a marriage is available to Catholics under some circumstances, this should not be labeled "a Catholic divorce," because the reasons for annulment do not contradict the divorce prohibition.

Nevertheless, the number of Catholic marriages which fail is at least 43%, since 28% of married Catholics get a secular divorce and 15% an annulment. Among Americans who have no religion, the divorce rate is 40% and among Protestants it is 39%.[38]

Although Judaism allows divorce, it is not taken lightly. Prior to the 10th century, only men could initiate a divorce, and this was done by simply handing a woman divorce papers. Since then, Judaism requires the consent of both parties for a divorce, and they must appear before a rabbinical court of three rabbis. That court will decide whether the reasons given by the parties are sufficient to allow the issuing of a divorce certificate, called a "get," meaning separation. Despite the possibility of obtaining a divorce, Jewish law and practice assumes that marriage is life long and consists of the joining of a woman and man into one soul in the presence of God.[39]

A number of studies have shown that the children of divorced couples are disproportionately likely to also get a divorce. Teenage marriage is strongly correlated with divorce, as are the family histories of both spouses.[40]

The Judeo-Christian tradition views cohabitation as adultery. Since the 1970s, there has been a steady increase of women and men living together without the benefit of marriage. There are some who argue that cohabitation allows the partners to discover whether they can engage in a secure marriage and avoid an eventual divorce. The evidence shows, however, that those who live together before marriage have twice as great a risk of divorce than those who married without a precedent cohabitation.[41]

The reasons why cohabitation fails to improve the chances of attaining a permanent marriage are, first, that cohabiters place very great emphasis on individualism and are less likely than some others to be committed to marriage as a permanent condition. Second, cohabiters are more accepting of divorce as an appropriate means to end a relationship.

Another characteristic of premarital cohabiters is that they are frequently the children of divorced parents, and therefore are more likely to accept becoming divorced themselves.[42]

Homosexual Marriage

These views of marriage exclude homosexual marriage between two men or two women. According to the Jewish Bible, homosexual marriage is an "abomination" (Leviticus 18:23 and Leviticus 20:13) and is punishable by death. While this prohibition does not mention women, later rabbinical sources condemned lesbianism also, although it was not considered a capital offense.

One reason for the rejection of homosexuality in Judaism is its failure to promote reproduction. So-called liberal Jews find this prohibition obnoxious and seek to discover Jewish sources for the acceptance of homosexuals in the Jewish community. This effort is related to the Conservative, Reconstructionist, and Reform movements in Judaism, which endorse equality for so-called gays and lesbians. Since the Bible is the very foundation of Judaism, it has become necessary for these denominations to get around the unambiguous biblical prohibition against homosexuality. This has been accomplished by arguing that homosexuals have no choice as to their sexual orientation and therefore its expression cannot be forbidden. In fact, in the Reform denomination, rabbis are encouraged to officiate at same-sex marriages. In the Jewish Reconstructionist movement, same-sex marriage is in fact considered a religious value. Likewise, the Conservative denomination in Judaism has voted to accept two responses to homosexuality. Thus, rabbis may choose not to allow homosexual marriages or to do so if they so see fit. Conservatives also ordain openly gay rabbis.[43]

It should surprise no one that Christian views concerning homosexuality rely largely on the Jewish Bible, that is, what Christians call the Old Testament. This is most in evidence within the Roman Catholic tradition. The Catechism of the Catholic Church clearly states that homosexual acts cannot be approved under any circumstances,[44] but Roman Catholicism considers homosexuality an innate condition and not a choice, and therefore it cannot be considered a sin. However, homosexual activity is seen as a moral disorder and homosexual acts are viewed as contrary to the natural law. The principal argument here is that homosexuality eliminates the gift of life from the sexual act. The Roman Catholic Church views homosexuality as a disorder. The word "disorder" in this connection refers to the proper ordering of nature, or, in this case, its rejection. The Roman Catholic Church opposes same-sex marriage, particularly because such marriages are not unfavorable for children and because of the view that legalizing such marriages damages society.[45]

It is common for American media to label all non-Catholic Christians "Protestants," although Anglicans and the Eastern Orthodox Church were not followers of Martin Luther and hence were never Protestants. There are numerous Protestant and other Christian denominations, so here we will consider only how a few of them view homosexuality.

The Anglican Church, including Episcopalians, has been sharply divided over the issue of homosexuality. The Church of England accepts same-sex marriages and allows homosexuals to be priests, but expects them to be abstinent.[46]

Because the Anglican Church has no communion-wide legislative body, a good deal of confusion arises within the denomination. As a result, the Lambeth conference of 1998 called homosexuality incompatible with Scripture and in 2003 the Episcopal Church approved Gene Robinson as Bishop of New Hampshire, although he is openly gay and non-celibate. Likewise, Mary Glasspool became the first open lesbian bishop to be consecrated in the Anglican Communion in the diocese of Los Angeles.[47]

The conflict concerning homosexuality within the Anglican Communion has led to the formation of the Fellowship of Confessing Anglicans, which represents more than two thirds of Anglicans around the world and rejects homosexuality. The Anglican Church in North America was formed in 2009. It consists of people who left the Episcopal Church in opposition to its approval of homosexual relations and homosexual bishops and a gay clergy.

The Baptists are the largest Protestant denomination in the United States. Of the several Baptist subgroups, the Southern Baptist Convention is the largest. Adherents believe that the Bible says practicing homosexuality is a sin. They hold that marriage and sexual intimacy may occur only between one man and one woman, for life, and that homosexuality is not valid. Similar views are held by the American Baptist Churches, USA, and The National Baptist Convention.

The Methodist Church is another mainline Protestant denomination. Their Book of Discipline includes all human beings as eligible to attend its worship services, but paragraph 304.3 of The Book of Discipline Statements holds that: "The practice of homosexuality is incompatible with Christian teaching. Therefore self-avowed practicing homosexuals are not to be certified as candidates, ordained as ministers, or appointed to serve in the United Methodist Church." In addition, paragraph 341.6 states that: "Ceremonies that celebrate homosexual unions shall not be conducted by our ministry and shall not be conducted in our churches."

In 2015, the Presbyterian Church USA approved the marriage of lesbians, homosexuals or gays, bisexuals, and transgender couples. The Presbyterian Book of Order was changed, and now it describes marriage as being between two people.

Reformed Churches (which follow Calvinist tradition more than Lutheran) adhere to the biblical view of homosexuality and cite Leviticus 20:13: "If a man lies with a man as one lies with a woman, both of them have done what is detestable." Therefore, a homosexual member of a Reformed Church will be placed under censure or excommunicated. According to the Reformed Churches, homosexuality is a sin.

Religious groups which view homosexuality as a sin are convinced that homosexuals have chosen that lifestyle and therefore will not support same-sex unions. They hold that people choose to be homosexuals. Research has shown that compared to women, men are significantly more likely to agree that homosexuality is a choice. As education increases, the belief that homosexuals choose their orientation decreases. Older individuals are less likely to support same-sex marriages than younger people, and people who view the Bible as being literally true are a good deal more likely to believe homosexuality is the result of choice. This is also true of people who attend worship services frequently. Evangelical Protestants are less likely to support same-sex marriages than mainline Protestants, and Reform Jews are far more likely to allow same-sex marriage that Orthodox Jews who reject such unions altogether. In sum it is evident that those who view the cause of homosexuality as controlled by the individuals themselves are less likely to agree to the right of homosexuals to obtain legal marriages.[48]

Americans who view themselves as "liberals" support the view that homosexuality is a biological trait for which the individual is not responsible. Although there is no evidence that homosexuality is inborn in any manner, it is an attribute of liberal ideology to undermine personal responsibility and to interpret almost all behavior as predetermined. So-called liberals therefore excuse criminal conduct on the grounds of poverty, although no one has ever found any connection between criminality and income, except that wealthy persons are more likely to commit white-collar crimes and poor people are more likely to commit physically violent crimes. However, crime is common in all income strata. The truth is that attributing inborn characteristics as cause of social behavior has been rejected and discarded since the days of Cesare Lombroso. Recent consultation with a well-known psychotherapist reveals that 21st century psychological thinking rejects the idea that homosexuality has biological roots. Instead psychotherapists view homosexuality as behavior which may well be related to parental conflict and other negative childhood experiences.[49]

Chapter 3: The Influence of Religion on Education

Protestantism

The early American settlers who had come to Massachusetts from England in the 17th century were probably the only Europeans who at that time taught women and girls to read. Some historians believe that women and girls were taught to read but not to write. This opinion is based on the view that colonial women used a mark instead of using a signature. They interpret this to mean that the women were not illiterate, although few of them could write.[50]

Both boys and girls were sent to private schools run by women in their own homes. Such schools were called dame schools, and accepted children as young as age three. The children learned the Lord's Prayer and were also taught to read from a so-called hornbook, which consisted of one page mounted on a board and covered by a thin sheet of animal horn.[51]

The Book of Psalms from the Bible was extensively published in the 17th and 18th centuries; reading the Psalms was not only an exercise in learning to read but also served to teach children to the Holy Scriptures, as the Puritans called them.[52]

Spelling books had appeared in England already in 1596, including one titled *The English Schoolmaster*, which was reprinted 54 times until 1737. Thereafter, a speller was published in the Bay colony in 1644.[53]

Among the Puritans, education was principally in the hands of parents and was viewed as a religious duty. The Boston minister Increase Mather was taught to read by his mother, whom he described as a "very holy praying woman." Undoubtedly, his mother, like all women in the Massachusetts Bay Colony, was deprived of emotional liberties and was forced to make religion her only purpose in life.[54]

The Puritans required that children become apprentices as early as the age of 10. These apprentices were sent to school so they could learn to read and write. The masters of these apprentices were legally obliged to teach them reading and writing, with particular emphasis on religious texts.[55] They were taught to read the Bible and to write adequately. Girls as well were taught to read "their catechisms," a Greek word meaning instruction.

The Puritans also believed that ancient languages were very important, so that they taught children to be proficient in Latin. Hebrew was also taught, as Hebrew was the language of the Old Testament, while the New Testament was written in Greek. In fact, some of the lectures at New College, later to become Harvard College, were given in Hebrew. The Puritan community believed it important to read the Scriptures twice a day in order to know God better.[56]

It was Puritan doctrine that the chief end of man was not worldly success but the glory of God. Therefore education was considered a necessary subservient means of religion, without which the colonies would soon sink into atheism.[57]

Nevertheless, the majority of women in Puritan colonies were unable to write despite the admission of girls to primary schools. In fact, in Massachusetts only about 40% of women were entirely literate throughout the 18th century.[58]

Boys, however, were far better educated than girls, although the emphasis in addition to religion was on being able to write both Latin and read Greek. Introduction to Latin and Greek began at a very young age for boys, beginning at age 6 in the so-called grammar schools.[59]

Although the Puritan clergy was anxious to maintain schools, this was not true of the general public. Many people felt that the schools cost too much. Furthermore, schoolmasters were paid very little, so that many were established farmers who kept school for only a few months a year.

This system continued among the Puritans until the American Revolution of 1775. After the revolution, a number of changes developed within the Puritan tradition of education. Thus, towards the end of the 18th century, the traditional grammar schools were largely abandoned in New England, so that by the end of the revolution, the grammar school tradition among the Puritans had entirely collapsed.

While classical learning was most important before the revolution, it was challenged after the revolution by practical and useful learning, including science, mathematics, geography, writing, and modern languages. These newer schools were called writing schools. As their enrollment increased, the grammar school enrollment decreased.[60]

Because Puritans were anxious to perpetuate the Christian religion in North America, they made immediate plans for the establishment of a college to train ministers of the gospel. Therefore, New College (shortly renamed for its earliest supporter, the Rev. John Harvard) began the training of ministers in 1636. The original motto of Harvard College was: "Truth for Christ and the church," which in the secular 20th century was abbreviated to the Latin word *veritas*.61

Today, during the second decade of the 21st century, one half of Americans adhere to Protestant Christianity. Catholics are represented by about 51 million Americans, although the Church includes all ever born into a Catholic family, leading to a count of 68 million.

During the first two centuries of English life in the United States, almost all citizens were Protestants. Therefore Protestant values such as self-reliance, individual freedom, hard work and the development of capitalism are entrenched in the American psyche. However, by the early 21st century, social cohesion is challenged by the millions of legal and illegal non-European immigrants, some of whom do not share that ethic. Protestant views of education as a means of self-improvement were the driving force behind the development of free public schools, the establishment of colleges and universities, and the enhancement of intellectual pursuits in this country.

In 1904, the German sociologist Max Weber published his influential book *Die Protestantische Ethik und der Geist des Kaptalismus*. In this book, Weber discussed how the Calvinist version of Protestantism led numerous followers of various Protestant denominations to engage in work in the secular world, leading to the development of capitalism. The principal argument of Weber's thesis is that activities dedicated to economic gain had moral significance for the Puritans, who rejected luxuries in favor of hard work and self-denial, resulting in increased profits, which through investments in business and enterprises, created capitalism. Protestant belief in predestined salvation led to looking for signs that one had been chosen by God. One of these signs was the self-confidence that came from economic success subsequent to promoting hard work and austerity. Calvinism forbade using hard earned money to buy luxuries. Even donating money to the poor was frowned on, as it was seen as furthering beggary. Calvinist Protestants believe that God impelled us to a secular vocation, called in German *Beruf*, literally meaning a calling.[62]

Protestants have traditionally held both economic and political power in the U.S.A.

Protestantism is Bible-centered, as is Judaism. Although there are numerous Protestant denominations in the United States, there are also thousands of unaffiliated Protestant churches, including mega-churches with 2,000 or more members.[63]

Judaism

There is a good deal of evidence that education was already highly esteemed in the Jewish community in Biblical days. This is exhibited by the verses "and you shall teach them diligently to your children,"[64] and "Hear, my son, the instruction of your father and forsake not the teaching of your mother."[65] Since then, the Jewish community created the Talmud, which may be compared to a vast, over 30-volume book consisting of all the lectures delivered by Harvard professors since its founding.

It is no exaggeration to say that education and religion were so intertwined in biblical days, as well as among the Eastern European Jews, that a distinction between religion and education really did not exist. There were in Eastern Europe and there are today in America young Jewish men who devote all their time to the study of Talmud while being supported by their wives or in-laws.[66]

The study of Talmud among the 9 million Jews at one time living in Europe served to bring about a sense of belonging among people living in widely scattered territories, although only a minority of Jews ever became Talmud scholars. It is important to recognize in this connection that advanced study of the Talmud or the Bible was open only to boys and not to girls, who were usually only trained in domestic occupations. In fact, among European Jews, only men executed the family rituals and synagogue ceremonies. Women were excluded and were not even required to attend synagogue services, where they were segregated in balconies or behind partitions, a practice still in use among Orthodox Jewish believers in America today. Talmudic study made Eastern European rabbis the role models of the Jewish community and gave them great prestige, so that these rabbis were in a position to enjoy a great deal of authority within their own community and throughout the Jewish world. In that world, those who could not or would not study the Talmud were obliged to financially support those who spent full time doing so. There are today a few Americans who choose full time Talmud study and who are supported by their wives' families in that endeavor.[67]

The vast majority of American Jews abandoned religious studies within a generation of arriving in America. Those who came between 1890 and 1924 were influenced by socialism, trade unionism, and class consciousness, as they began American life on the bottom of the economic ladder. In the next generation, Jews born in America entered the sciences, business administration, law, and medicine, as religion was gradually reduced to a secondary interest, if it was practiced at all.

While study of the Talmud was always confined to a few exceptionally competent youngsters, Jewish boys in Eastern Europe were confined to schools beginning at age three to five. Such an elementary school was called a cheder, the Hebrew word for room. A teacher in a cheder puts the child on his lap and teaches him the Hebrew alphabet by having the child repeat the names of the letters after the teacher pronounces them. The letters are read to the child forward and backward. Subsequently the teacher reads a few verses from the Hebrew Bible as the child is asked to repeat. The child is given honey cake after achieving a certain level of Hebrew education.[68] This religious education was compulsory in Jewish communities, although unknown among Christians. In addition to such elementary and secondary schools, there were in Eastern Europe Jewish schools of higher education, best considered seminaries, which trained advanced scholars.

In Eastern Europe, and to a far lesser extent in the United States, young Jewish men attended so-called "yeshivas," which are institutes of higher education in the sacred books, particularly the Talmud. Many of these schools of higher education were founded in the 19th century in Russia. Some even survived the Soviet drive to replace all religions with a rational, secular worldview. Graduates of these Talmud schools had few skills that could be used in the secular world to earn a livelihood and or support the family. This was because the curriculum consisted almost entirely of the study of rabbinic literature and the study of Responsa for Jewish observance. Jewish law was also taught in the yeshivas, although it could not be applied in the United States. In addition, ethics, mysticism, and philosophy were taught in these yeshiva schools, which were undoubtedly of academic interest but had little application in the civil world.[69]

These advanced scholars were the predecessors of reform in Jewish education. Within a generation of arriving in America, many of these Jews replaced religious study with secular learning. Religious education was conducted and still is in the hands of a Jewish Board of Education.

There can be little doubt that secular learning among American Jews is related to the traditional scheme of learning among their European ancestors. The American Jewish community was also able to take advantage of public education from the grades through graduate universities because of the high urbanization of American Jews.

As of 2018, Jews have the highest number of years of schooling among the American population. The average years of formal schooling for Jews is 13.4 years, followed by Christians, whose average formal schooling is 9.3 years, while the unaffiliated have an average amount of schooling of 8.8 years. It is it is also noteworthy that Jewish women also averaged 13.4 years of schooling, equal to men. This is remarkable because in Eastern Europe, Jewish girls and women were hardly educated. Among the youngest Jewish adults, women spend one more year in school than men. At present (2018) 39% of Christian Americans and 75% of Jewish Americans hold a college degree.[70]

Judaism has hardly benefited from this level of educational achievement, because it is principally of a secular nature. It is therefore important to the Jewish community in America that Jewish studies became an academic discipline in American secular and Christian universities in the 1960s. These college departments of Jewish studies developed so far that some of them now even offer graduate degrees, leading to master's degrees and doctorates. A good number of Christian colleges seek to understand the relationship of Christianity to Judaism, while others have become Christian Zionists, reflecting support for Israel.

Some of the American colleges offering undergraduate courses and even advanced studies in Judaica include the State University of New York at Albany, as well as the State University of New York at Buffalo and the State University of New York at Binghamton. It is significant that these are universities that are tax supported and public. Hebrew language courses are included in these programs, as are courses in Jewish history, philosophy, and literature. Even the University of California at Berkeley offers a joint doctoral program in Jewish studies in collaboration with the Graduate Theological Union, despite a large anti-Jewish contingent among faculty and students. Harvard University teaches Judaica at the Center for Jewish Studies. Other universities which offer Jewish studies are Indiana University, the University of Michigan, and New York University, which has acquired money from the Skirball Foundation, leading to an extensive number of studies in Jewish history, modern Jewish history, biblical studies, Middle Eastern studies, and Talmudic literature.

The number of colleges and universities including Jewish studies and their curriculum is considerably larger than what can be represented here. It is also important that numerous Catholic and other Christian universities and colleges include Judaism in the form of courses or lecture series. A good example is Holy Cross.

It is therefore most evident that Judaism has had a major influence on the education of Americans, a condition also visible among Roman Catholics.

Catholicism

In the 21st century, Catholics have become so much part of the American life and experience that it is hard to understand the hatred with which Irish Catholic immigrants were met in this country in the 19th century. This anti-Catholic anger on the part of the Protestant majority was largely derived from the Protestant orientation of the public school system.

Catholics, who began to arrive in the United States in large numbers during the second half of the 19th century, objected to having all schoolchildren recite Protestant prayers at the beginning of the school year and reading from the King James Version of the Bible. That Bible was named after James VI of Scotland, who had become James I of England in 1603 after the death of Elizabeth I, who had no children. James had appointed a number of scholars to translate the Bible from the Hebrew into English. Catholics instead read the Douay version of the Bible, produced by English Catholic exiles then residing in France. That Bible was a translation from the Latin Bible dating from the fourth century, when it had been translated from the Hebrew into Vulgate Latin.

Distinctions of this kind may seem spurious today but they meant a great deal in 1844, when riots broke out between Protestants and Catholics in Philadelphia. Protestants believed in a Papist conspiracy, reputedly designed to force all Americans to become Catholics. Such views were supported by the American Protestant Association in Philadelphia. Protestants marched through Catholic neighborhoods and celebrated the battle of the Boyne in 1690 when Protestants defeated the Catholics in Ireland. This provoked Catholic anger, even as some documents used in schools portrayed the Pope as the Antichrist. Anger concerning these religious disputes led to fighting in the streets, including the use of firearms and the wounding and death of a number of the contestants. Catholic churches were burned down, as were the homes of a number of Catholic citizens. The riots lasted from May through July 7, 1844. It took the National Guard to restore order.[71]

In view of these anti-Catholic sentiments throughout the nation, the Catholic Church organized its own educational system from elementary school through universities. These schools have declined substantially to the 21st century, as secularism has become more prominent in the United States.

The National Catholic Educational Association issues an annual report concerning enrollment in American Catholic schools. This indicates that from the mid-1960s, when there were 5,200,000 students enrolled in 13,000 elementary and secondary Catholic schools, there were in 2017 only one half as many students enrolled in only 7000 student schools with 2.1 million students. This sharp decline in Catholic education may be attributed to a number of factors. These include a considerable drop in the number of nuns in teaching orders, which were at one time the most important resource supporting Catholic education in the United States. Furthermore, immigration of Catholics from Europe has dropped dramatically in the late 20th century. In addition, many American Catholics can no longer afford the cost of private education. Even more important than all of these factors is that many Catholics are no longer interested in their school system and prefer to send their children to public schools. This failure to support the Catholic school system is associated with a major change in attitudes among Catholics concerning their Church. Many Catholics are no longer interested in participating in Catholic practice and have become indifferent to Catholic teachings. This is true despite the fact that Catholics have been very successful, as have Jews, in achieving academic results far better than is true of public schools.[72]

Both the Jewish and Catholic school graduates are more devoted to their religion than are public school graduates. Members of both religions are more likely to support their community financially and are more socially responsible in giving to the poor and the needy.

Catholic schools seek to resist the secularization of American culture, which affects all religions to the effect that secularists expect members of religious denominations to be intolerant and unenlightened. In the 21st century, secularists largely view members of religious communities to be un-American. It is noteworthy that both Jewish and Catholic schools originated at the end of the 19th century and the early 20th century, when both religions depended largely on small donations from poor immigrants. The grandchildren of these immigrants, who are financially far better off than their grandparents, are less likely to support Jewish or Catholic schools.[73]

Religion-controlled schools have produced better educated graduates than public schools, yet these schools have declined as religion has been marginalized. A number of Catholics and Jews have recognized that long-term financial security is necessary if religion-based schools are to continue. Such schools need to support the culture, identity, and religion of their supporters. It is evidently not sufficient from the religious point of view that such schools be operated by Christians or Jews. Instead, such schools, in order to survive, need teachers knowledgeable about the traditions of their constituencies. There are those who demand that religion controlled schools inject religious tradition into all academic subjects and that teachers and others in support of religious schools conduct their private lives in a manner reflecting their religious traditions. There was a time when American Catholic schools were taught almost exclusively by nuns and some priests. This has changed a great deal in the 21st century, as the number of nuns and priests has decreased substantially.

In 1965 there were about 180,000 religious sisters in the United States. By 2015 there were only 50,000 nuns in the United States, a drop of 72% in one half-century. The decline in the number of priests from 59,000 to 38,000 between 1965 and 2015 constitutes a 35% drop. Because of these reduced numbers, Catholic schools are now principally staffed by lay teachers and by teachers who are not Catholics.[74]

American Catholicism has not only been forced to face increased secularization, but has also been plagued by scandals surrounding sexual abuse of children in Catholic schools.

Chapter 4: The Influence of Religion on the Government

Symbolic Religious Interaction

The First Amendment to the Constitution of the United States begins with the words: "Congress shall make no law respecting an establishment of religion or prohibiting the free exercise thereof." Over the years, the United States Supreme Court has vigorously supported this amendment. Nevertheless, religion is present in American life and continues to be intertwined with government affairs. Thus, religious symbols are common in American life. Politicians elected to public office generally swear on the Bible to uphold the Constitution of the United States. It is also usual to end such an oath with the words "so help me God." Recent Presidents and other officeholders will often end their speeches by invoking the deity. This was not always the case. George Washington did refer to "that Almighty Being" during his inaugural address in 1789, however, the second president John Adams and his successors Thomas Jefferson and James Madison never once mentioned God in their inaugurals. It was 30 years later before God was invoked at such an occasion by James Monroe, who sought to placate the then current and powerful Great Awakening. Then in 1881 Chester Arthur added the phrase "so help me God" to the presidential oath. In the 21st century presidents have gone out of their way to mention God. President Obama mentioned God five times in his inaugural address and President Trump did the same. In the 20th century, only Theodore Roosevelt did not mention God in his inaugural address, and in the 19th century it was Rutherford Hayes who failed to invoke God.

The military is sworn in using similar phrases relating to the belief in God. American coins and paper money include the phrase "In God We Trust." In addition, the American dollar bill includes the phrase "Annuit Coeptis" or "He favors our undertaking." The introduction of these phrases into American money began in the 1830s, when Congress prescribed these mottoes. In 1864 Congress passed an act which changed the one cent coin as well as the then in existence Gold Double Eagle coin and the silver dollar coin, as well as several other denominations, to include the phrase "In God We Trust."[75]

In some smaller communities around the country, a sculpture displaying the 10 Commandments is located in front of courthouses or even inside. This practice has been challenged in the courts as violating the First Amendment to the Constitution. Religious symbols are also commonly exhibited in the form of artistic expressions and are often worn as amulets, believed to protect the wearer or the drivers of cars who have hung such symbols from their rearview mirrors.

It is usual for presidents of the United States to host an annual prayer breakfast in the company of clergy of various religions and denominations. Speeches by officials as well as candidates frequently include verbiage concerning the speakers believe in God. In sum, it appears that despite widespread secularization, religion is very much on the minds of Americans, so that the Supreme Court of the United States has been called upon repeatedly to settle disputes derived from interpretations of the First Amendment to the Constitution which prohibits making any law concerning religion but also requires that nothing be done to hinder the free exercise of religion. This seemingly contradictory requirement has led to innumerable disputes which have occupied the Supreme Court of the United States over many years.

Some Supreme Court Decisions

Thus, education is not the only area in which the Supreme Court has ruled concerning the actions of government with reference to religion. On July 30, 2014 the Supreme Court ruled that requiring family owned corporations to pay for insurance coverage for contraception under the Affordable Care Act violates a federal law protecting religious freedom. The ruling, which applies to two companies owned by Christian families, opened the door to challenges from other corporations concerning laws which violate religious liberty The decision concerned a chain of craft stores called Hobby Lobby and Conestoga Wood Specialties, the latter of which makes wood cabinets. The owners of both corporations say they run their business on Christian principles. Both owners objected to providing contraception coverage for their employees. The court held that companies' religious rights need not be infringed because the government could pay for the coverage or employ a method used for certain nonprofit religious organizations which require insurance companies to provide the coverage.

Because The Affordable Care Act requires employers to provide female workers with insurance coverage for several methods of contraception, the companies objected on the grounds that inter-uterine devices and "morning after" pills constitute abortion. The court decided the case under The Religious Freedom Restoration Act of 1993.[76]

That law sought to prevent government from burdening religious exercise without compelling justification. The law requires that a person whose religious exercise has been burdened in violation of this law claim it as a defense in a judicial proceeding and obtain appropriate relief against a government body. The law further asserts that the term "government" includes a branch, department, agency, instrumentality, or official of the United States, a state, or a subdivision of a state.[77]

It was The Religious Freedom Restoration Act which led to the United States Supreme Court rule in May 2016 that *The Little Sisters of the Poor* would not have to pay millions in IRS finds for refusing to violate their religious beliefs. The ruling vacated lower court rulings against the Little Sisters and accepted the government's admission that it could meet its goals of providing contraception to women without involving The Little Sisters or using their plan.[78] There are numerous additional Supreme Court decisions concerning religion. Only a sample can be mentioned here. Among these is *Texas Monthly, Inc. v. Bullock.* This case involved the legality of a Texas statute that exempted religious publications from paying state sales tax. The court held that the lack of a sales tax on religious literature was in effect a subsidy to the religious writers. If the religious writers did not pay a tax, then secular writers would have to. The court ruled that the state violates the establishment clause and the free press clause by excluding religious publications from praying taxes. The statue was therefore stricken down and the state of Texas ordered to collect the sales tax from the religious publications.

Town of Greece v. Galloway was decided by the Supreme Court in 2014. This case dealt with the custom on the part of the town board to begin all meetings with a prayer delivered by Christian clergy. Galloway argued that this practice violated the establishment clause in the First Amendment. However, the court ruled that no one was coerced to participate in the prayer which was for the board only and that therefore it was constitutional and could continue.[79]

In 1985 the Supreme Court in *Thornton v. Caldor* decided that an employee could not impose his opinion on others as to what constitutes a Sabbath prohibition to work. This case involved a Christian believer who sought to be excused from work on Sundays, a day on which his employer opened its stores. Thornton contended that his First Amendment rights were infringed because he was not allowed to skip work on Sundays.[80]

Kiryas Joel is a small town in New York State founded by a sect of fundamentalist Jews whose religious observances include a total abstinence from work on the Sabbath (or Saturday), the wearing of black clothes, the observance of biblical and Talmudic minutiae, and in the exclusion of persons not belonging to the community. Kiryas Joel citizens established a Board of Education and a school district pertaining only to schools consonant with their religious beliefs. In 1994 the Supreme Court held such a school board in violation of the First Amendment to the Constitution.[81]

In 1986 the Supreme Court denied a Jewish Air Force officer the right to wear a skullcap when in uniform on the grounds that the free exercise clause applies less strictly to the military than to ordinary citizens. The case involved Simcha Goldman, a rabbi and clinical psychologist, who had entered the United States Air Force as a commissioned officer. Goldman wore a skullcap, also known as a yarmulke, at all times. He was ordered by a superior officer to remove this headgear on the grounds that it violated Air Force regulations which stated that headgear were not to be worn while indoors except by armed security police. The Supreme Court agreed with this regulation and refused the appeal of Goldman. Thereafter, Congress included in The National Defense Authorization Act of 1988 a provision to the effect that a member of the Armed Forces may wear an item of religious apparel while wearing the uniform of the armed forces. This bill became law, having been signed by President Ronald Reagan.[82]

Good News Club v. Milford Central School is a case in which the Supreme Court held that exclusion of The Good News Club from the Milford school district was unconstitutional despite the promotion of Christianity by the club. The court held in 2001 that instruction related to morals and values from a religious perspective does not taint that instruction so as to alter the viewpoint such instruction takes. The court held that the Good News Club "seeks nothing more than to be treated neutrally and to speak about the same topics as are other groups."[83]

In 2012 the Supreme Court ruled that a teacher dismissed by a church related school could not be reinstated by The Equal Employment Opportunity Commission, who claimed that the teacher was fired for complaining to the commission. The court relied on the First Amendment to the Constitution to the effect that government cannot determine who may teach or may not teach in a church or church related school.[84]

In 2017 the Supreme Court ruled that churches have the same right to seek state money for new playground surfaces and other non-religious needs as secular groups. The court said that a Lutheran Church was wrongly denied a state grant for its preschool playground. By a vote of 7–2, the court sided with Trinity Lutheran Church of Columbia, Missouri, which had sought a state grant to put a soft surface on its preschool playground.[85]

The Rights of Prisoners

Prisoners in state and federal institutions are the responsibility of government. Therefore, the dispute concerning the dietary laws of Jews and Muslims alike have occupied prison administrators not only because kosher food costs more than double what is normally provided to prisoners but also because prison guards and administrators are generally ill disposed towards Jews.

The Hebrew word "kosher" means "fit" or proper, and refers to the biblical ordinances concerning what believing Jews may eat or must avoid. Two examples would be the prohibition found in the Bible of eating any animal which does not chew the cud and has a "cloven" hoof. The pig is one example of such an animal, and there are others. Kosher food is also defined as food that is either a meal containing meat or one that involves milk. Meat and milk may not be eaten at the same time. This prohibition is based on the biblical verse: "You shall not cook a kid in its mother's milk," which is found in the Bible five times. Kosher is far more complicated than this and involves many additional regulations. Although the cost of kosher food is greater than the cost of normal prison food, the difference in expenditure among all the prisons of the United States is not very big, because the Jewish population among American prisoners is only 1.7%, which reflects the proportion of Jews in the general American population. However, once a few Jewish prisoners were accommodated and received kosher food, a number of other prisoners who were not Jewish demanded the same privilege. This was usually denied by prison administrators because of the significant extra cost. The failure of prison administrators to furnish prisoners kosher food became a legal issue in 1987, and two decisions by the Supreme Court supported a constitutional right of prisoners to exercise their religion freely. These two cases are *Turner v. Safely* and *O'Lone v. Estate of Shabbaz*. Consequently, 35 states and the federal prison system offer kosher food to prisoners, even if they are not Jewish.[86] Some think it tastes better, others believe it is safer than standard issue prison fare, and, finally, kosher food comes in packages, which makes it possible to trade or sell it among inmates. Kosher meals consist of factory sealed cut vegetables, frozen or nonperishable dishes like lasagna, and whole fruits and vegetables. These kosher meals are provided under the Religious Land Use and Institutionalized Persons Act of 2000, which guarantees religious freedom, including religious services and kosher or, in the case of Muslims, halal food.

Jews make up just one sixth or about 4,000 of the 24,000 inmates who eat kosher food in American prisons. Since kosher food costs more than double what regular fare costs, it costs the taxpayers millions of dollars to feed all those who want to eat kosher.

Because most American prisons are run on the state level, the rules about religious practice and diet differ among the 50 states. The federal corrections system houses some 4127 individuals receiving Certified Religious Diet out of the total of 217,000 inmates. The diet costs $2.33 per meal, as opposed to $.90 for regular prisoners. In California, Jewish chaplains oversee kosher programs, which are fed to about 800 people out of about 140,000 inmates. California spends about $2 million per year on kosher food.

In Indiana, the excessive cost of the religious dietary program led the Department of Corrections to serve kosher eating inmates a vegan diet instead.[87]

The U.S. Department of Justice sued the state of Florida in 2012 for failing to accommodate prisoners' requests for kosher food. The state had announced that it would provide kosher food at the Union Correctional Institution but then delayed the program. The Florida Department of Corrections measured the sincerity of the religious conviction of those seeking to eat kosher food. The Florida Department of Corrections then argued that there was no way of adequately determining which prisoners were requesting kosher food for religious reasons and who wanted kosher food because it is considered more palatable than regular prison food. The state then attempted to escape the demand for kosher food because each meal cost at least four dollars per day while ordinary cost of each meal is only $1.52 per day. However the 11th circuit court said that these concerns were unfounded, leading to a court decision entitled *United States v. Secretary, Florida Department of Corrections* compelling Florida to provide kosher food to those who seek it.[88]

The Rights of the Military

Not only prisons, but also the military, involve the US government with the institution of religion. Because the armed services include chaplains of various faiths who have officers' ranks, the uniforms of these chaplain officers include insignia designating the religion they represent. The vast majority of chaplains are Christians and therefore exhibit a cross on their uniform lapel. Jewish chaplains, who serve a much smaller contingent in the military, exhibit a small replica of the tablets of the 10 Commandments. These symbols indicate that religion is indeed present in the military, and is supported in part by the US government.[89]

American military installations and cemeteries include chapels of various faiths. In Honolulu, Hawaii, there is a military cemetery located on a hill. A chapel is attached to the cemetery. It displays three insignias concerning the Christian, the Jewish, and the Buddhist faiths, because members of all three traditions are buried there. There are of course numerous additional military chapels maintained at the military academies such as West Point, New York, The Naval Academy, and the United States Air Force Academy. In addition there are several memorial chapels maintained by the military. Included are the Pearl Harbor Memorial Chapel and the Submarine Memorial Chapel, also located at Pearl Harbor.[90]

These and other symbols of religious significance remain part of American existence and life without respect to the First Amendment of the Constitution.

In 2014 The Population Reference Bureau reported on religious preferences of military personnel. That report found that 35% identified as Protestants and 22% as Catholic/Orthodox. Other Christians constituted 11%, so that Christians were 68% of all military personnel at that time. Because the Jewish population of the United States is only 1.8% of all Americans, the Jewish contingent in that study was one half of 1%, which is also true of Muslims, Buddhists, and Hindus. Atheists and those without any religion were 21% of those surveyed. This leaves 11% not accounted for in this study.[91]

Those who have no religion and are serving in the armed services of the United States are frequent victims of religious discrimination and coercive proselytizing (Greek=newcomer or stranger). Since the armed services rely almost entirely on coercion and force, there are those who use the military environment as a means of forcing their religion on those who don't want it.

The problem of coercive proselytizing in the military became a public issue in 2005 when it was discovered that cadets at the Air Force Academy in Colorado Springs sought to force evangelical Christian beliefs on cadets practicing a different religion or who chose not to practice any religion.[92]

The New York Times has published several articles dealing with the problem of military proselytizing. This included the unethical appearance of seven high ranking uniformed military officials in a video promoting a so-called Christian Embassy. This video sought to evangelize among military leaders, politicians, and diplomats in Washington. This kind of coercion was publicly revealed by an Air Force Academy chaplain, Capt. MeLinda Morton. Morton spoke to an Air Force task force which came to the Air Force Academy to investigate accusations that officers, staff members, and senior cadets inappropriately used their positions to push their evangelical Christian beliefs on Air Force cadets. Captain Morton, who is a Lutheran, told the *New York Times* that her willingness to expose the bigotry at the Air Force Academy means "the end of my Air Force career."[93]

An organization called Officers' Christian Fellowship operates in almost all American military bases worldwide and counts 15,000 US military personnel around the world as members. This organization is dedicated to co-opting military resources and personnel to market Christianity until the entire military society becomes a community of believers for the Christian God. These activities directly contradict and undermine the First Amendment to the Constitution of the United States which these military personnel have sworn to uphold. Despite this oath, assignments and promotions based on religious membership rather than merit have occurred in the armed forces, as has endorsement of religion.[94] There are reports that military leaders worked in conjunction with the military chaplaincy, forcing soldiers to attend religious services and encouraging them to abide by religious laws proselytizing their fellow soldiers.[95]

Christian chaplains have usually avoided intervention when non-Christians are ostracized, harassed, denied promotions, or threatened with physical violence for religious reasons. Chaplains have been willing to participate in remarks about belief systems, including the statement that "there are no atheists in foxholes" and allowing commanding officers to deny privileges to monotheists that are routinely available to religious members of the Armed Forces, such as meeting passes.[96]

An effort to countermand the Influence of fundamentalists on armed services personnel has been made by the Military Religious Freedom *Foundation*. This foundation was created by Michael L Weinstein, a lawyer and honor graduate of the United States Air Force Academy. A registered Republican, Weinstein spent three years working for the Reagan Administration as legal counsel. Weinstein is the founder of the Military Religious Freedom Foundation. Weinstein wrote a book entitled: *With God on Our Side*.97 This book exposes the systematic problem of religious intolerance throughout the United States Armed Forces. In 2012 Weinstein released another book: *No Snowflake in an Avalanche — The Military Religious*

Freedom Foundation. This book deals with The Military Religious Freedom Foundation in its effort to defeat the fundamentalism and religious coercion in the military. The Military Religious Freedom Foundation has been described "as the leading voice protecting church state separation in the military." The foundation has also been nominated for the Nobel Peace Prize.

In response to the complaints by the Military Religious Freedom Foundation, the Air Force Academy sponsored an Ask an Atheist Day. This activity promptly led to complaints by Christians and others including Michael Weinstein, who now objected to the atheist event. It is evident from these experiences that the Founding Fathers were most wise when they determined in the First Amendment to the Constitution that: "Congress shall make no law respecting an establishment of religion..."

The Pew Forum on Religion and Public Life is concerned with the role of religion in the military. This concern relates to the funding of chaplains by the Continental Congress as early as the beginnings of the nation. At that time, and for over a century later, almost all Americans were Protestants, and diversity of religion was hardly known in this country. In the 21st century this is quite different, as the nation has become much more religiously diverse. Consequently numerous disputes have arisen concerning men and women in the various branches of the military. These controversies arise because freedom of religion is one of the cornerstones of American democracy. Yet, all service academies used to require everyone to attend religious services until the District of Columbia Circuit found this requirement unconstitutional in *Anderson v. Laird* (1972). Despite this, the Naval Academy still holds pre-meal prayers, and attendance at these meals is required. A similar requirement at mealtime prayer at the Virginia Military Institute was held unconstitutional by The Fourth District Circuit Court of Appeals in *Mellon v. Bunting.* Controversy also has erupted over whether those in authority over military personnel are too aggressive in promoting religious activities.

The presence of chaplains in the military also presents a constitutional paradox, as the First Amendment's establishment clause restricts the government's authority to fund and endorse religion. Yet the military funds chaplains who promote religious messages. The government pays the chaplains' salaries and pays for the place of worship and even for the worship materials themselves. This contradiction is explained by showing that in the case of the military, it is government action that prevents military personnel from having access to religious resources. The interpretation here is that in these situations, the government is not sponsoring religion nor promoting it but is merely responding to a religious need. In *Abington School District v. Schempp*, the Supreme Court held that Bible reading in public schools is unconstitutional and that those who wish to read the Bible can do so outside of school hours at any time. Several justices remarked in that connection that the military is an exception to this rule because military personnel have no choice but to remain within the jurisdiction of the military and therefore have no other opportunity to read the Bible and practice their religion.

Recently, controversy has arisen over prayers at public events such as the ceremony for a change of command, at which the military asks a chaplain to give an invocation. The controversy centers on the issue of whether a chaplain may provide faith specific prayers such as, "in Jesus' name," which offends non-Christians.

Because the armed services treat enlisted personnel like slaves of the officer corps, officers continue to believe that they have a right to impose their religious beliefs on those who are subordinate to them. It is therefore highly likely that more litigation concerning religion in the military will increase in the next few years, as enlisted personnel are no longer willing to relinquish their constitutional rights to the military hierarchy. Nevertheless, the Supreme Court has a history of refusing to hear complaints by military personnel. Furthermore, there is a possibility that pressure from Congress will alter some of the behavior of officers towards enlisted women and men with reference to religion.

The Religion of Congress

On November 8, 2016, the voters of the United States demonstrated that they are the true government of this country. It was on that day that Donald Trump was elected president, having achieved a majority of the electoral vote. Trump's victory did not become visible until the early hours of November 9, to the consternation of the media and the Democratic Party it became evident that the voters are the decision-makers in this country.

The government of the United States includes 435 members of the House of Representatives and 100 senators, together making 535 Members of Congress. Of these, 91% described themselves as Christians. Among the 293 Republicans elected to the 115th Congress, all but two identify as Christians. These two are Lee Zelden of New York and David Kustoff of Tennessee, who are Jewish. Of the 242 Democrats in Congress, 28 are Jewish, three are Buddhists, three are Hindus, two are Muslims, and one is a Unitarian Universalist. It is noteworthy that the total percentage of Protestants in Congress has dropped from 75% in 1961 to 56% in 2017. Meanwhile the share of Catholics in Congress has increased from 19% to 31%. Fully two thirds of Republicans in the new Congress are Protestants, while 27% are

Catholics. Among Democrats, 42% are Protestants and 37% are Catholics. Catholics, Protestants, and Jews have greater representation in Congress than in the general population. For example, Jews, with only 1.8% of the United States adult population, account for 6% of Congress. The unaffiliated are the most underrepresented. They account for 23% of the general public but only two tenths of 1% of Congress. In fact, only one member of Congress describes herself as religiously unaffiliated. It is evident that a good number of Americans who are not interested in religion for themselves nevertheless require that their representatives are religiously involved. It is probable that a good number of politicians will claim religious affiliation because it is politically sound policy even if they themselves are not interested in religion.

Both the House and the Senate have Protestant majorities, but there are differences among Protestant denominational families. Baptists are more numerous in the House than in the Senate, while Presbyterians and Lutherans account for greater shares of the Senate than the House.

It is significant that although Jews are only 1.8% of the American population, they are 5.1% of representatives and 8% of senators.

A Gallup poll concerning presidential candidates resulted in the willingness of 94% of the electorate to vote for a Catholic president and 91% of the electorate willing to vote for a Jewish president. While the United States has already had a Catholic president, no Jew has so far been elected to that office. However, the Jewish senator Sanders of Vermont has demonstrated that Americans from all over the United States are willing to vote for a Jew for president when in May of 2015 he announced his candidacy. As a result his campaign drew large crowds and innumerable votes all over the United States even as it was widely advertised that he is of the Jewish faith.

All of this demonstrates that the American people have set aside many previous prejudices concerning officeholders and are evidently willing to be governed by people of all faiths and both sexes respecting only their political views and without regard to religion, ethnicity or gender.

Chapter 5: The Influence of Religion on the Economy

Although religion is generally associated with belief in supernatural beings such as God and angels, as well as supernatural events, religion is also a part of *the* economy. This is visible when we consider that, according to the Bureau of Labor Statistics, there are 46,510 clergy in this country, who earn an average salary of $47,736.[98] Their $2,220,000,000 salaries are part of the US gross national product.

In addition to the clergy, religious institutions employ 91,630 workers earning an average of $42,950. The total employment associated with religion is 238,140.[99]

Religion is therefore an American industry and its impact on the economy is far greater than the wages paid to those who are clergy.

Judaism

Religious conduct consists largely of ceremonial behavior, which relies on a variety of objects associated with beliefs concerning them. A number of such examples are available. Jews of all denominations venerate the Torah, which is both a physical object and a concept. The word Torah is translated as "instruction or guidance." It may refer to a handwritten scroll containing only the five books of Moses in Hebrew.

The word "Hebrew" is an Anglicized form of the Hebrew word "Ivri," meaning to ford or cross a river. The word comes from Genesis and is associated with the patriarch Abraham, who was told by God to leave his father's house in Chaldea and to cross the river Euphrates to go to a land "which I (God) will show you".[100]

The Torah scroll may cost as much as $24,000 to $55,000, depending on who copied it, its age, quality of the parchment, and a number of other considerations such as the beauty of the script.[101]

There are a number of other objects used in the course of observing Jewish ritual. Included are a seven-branched candelabrum, prayer shawls, skullcaps and, among conservative and Orthodox Jews, leather straps wound about the arm and the head during weekday morning prayers. These leather straps are attached to two small boxes, one worn on the head and the other on the upper left arm during prayer. These "Tefillin" contain verses from the Torah. Tefillin cost between $300 and $1000.

Another aspect of Jewish practice which contributes to the religion industry is kosher meat. Because the biblical prohibition concerning eating only animals which have a cloven hoof and chew cud, observant Jews not only avoid eating non-kosher meat, but also adhere to a number of additional requirements defining what is kosher and what is not. This includes totally separate dishes for the consumption of meat or milk products. In addition, totally separate dishes are used during the Passover celebration lasting a week. Some fish are considered kosher while shellfish are prohibited. In sum, there is a kosher food industry in the United States whose adherents pay almost double to eat according to Jewish law.

One of the most costly events in Jewish life is the bar mitzvah (son of the commandments) or bat mitzvah (daughter of the commandments) celebration. It is traditional to celebrate the 13th birthday of a boy or the 12th birthday of a girl by means of the religious service in which the celebrant reads publicly from the Hebrew Scriptures and gives a prepared speech concerning a biblical theme. Friends and relatives will reward the child with some gifts as he or she becomes an adult responsible for observing Jewish law. The cost of all this is minimal if it is celebrated within the confines of a synagogue. A bar or bat mitzvah can occur on any Monday, Thursday, or Saturday because during those three days of the week traditional Jews recite portions of the Torah.

In the United States, however, the bar or bat mitzvah celebrations have frequently become outlandish parties unrelated to the Jewish religion and designed to exhibit the financial success of parents. Children who are the center of attention in these opulent parties learn nothing about Judaism. Those who have the money and are willing to spend it on these adolescent celebrations spend upward of $10,000 and in some instances as much as a hundred thousand dollars proclaiming their financial success. In 2008, the *New York Post* reported on a bat mitzvah celebration costing $1 million. The entertainment was furnished by a so-called rock star. In South Florida there are a number of bar mitzvah planners who satisfy parental narcissism. Few Jewish children who have been the victims of this kind of ostentation know anything about Judaism or care to know it.

Christianity

Because Christianity is directly derived from Judaism, it is no surprise that a number of sacred objects and traditions in use by the Catholic Church are essentially Jewish. On numerous occasions, the Popes have emphasized this relationship. On October 27, 1965, the members of Vatican II adopted The Conciliar Declaration *"Nostra Aetate"* to the effect that numerous ties exist between Christianity and Judaism and acknowledge the Jewish origin of the Christian faith.

This declaration was followed by various Protestant denominations giving this attitude considerable emphasis, to this day.[102]

Physical objects used by Catholic priests in celebration of their religion include the vestments worn by priests during the service called a Mass. The word "Mass" is derived from the Latin "missa" meaning "dismissed." These vestments (Latin for "clothes") are derived from Exodus 28:2, describing the manner in which the Jewish high priest and his descendants were to be dressed.

In the 21st century, there are 39,600 Catholic priests officiating in the United States.[103] All of these priests need liturgical vestments. These are quite expensive. For example, a prayer shawl, also called a stola, costs around $432. A Cape costs $456 and various other garments used by priests during the mass ceremony are equally costly. Since priests do not receive a salary, these expenses must be borne by the Catholic followers and believers who make up the Church.

Christmas

The most expensive and widespread religious contribution to the American economy is the annual Christmas celebration, which has principally become a secular event. It has been estimated that Americans spend more than $1 trillion during the Christmas season. This phenomenon is best understood by recognizing that Christmas in America has largely become a secular holiday with minor religious overtones. This means that Christmas has become a concept related to the acquisition of material objects. The evidence for this is rather overwhelming. For example, a number of business establishments have recently resorted to advertising "Christmas in July." Since the holy day of Christmas is celebrated on 25 December, this advertisement means that the acquisition of a car or other material object at a reduced price constitutes the substance and meaning of Christmas. Other examples of a similar nature are the annual appearances of department store Santa Clauses. These bearded actors ask little children and sometimes older "children" about the meaning of Christmas. The almost inevitable answer is: "I want a baseball glove," or "I hope I get a model train." Hardly anyone mentions the birth of the Christian God.[104]

This means that the average American spends $805 during the holidays for gifts. In addition, that average person will travel 275 miles, adding to the expenses of the holiday. It has been estimated that 26.3 million real trees are purchased during the Christmas season. 6 million of these trees come from Oregon. An additional 16 million artificial trees will also be in use. United Parcel Service ships approximately 630 million packages during any Christmas season. Because toys and games are most popular, gift, toy, and game stores increase their staffs by 38% beginning in November.

Christmas card purchases total 1.6 billion annually, or about five cards for every US resident. More women than men buy clothing or clothing accessories, home improvement items, and jewelry and beauty items. Men buy more tools, sporting goods, electronics, and computers.

In each Christmas season some 50 million chocolate Santas are made and sold. Some 46% of holiday shopping is done online.

Public opinion polls have concluded that 94% of Americans celebrate Christmas.[105] Since Jews, Muslims, Hindus, Buddhists, and other religions are minimally represented in the United States, it is reasonable to conclude that everyone other than members of these minuscule religious communities are Christians. Yet if we look at church attendance, we find that according to Life Way Research, only six out of 10 Americans attend church even at Christmas. On any ordinary Sunday this attendance is far lower, so that it is not unreasonable to suggest that Christmas is largely a secular holiday and that its religious meaning has been marginalized in the United States.[106]

Sacred Spaces

Throughout the existence of mankind, sacred buildings have been constructed in honor of the deities. The ancient Jews maintained a Temple in Jerusalem which contained a space known as the holiest of the holy. In ancient Athens and in ancient Rome a pantheon was maintained in honor of all the gods. In India, the Buddhists constructed the Borobudur in commemoration of the Buddha, and the Egyptian pyramids testified to the Pharaoh Gods of that ancient world.

Americans likewise have constructed large and ostentatious buildings, sometimes called cathedrals, in honor of the Christian God. "Catedra" is a Greek word for seat. The large churches called cathedrals are the seats of the bishop in a Christian diocese.

Although the largest cathedral in the United States is St. John the Divine in New York City, there is no better example of an American cathedral than the Episcopal Cathedral in Washington DC. It took 85 years, from September 29, 1907 to September 29, 1992, to construct this building at a cost of $65 million. The Cathedral stands on 30 acres bought in 1898 for $245,000, a sum equal to $6,767,000 in 2016. More land was purchased after 1898, so that the Cathedral finally occupied 57 acres at a cost of $291,427 in 1898 dollars.

There are 288 stone angels atop the two west towers. The largest stained-glass window is 26 feet in diameter, and the central tower rises 676 feet above sea level, making it the highest point in the District of Columbia. There are 53 bells in the towers, of which the largest measures 8'8" in diameter and weighs 24,000 pounds. There are 112 gargoyles attached to the walls, and 215 stained-glass windows in the Cathedral. One window, the West Rose window, holds 10,500 pieces of glass, and there are 10,650 pipes in the great organ.

This partial description of the National Cathedral demonstrates that religion is indeed an industry in the United States. Evidently the 320,000 churches in this country provide a considerable amount of employment not only to clergy and others directly on the payroll of a church, but also to all those who construct them, who make the stained-glass windows, who provide music and food to those who celebrate there, and many others whose income is augmented or totally dependent on the religion industry in this country.[107]

Lackawanna, NY, is the site of a Roman Catholic church called Our Lady of Victory Basilica. The Basilica contains numerous statues and employed sculptors and other artists. It was built at a cost of $3.5 million in 1921, a sum equal to $48 million in 2017, when the average church of 17,000 sq. ft. costs approximately $1.78 million. Church construction employs a good number of construction workers as well as architects, sculptors, and artists and others.

St. Patrick's Cathedral in New York City has recently been restored at a cost of $175 million, with 200 people working to restore the pictures, statues and other aspects of this vast building that was first begun in 1888. Restoration is very expensive and requires numerous specialized skills on the parts of those entrusted to carry out this sacred task.

The largest Jewish house of worship is Temple Emanuel, located in New York City. It is the largest synagogue in the world. The congregation was founded by 33 German Jews in April 1845. The congregation had numerous locations around New York until it finally settled at 65th St. and Fifth Avenue in 1929.[108] The hall of the synagogue seats 2500 persons.

The interior sanctuary of this temple includes the ark at the front and is depicted like an open Torah scroll. The doors of the ark are the tablets of the law and hanging in front of the ark is the eternal light, symbolic of God's eternal presence.

Sacred Scriptures

The religions of literate peoples usually rest on books and other literature held sacred by the followers of the religion. These scriptures are generally attributed to a deity or God. This is true of the Hebrew Bible as well as the Greek New Testament.

The word Bible is derived from the name of a city in ancient Phoenicia located in an area now called Lebanon. The Greeks called the city Byblos. The Greeks imported palm leaves from Byblos, dried them, and then wrote books on the wide dried leaves. The finished books were rolled up in scrolls and preserved in libraries. Therefore all books were called Byblos, a word which in English became Bible.

It has been estimated that Americans bought some 25 million Bibles in any one year, spending approximately one half billion dollars. There are numerous translations of the Hebrew Bible into English and all the languages of mankind. Since the New Testament was written in Ancient Greek, which differs from modern Greek, that book too has been translated numerous times. No two translations are identical, of course. English renditions of Hebrew cannot correspond to renditions of ancient Greek. It is likely that new translations will continue to be produced as the English language changes over the years.[109]

Religion Inspires Art

Sculpture and painting are of considerable importance to religious communities. While portrait painting has been largely supplanted by photography, this cannot be the case with sculpture.

In Dallas, Texas, there is a Museum of Biblical Art. Until recently there was also a biblical museum in New York City, which has closed.

These museums are American versions of the numerous European art museums which have served for centuries to make the unseen visible. Religion deals largely with beliefs in supernatural beings and miraculous events which cannot be experienced by the believers. Therefore paintings and sculptures have been employed to demonstrate the existence of deities, angels, devils, and other products of the human imagination. Painters have painted such miracles as the parting of the Red Sea, the arrival of sacred persons in heaven, miracles of every kind, and numerous scenes described in sacred Scriptures but not otherwise visible.

The museum in Dallas includes a National Center of Jewish Art, Via Dolorosa sculptures, The Resurrection Mural, The Hand of God, Adam by Michelangelo Buonarotti, and an exhibit called Holocaust Heroes. The museum includes works by Marc Chagall, Andy Warhol, Joan Sargent, and numerous others.

In November 2017 the Museum of the Bible opened in Washington, DC, with assets of $474 million. This 430,000-square-foot museum has 40-foot-tall bronze doors. There are three permanent sections and spaces for temporary exhibits. On the first floor are located two libraries. On the second floor is an exhibit entitled The Impact of the Bible, on the third floor is the Nazareth Village, on the fourth floor is the history of the Bible, on the fifth floor there is a 500-seat theater and a 100-seat lecture hall as well as classrooms and offices, and on the sixth floor are biblical gardens and a restaurant.[110]

Sculpture

Roman Catholics as well as Episcopalians and some other non-Catholic Christians rely extensively on the use of monuments and pictures to promote their message. Many families place sculptures on their property or inside their home depicting saints and other religious personalities. Some churches, and particularly large cathedrals, contain numerous statues of saints and others, which some believers regard as the actual supernatural being. Monuments and statues are "big business" in this country, although those who produce them are seldom paid more than $50,000.

Religious Paintings

Favorite Christian religious paintings include pictures of the Last Supper, the Virgin with Angels, The Good Samaritan by van Gogh, and the Annunciation by Botticelli. Prints of pictures by famous artists are quite popular, particularly among Catholics. The Ascension, the Immaculate Conception, The Resurrection, and a large selection of other pictures are labeled spiritual paintings and produce a good-sized income for those who deal in them.

Religious Music

Religious music is another part of the religion industry. Included in this industry are gospel singers. Some of these gospel singers have become famous and exceptionally successful popular singers, such as Elvis Presley, Tom Jones, and Alice Cooper. While these artists earn large sums, the average pay for singers, according to the Bureau of Labor Statistics is $25 an hour. The Bureau reports that in 2016 there were 173,000 such jobs in the United States and that the job outlook for this occupation was poor.[111]

There is also religious music which accompanies church and synagogue services. For centuries, major composers like Beethoven, Mozart, and Verdi have composed music pertaining to the Catholic mass. This music has been composed almost entirely by Europeans. However, in 1971, as mentioned previously, the widow of President John Kennedy, Jacqueline Kennedy, commissioned the composer Leonard Bernstein to compose a Mass in memory of the murdered president. Bernstein's composition is called a Mass. This is a bit unusual as it depicts the conflict between believers and nonbelievers. In the end, however, a hymn called "Sing God a Secret Song" restores the faith of everyone, as they sing in Latin "Pax te cum," peace be with you. There are those who find it peculiar that Mrs. Kennedy asked a Jewish composer to produce a Mass. That, however, overlooks the fact that the mass was written in honor of a Jew.[112]

Jewish synagogue practice includes the employment of a Cantor who leads the congregation in the prayers and songs included in the daily and Sabbath services. These cantors generally have an exceptionally good voice and have graduated from a cantorial school associated with a theological seminary. According to the American Conference of Cantors, the average salary of cantors is between $80,000 and $90,000 a year. There are also a few cantors with operatic voices who are singing for an exceptionally large and wealthy congregation who may earn as much as $150,000 a year.

The Jewish Theological Seminary includes a College of Jewish Music and a cantorial school. The College of Jewish Music awards a master's degree in sacred music and the cantorial school awards a Cantor's diploma. Candidates for a cantorial diploma must attend both programs, requiring five years of full-time study.[113]

TV Evangelists

The income of Christian clergy is indeed meager. There are, however some Christian preachers known as television evangelists (good messengers) whose income is astounding. Yet, those who use a private jet may well have no choice if they are preaching in Hong Kong with a stopover in Hawaii. Such a schedule also requires a private pilot and money to operate the plane. Such famous evangelists as Billy Graham or Joel Osteen would be mobbed at airports needing additional security if they traveled commercially. Evidently they have no choice but to use private planes. Then there are high salaries which are resented by the media. Yet some of these preachers have more than 700 employees worldwide and therefore must be paid commensurately in order to find executives able to manage such huge enterprises. Like many universities such as Harvard, Yale, and Princeton, some of these evangelists have large endowments to finance their messages in the future. Therefore it is entirely possible for high paid evangelists to be honest, despite what appears to be excessive financial gain.[114]

Nevertheless there are those among the evangelists who have a garage full of luxury cars, expensive paintings, and millions hidden away in personal bank accounts.

In the 1980s and 1990s, a number of the most prominent television evangelists were discovered to have been dishonest and in fact "white-collar criminals." These preachers had resorted to numerous schemes by which to enrich themselves at the expense of their followers.[115]

Among those whose income for preaching Christianity has attracted the attention of the federal government is Benny Hinn, who has a television show that airs in over 100 countries. Hinn claims to have seen people get healed from crippling diseases by religious incantations and even claims to have seen a dead man resurrected. Hinn's ministry collects more than $200 million a year, and his salary is a half a million a year. He stays in hotel rooms that cost thousands of dollars a night and drives luxury vehicles.

Joyce Meyer is a TV evangelist who owns five homes, including homes with eight car garages, a large fountain, a gazebo, a putting green, a pool, and a pool house with a $10,000 bathroom.

Kenneth Copeland is an evangelist who lives in an immense mansion. He has acquired a $20 million Cessna Citation private jet, and he owns an airport to accommodate his airplanes.

The evangelist Eddie Long owns a million-dollar home on a 20 acre lot, drives a Bentley, and collects a host of other benefits as well.

Randy and Paula White earned millions by means of their ministry. They own million-dollar houses across the country. Investigated by the United States Senate, they refused to submit their financial records to the Senate committee.

Joel Osteen is perhaps the most successful of the TV evangelists in the United States. It has been estimated that Osteen reaches 7 million people worldwide by means of his televised sermons. Osteen is the pastor of the Lakewood Church of Houston, Texas. The son of a minister, he began his career in 1999 after the sudden death of his father. Although Joel Osteen studied briefly at Oral Roberts University, he did not graduate, as he worked alongside his father as the publishing supervisor. He authored seven books and toured the world with his message. Osteen has been in England, Northern Ireland, Israel, and Canada. His weekly sermons attract 40,000 people. Because of his success, Osteen has attracted criticism from those who consider his sermons not in concert with Christian orthodoxy.[116]

Televangelists and pastors of mega-churches have large incomes which many of them spend on expensive cars and expensive homes and numerous luxuries. All of these expenditures contribute to the American economy and are part of the religion industry in this country.

The Protestant Ethic and the Spirit of Capitalism

Religion is an important American industry. This industry employs clergy, financial experts, artists, and numerous other workers, including stonemasons, real estate agents, teachers, civil engineers, and a host of other professions. In the United States, these religion inspired efforts are mainly the outcome of Protestant beliefs as well described by the German sociologist Max Weber.[117]

Although religion has been challenged by science since the days of Thomas Jefferson, religion exhibits so many functions other than belief in a deity or supernatural events that there is no chance of it disappearing.

Religion may be described as a means of relating man to man and men to the universe. An example of this definition is the so-called Ten Commandments, including commandment number one, which begins with the phrase "I am the Lord your God who brought you forth out of the land of Egypt." The fifth through the tenth commandments relate man to man, as, for example, "You shall not kill."[118]

It is, however, evident that a good number of secularists who care little for biblical injunctions nevertheless deal with the economic consequences of religion, even as religion influences the American economy.

Since the American economy is based on capitalism, which may be defined as a means of securing profits, it is important to discover the origin of capitalism. Religion certainly contributes to the capitalist enterprise. In fact, Max Weber discovered that one of the major contributing factors leading to capitalism was the Protestant Reformation and in particular its Calvinist interpretation. Weber did not claim that Protestantism is the only source of capitalism. However, he did write that the Protestant ethic was greatly influential in promoting the capitalist enterprise.[119]

In the 21st century, capitalism is largely divorced from religion. Nevertheless there is a good deal of evidence that Puritan ethics influenced the development of capitalism. This came about because the Protestant Reformation dignified all work as adding to the common good. It was claimed that work was blessed by God no matter how humble, no matter what kind of labor. This belief is usually called the work ethic, which holds that all work is a "calling," leading to the spirit of capitalism, which may be defined as the rational pursuit of economic gain accomplished by means of planning, hard work and self-denial.[120]

All this, which is a matter of individual responsibility, leads to eventual salvation according to the Protestant ethic; that differs from the Roman Catholic position, which holds that salvation is attained by means of the Church and sacraments, subject to clerical authority.

The Calvinist interpretation of salvation claims that God chose some people for salvation and others for damnation. It therefore became the duty of believers to display self-confidence and material success as evidence of having God's grace and as a sign of having been saved. Luther taught that vocation came from God and was not limited to the clergy or Church but applied to any occupation or trade. Therefore, Protestants rejected paralyzing asceticism as practiced among some Catholics. Instead, Protestants were taught to follow a secular vocation with as much zeal as possible, thereby accumulating money. Calvinists prohibited wastefully using hard earned money and identified the purchase of luxuries as a sin. They also viewed failure to work as an affront to God and frowned upon donating money to the poor, as that was seen as furthering beggary. Max Weber commented that individuals began to accept the uniform products produced by industrialization because expensive luxuries were disdained.

Weber did not argue that the Puritan religion is the only factor producing capitalism. He recognized that scholarship, the rational systematization of government administration, and an increase in individual economic ventures were additional factors in promoting capitalism. It is however evident that religion has impacted capitalism in a major way and has contributed considerably to its survival. Religion is an industry which contributes to the overall economic condition of the United States and also serves numerous functions other than belief in the supernatural, which has been challenged in the United States for over 200 years.

CHAPTER 6: THE INFLUENCE OF RELIGION ON PHILANTHROPY

Religion and Medical Practice

The Greek word "philanthropy" means love of man. Therefore those who contribute financially or otherwise participate in efforts designed to help those in need are called philanthropists. The Judeo-Christian tradition of helping those who need help is rooted in the Bible. Chapter 19 verse 18 of Leviticus ends with the words, "and you shall love your neighbor as yourself." That commandment is undoubtedly exceedingly difficult to fulfill, although there are Americans in every generation who have sacrificed their lives for the sake of others and who have shown in other ways willingness to accept this dictum, thereby practicing philanthropy.

Included in the concept of philanthropy is the maintenance of hospitals, evidently designed to help those who are ill or injured.

According to the American Hospital Association, in 2013 there were 5,564 hospitals in the United States. A good number of these were founded by religious communities, although 46% of US hospitals are for-profit businesses. According to the Catholic Hospital Association, 41% of American hospitals are Catholic hospitals or are associated with other religious communities, including 34 Jewish hospitals, reflecting that the percentage of Jewish Americans is only 1.8%. Almost all Protestant denominations also sponsor American hospitals.[121]

While Catholic hospitals have increased in number and percentage over the last 10 years, the number of all other hospitals has declined. This decline is in part related to mergers of Catholic hospitals with secular hospitals.

Catholic doctrines affect patients in these hospitals, as the US Conference of Catholic Bishops has developed a directive to the effect that Catholic hospitals ban elective abortion, sterilization, and birth control. Also restricted are fertility treatments, genetic testing, and end of life options. Crisis care for women suffering miscarriages or ectopic pregnancies are also limited by this directive, as is emergency contraception after sexual assault.[122]

Some small communities have only one hospital. If that hospital is Catholic, then non-Catholics are obliged to conform to Catholic religious beliefs. Therefore the American Civil Liberties Union has filed a lawsuit against the Catholic bishops in order to prohibit the enforcement of Catholic practices on non-Catholics.[123]

Religion is not absent from secular hospitals. There is hardly a hospital in the United States that does not provide a chapel allowing patients and relatives of all religions to pray or meditate. More recently numerous hospitals have altered their chapels to become interfaith meditation rooms. This effort to provide meditation rooms in hospitals began in California at Kaiser Permanente facilities in Sacramento. The meditation rooms have stained-glass windows depicting nature scenes. The growth of these meditation rooms reflects the willingness of hospitals nationwide to accommodate Americans of various faiths, as well as those who have no faith.[124]

Visiting the sick is regarded as one of the most important functions of religious communities. Therefore the clergy are constantly visiting members of their congregations who are hospitalized. In addition there are chaplains who are full time hospital employees ministering to patients, family members, and other caregivers within the hospital setting. Many of these chaplains work in an interfaith denominational setting.

According to the Bureau of Labor Statistics, hospital chaplains counsel patients who are undergoing surgical procedures, dealing with end of life issues, have suffered traumatic accidents, and they offer comfort and support to patients' families. They may also be called upon to deal with angry visitors, emotionally distraught friends and family, and other emergency conditions. Such chaplains also conduct religious services in the hospital chapel and deal with memorial services and weddings. These chaplains also provide support to fellow staff members. Hospital chaplains need to work well within a team environment. This means that these chaplains must be able to deal with different cultures and persons of different faiths. Like all clergy, such chaplains are held to a high standard of ethical behavior professionalism and, very importantly, confidentiality. Chaplains must maintain a calm demeanor in the face of many distraught individuals, making their work quite stressful.

Hospital chaplains are expected to have a bachelor's degree in counseling, theology, or a related field. Some large hospitals require that chaplains hold a Master of Divinity degree, be endorsed by a recognized religious institution, and be a member of a professional organization such as the Association for Clinical Pastoral Education.

According to the Bureau of Labor Statistics, the average salary for clergy working in hospitals is $50,430 annually, a salary far too small to support a family.[125]

Religion and Aid to the Poor

#The Salvation Army was founded By William Booth in 1865 in England. It has since then come to America and spread throughout the world. Booth was a Methodist minister who sought to intervene on behalf of the poor. To achieve this, Booth recruited followers willing to abstain from alcohol and tobacco and to accept the Army's moral code. Booth fulfilled his mission as a general, attacking homelessness, hunger, and misery of all kinds. He organized his followers as an army and used military labels to designate the ministers in the Army. Those working full-time for the Army held ranks such as Major. The whole purpose of the Salvation Army is the alleviation of misery. To that end the Army cooperates with international relief agencies and governments. The top commander of the Army at this time is General André Cox, who was elected to that post in 2013.[126]

The Salvation Army targets homelessness and hunger. The leading causes of homelessness are lack of affordable housing and an insufficient income. For some years now, approximately one in four Americans has had an extremely low income. This affects at least 10½ million Americans, even as they were only about 6 million rentals available in the country. Extremely low income prevents nearly 70% of the homeless to find a place to stay. It has been estimated that 75% of those with extremely low incomes end up with less than half of the income to pay for such necessities as food, medicine, transportation, or childcare.

Efforts by the Salvation Army to prevent homelessness are confronted by what has been called the foreclosure crisis. Related to this is that a good number of Americans living in rental homes are evicted for failure to pay rent. Since 2008, there has been a 61% rise in homelessness in this country.[127] One reason for this is domestic violence, which is a leading cause of homelessness for women. Unemployment, poverty, and low wages impact homelessness as well. Added to this are mental illness and substance abuse.

The clientele of the Salvation Army are 63% male and 37% female, based on sheltered adults. 39% of these adults are white and non-Hispanic, 9.5% are white and Hispanic, 39 ½% are African-Americans, and 7.2% are of multiple races. 63% of Salvation Army clients are single and 39% are disabled. 23% are under the age of 18, and 3.2% are 62 years old or older.[128]

Single mothers with small children are the majority of homeless families dealt with by the Salvation Army. About 2 ½ million American children are homeless at any one time.

Because more than 49 million people in the United States face the threat of hunger every day, the Salvation Army serves more than 56 million meals to anyone in need at its numerous soup kitchens, sit down meal programs, and food pantries.[129]

The Society of St. Vincent de Paul is an international voluntary organization in the Catholic Church. It was founded in 1833 for service to the poor. The society offers material help to the poor or needy. It has thrift stores which sell donated goods at a low price and raise money for the poor. It also has a great variety of outreach programs sponsored by local churches. Founded in France to help impoverished people living in the slums of Paris, the society came to the United States in 1845 and established itself in St. Louis, Missouri.[130]

A Jewish service organization called "Mazon: A Jewish Response to Hunger" seeks to alleviate hunger in America. Mazon (Hebrew for "food") estimates that 42 million Americans — about one in eight people — experience hunger. The organization supports a multimedia exhibit housed in an expandable semi-trailer. Inside is an exhibit showing portraits taken over the course of three years in every region of the United States. It has voice-overs gleaned from hours of interviewing, showing that hunger is not partisan. It affects children and old people, families and singles, and women and men of all races and locations. The photographs were taken by photographer Barbara Grover, who crisscrossed the United States visiting soup kitchens, food stamp offices, and people's homes. The exhibit is called "This Is Hunger." Visitors are asked, with the help of a placemat that lists food items and their costs, to plan a balanced dinner for the Supplemental Nutrition Assistance Program which costs $1.40 per person per meal. The exhibit includes three iPads where people can sign the petition urging Congress to retain the Supplemental Nutrition Assistance Program. Nearly 1,000 American synagogues participate in this effort, and are encouraged to make a financial contribution to alleviate the hunger of people they have never met in order to fulfill the commandment: "you shall love your neighbor as yourself."[131]

Homelessness

Religious communities seek to alleviate the pain of being homeless in America. It has been estimated that there are 1,750,000 homeless people in the United States on any one day, whose average monthly income is $348. Twenty-eight percent of the homeless do not get enough to eat each day, although 44% do paid work during any month. It turns out that 66% of the homeless are alcohol or drug abusers and/or have a mental disease. 40% of homeless women are single or have no partner. 40% of the homeless are veterans.

In 2016, 31 million Americans lived in hunger or on the edge of hunger. 12 million American children lived below the poverty level. And 9,300,000 children receive food stamps annually. Homelessness is caused by domestic violence for 46% of all homeless people. 30% of all homeless people have been homeless for more than two years.[132]

Although 66% of all the homeless are drug dependent or alcoholic, there are a good number of homeless men and women who are working but do not have enough income to pay rent and are therefore dependent on homeless shelters every night.

An example of this situation is "Jim," whose experiences mirror those of many others now in homeless shelters. After his divorce, this gentleman worked for 14 years in low-paying jobs which provided barely enough to pay rent. In all those years a number of unexpected events forced him to give up his apartment and live in the streets. He was laid off once and also became ill. His brother needed financial help. During the course of all these emergencies, "Jim" never had any resources other than low-paying jobs.

Another example of the homeless workingman is Kenneth Lindo, who worked as a messenger on Wall Street earning $5.50 an hour. He is unable to afford the weekly rent of $140 for a Harlem room. He was forced into a men's shelter in Manhattan.[133]

Jewish Efforts for the Homeless

Three Jewish denominations in New York City have provided 20 beds for the homeless. In addition, several other Jewish denominations have also participated, according to The New York Board of Rabbis. Further, the Federation of Jewish Philanthropies has opened numerous shelters in synagogues for the homeless. In addition, the Federation of Jewish Philanthropies has opened a housing facility on Ward's Island for people newly released from various state institutions who otherwise would most likely be homeless. In addition to these Jewish efforts, 16 churches in

New York house 109 homeless people every night, and 10 more religious institutions plan to open additional facilities, increasing the number of beds for the homeless to 340 in New York. New York City provides beds, linen, transportation, and technical assistance to religious organizations that want to shelter the homeless. Normally the homeless in New York showered and were fed at city sponsored centers. Under an agreement with The Coalition for the Homeless, the city of New York will give shelter to any homeless man or woman who asks for it.[134]

Catholic Charities has had a major impact on the prevention of homelessness in the United States. The goal of the Catholic homeless effort is prevention. This prevention program is to ensure that vulnerable people have a home, either in the form of temporary shelter or long-term housing. These programs provide eviction prevention support in the form of rental assistance for back rent, security deposits, and referral to appropriate community agencies. Catholic Charities also sponsors The Family Eviction Prevention Collaborative, which deals principally with the rental assistance for low income families, at-risk families, and individuals. Catholic Charities also sponsors Progress of People's Development Corporation, which transforms vacant land and buildings into affordable housing units and, as a result, transforms the lives of individuals and families.

Catholic Charities' Progress of Peoples has completed more than 3600 units of housing in New York City, including 2186 units of housing for low income older adults, 1069 units of family housing, and 433 units of supportive housing for the formerly homeless and individuals suffering mental illness or behavioral difficulties. 90% of all tenants in the Catholic single occupancy family and senior housing had incomes below 30% of the annual median income in New York.

Catholic Charities is nationwide and has numerous additional programs beyond housing. Catholic Charities supports a vast network of soup kitchens and food pantries, emergency shelters, temporary and transition role housing, and permanent affordable housing to help homeless families and individuals.

Catholic Charities also helps physically disabled people. This includes those who need to adjust to recent blindness, developmentally disabled children, and emotionally disturbed adults needing intensive care.

Catholic Charities also helps immigrants reunite with their families, obtain proper work authorization, learn English and civics, and prepare to pass citizenship exams. Catholic Charities also helps immigrants avoid exploitation by unscrupulous practitioners.[135]

Although the Koran teaches its followers to kill Jews as well as other unbelievers (Qur'an 17:33), the Jewish communities in the United States have been most active in helping Syrian Muslim refugees who arrived in the United States in 2016 and 2017. There is a Jewish Coalition for Disaster Relief which feeds and houses Muslim Syrian refugees.[136]

Episcopal Housing Corporation is a nonprofit organization founded in 1995. This corporation develops affordable housing to families with very low incomes and with recently overcome homelessness or substance abuse addiction. The corporation also works to develop facilities such as community centers that help strengthen entire communities.

Drug and Alcohol Addiction

In August 2017, President Trump declared the United States' worsening epidemic of opiate overdoses as a national emergency. This announcement came about because of an urgent recommendation from the national commission on the opioid epidemic. As usual, Democrats criticized this declaration for political reasons, although the president's declaration was caused because 52,000 overdose deaths occurred nationwide in one year as a result of the use of heroin and Fentanyl.[137]

The Federal Drug Administration reports that 2.6 out of every 1000 USA residents 12 years old or older used heroin. That is a 63% increase in the rate of heroin use since 2002. The rate of heroin abuse and dependence climbed 90% over the same time, according to the US FDA and the Centers for Disease Control. This means that a half million people used heroin each year, an increase of 150% since 2007. Young men are the principal uses of heroin, although women and people with private insurance and high incomes had an equal rise in drug use over the past 10 years. 96% of people who used heroin also use other drugs such as cocaine, marijuana, or alcohol. 61% of heroin users use at least three different drugs. There's also a strong relationship between the use of prescription painkillers and heroin. People who are addicted to narcotic painkillers are 40 times more likely to misuse heroin.[138]

Religious communities are therefore faced with an immense problem far worse than the alcohol epidemic which is already a principal user of private and public resources.

Christian Rehabilitation

The National Institute of Drug Abuse has supported a study by William White and Alexandre Lauder concerning the relationship between addiction counseling and spirituality. Because the word spirituality seems to have no scientific basis, it is suspect by those seeking to help addicts overcome their disabilities. However, William White and Alexandre Lauder claim that they can use scientific methods to define spirituality and measure its influence on the course of addiction and recovery. There is the Brief Multidimensional Measure of Religiousness/Spirituality and the Religious Background and Behavioral Scale. These instruments measure such dimensions as belief in a higher power, daily rituals of meditation or prayer, life purpose and goals, balance and wholeness, personal values such as honesty, humility, passion, forgiveness, tolerance, and personal relationships. Scientists are using instruments to answer several questions about spirituality and addiction. These questions are:

Does a spiritual void in one's life heighten vulnerability for the development of a substance use disorder?

Do self-defined spiritual experiences play a role in recovery initiation and, if so, what are the active ingredients and measurable effects of such experiences?

Does spirituality play a role in recovery maintenance, and, if so, are these dimensions different than those that influence recovery initiation?

What is the relationship between spirituality and religiosity as they interact over the course of addiction and recovery?

Does a focus on spirituality within recovery mutual aid societies and the professional treatment of substance abuse enhance long-term recovery outcomes?[139]

There are those in the counseling community who claim that there are some consistent findings of a scientific nature concerning spirituality and addiction. It is well known that individuals with a high degree of religiosity are less likely to consume alcohol and other drugs than those without such involvement. Several studies also have confirmed that people with lower levels of religiosity, and lower levels of meaning and purpose in their lives, are at increased risk for substance abuse. Researchers also found that a religious orientation to recovery is associated with a higher quality of life, optimism, social support and lower levels of stress and conflict.[140]

Lauder and White found that religiosity reduces the risk of relapse and may be serving as a protective buffer against the stress of recovery.[141]

There are in the United States numerous Christian rehabilitation centers which advertise that they are judgment free and based on forgiveness. These centers use the 12 step model adopted from Alcoholics Anonymous as well as teachings from the Bible, including "surrendering to a higher power." In an effort to facilitate self-improvement, group support is provided. This is essential because, according to Christian Rehabilitation, addiction is a physically dangerous disease and cannot be managed alone. Therefore recovery requires assistance from trained medical addiction specialists and physicians. Christian Rehabilitation considers addiction a medical disease centered inside the brain, in that addictive drugs and alcohol alter the structure of the brain that can hinder self-control. Christian-based rehabilitation treatment plans follow a singular purpose to recover with the aid of a higher power. This belief is expected to give the addict the strength needed to recover.

Christian rehabilitation holds that self-control must be developed over time. To attain self-control, Christian-based rehabilitation offers and arranges detoxification programs, types of therapy, and aftercare that supplement medical addiction treatments.[142]

Catholic Charities and Substance Abuse

Although the Catholic population of the United States is only 23% of all Americans, Catholic Charities is evidently the leader in the treatment of opiate addiction in this country. Treatment for these addictions is accorded to anyone without respect to religious affiliation.

The Catholic Church operates opiate addiction treatment centers all over the United States. They treat those suffering from addiction to illegal opioids like heroin, as well as prescription drugs like oxycodone. These centers combine physical as well as mental and emotional support to help stop addiction. Physical support often includes medical detox and subsequent medical support including medication. Medical support includes in-depth therapy to address the underlying causes of addiction.[143]

Evidently the goal of treatment for alcoholism is abstinence. This is difficult to obtain, particularly among those with poor social support, poor motivation, or psychiatric disorders. Such addicts tend to relapse within a few years of treatment. Treatment success is measured for addicts by long periods of abstinence, reduced use of alcohol, better health, and improved social functioning. Catholic Charities employees the 12 step program of Alcoholics Anonymous.

Drug and alcohol addiction usually takes a heavy toll on the body of the addict even as the body needs the substance to function. Detoxification therefore is the process of removing drugs and/or alcohol from the body, a process that can be lethal if mismanaged. That is why Catholic Charities employs licensed physicians and mental health and other substance abuse professionals. One drug meant to help with long-term treatment for opioid addiction is buprenorphine.[144]

Catholic Charities also offers outpatient programs for those addicts who wish to live at home and/or who are working on going to school. These outpatient programs will need mental health rehabilitation or drug rehabilitation.

Catholic Charities also offers trauma therapy, which addresses traumatic incidents from a client's past. Trauma (Greek=wound) is often one of the primary triggers and potential causes of addiction. Traumas can stem from child sexual abuse, domestic violence, having a parent with a mental illness, losing one or both parents at a young age, or a number of other factors. Trauma therapy allows the patient to deal with his past with the help of mental health professionals.[145]

Catholic Charities also operates Covenant House International. This agency provides shelter, immediate crisis care and services for runaway youth. Most of these Covenant Houses provide for youth age 14 to 20, although some deal with children as young as age 13 and adults up to age 24. Covenant House helps, educational support, college scholarships, jobs and skills training programs, drug abuse treatment, legal services, mental health services, street outreach, and aftercare.

In in the 1960s, the Rev. Bruce Ritter, a Franciscan priest, resigned from his position as professor at Manhattan College and began a ministry serving the city's poor. He was joined by father James Fitzgibbon. They moved into a dilapidated tenement building in New York's East Village together with some friends, former students, and neighbors. They then began an effort to help homeless runaway youth. In 1972, Father Ritter and others founded Covenant House. By using established fundraising methods, Covenant House was able to use the money to shelter homeless children in lower Manhattan and Staten Island. Thereafter, Father Ritter announced creation of a multiservice center near the Port Authority bus terminal. Thereafter Covenant House branched out to other cities under the leadership of Sister Mary Rose McGeady.

Covenant House supports a research institute that provides research and public education about all aspects of the homeless youth population. The Institute also calls attention to issues that affect the homeless, runaways, and at risk youth. It trains leaders in the social service field and trains the youth that Covenant House serves in advocacy techniques.

Covenant House operates a free confidential crisis hotline that operates 365 days a year. Crisis counselors utilize a database of 30,000 social service and child welfare agencies to connect callers with immediate assistance in their locations. In one year, Covenant House may receive 51,000 or more phone calls from children, parents, and caregivers dealing with running away, suicide and abuse.[146]

During the eight years of the Obama administration, there was a considerable increase in homeless children and adults. It has been estimated that there are 1.4 million children who are homeless in this country every year. Of these, 1,166,000 are enrolled in public schools. This is a 71% increase since the 2007 school year. The increase in homeless children occurred mainly in 31 states. Since not all school districts report to the United States Department of Education, this estimate is an underestimate. Furthermore, this number does not include preschool children or infants and toddlers. Most homeless families, 90% of them, are single parent families, usually headed by a mother. Over 45% of children who are homeless do not attend school regularly. Many of the homeless feed themselves from garbage cans, ride subways all night, sleep on sidewalks, or hang out in parks. They have a markedly elevated death rate, are very often ill, and have a 2 ½ times higher risk of death during any year than the general population.

All of this and more demonstrates the need partially met by Catholic Charities and other charities supported by religious communities in this country. It is nevertheless impossible for religious communities alone to eradicate this atrocious problem, which could easily be solved if much of the money wasted by government bureaucrats were applied to those who need it the most and who are usually invisible to politicians, media employees, and others who don't want to hear about the pain and suffering of their fellow citizens.

Jewish Efforts

Jewish alcoholism is almost unknown, but drug addiction among Jews is as common as it is in the general population. Jews view alcohol, and particularly wine, as a sacred substance which introduces the Sabbath and other Jewish holy days. Therefore, excessive drinking is unusual among the Jewish community. Jewish drug addiction, however, is a traumatic situation which alienates family members and negatively impact physical and mental health. Therefore, the Jewish community maintains drug rehabilitation centers intending to help Jewish people overcome their addiction. These drug rehabilitation centers begin with detoxification and healthcare. They therefore do not differ from those employed by Catholic Charities and others. Jewish drug rehabilitation involves individual and group therapy sessions, trauma counseling, anger management, relapse therapy, and drug abuse education.

Jewish drug rehabilitation also involves eating kosher food. Indeed, non-Jewish centers sometimes are also willing to provide Jewish patients with kosher alternatives. The Jewish drug rehabilitation centers accommodate a diverse kosher diet, which it is believed will give the patient the needed nutrients to recover from malnutrition, which is common among drug users. It has been discovered also that a well-balanced diet improves emotional moods, increases the energy level, and leads to a healthier lifestyle.

Jewish drug rehab centers include religion and faith as part of the recovery process. These centers hold religious services in the center and/or find a synagogue in the area which will accept drug addicts. William White and Alexander Lauder have demonstrated that religious belief helps in quitting drug addiction and makes it easier to stay clean and sober after rehabilitation treatment.[147]

CHAPTER 7: THE INFLUENCE OF RELIGION ON AMERICAN MUSIC

The Jewish Experience

Although Jewish Americans are less than 2% of the American population, the overwhelming number of American songwriters are followers of Judaism. Commercially successful American songs written in the 1930s and 1940s were written mostly by Jews, with Cole Porter a major exception. Yet even Cole Porter reputedly told Richard Rodgers that in order to succeed, "I'll write Jewish tunes." No doubt the most prolific of all the Jewish songwriters was Irving Berlin, who wrote 1,500 songs and lived 101 years.

A good deal of the music written by these composers was heavily influenced by synagogue music. An example is Gershwin's "Swanee," which is derived from Stephen Foster's song "Old Folks at Home," and "It Ain't Necessarily So," which apparently came from the blessings over the prophetic readings during the Sabbath service.[148]

Likewise, "Rudolph the Red Nose Reindeer" by Johnny Marks, "Silver Bells" by Livingston and Evans, "Let It Snow, Let It Snow, Let it Snow" by Kahn and Styne, "The Christmas Song" by Mel Tormé, and other popular Christmas tunes, were written by Jews.

An example of the American secular religion is Irving Berlin's song *God Bless America*. This song was at first denounced as un-American because Irving Berlin was Jewish. Yet, this song was played at numerous sporting events and was played by the Brooklyn Dodgers at every home game. The song appeared in the film *This Is the Army* starring Ronald Reagan, and it became a source of revenue for the Boy Scouts and Girl Scouts, as Berlin assigned all profits from the song to those organizations.

In more recent years, the most successful of Jewish influenced musicals on Broadway was composed and written in 1964 by Jerry Bock and Sheldon Harnick. They produced the play "Fiddler on the Roof" on Broadway, which was nominated for 10 Tony awards, winning nine. It was cited for best musical and book, and in 1972 won a special Tony because it became the longest running musical in Broadway history. The play was also made into a movie, and translated into numerous languages playing all over the world.

This musical is the first musical to surpass 3000 performances, winning a special Tony award on becoming the longest running musical in Broadway history. It also became an international hit in Europe, South America, Africa and Australia. In Germany there were over 100 productions of this musical and there were 292 performances in France. The Stratford Festival in Canada produced the musical in 2013. In 1971 a film version was released.[149]

This play deals with a poor Ukrainian Jew who can barely feed his family as a milkman in 19th century Russia. It is heavily influenced by the Jewish religion has the principal protagonist constantly speaks to God as he pulls his delivery wagon around the town.

This unusual and outstanding theatrical performance is based on a number of stories written by Solomon Rabinovich, who use the pen name Sholem Aleichem which is Hebrew for "peace be with you."

Throughout this musical play, the lead actor constantly consults God, whom he seems to know intimately. The play is indeed heavily influenced by the Jewish religion, and exhibits 17 musical numbers, including "Tradition," "Matchmaker," "If I Were Rich Man," "Sunrise, Sunset," and a number of others.

The play exhibits numerous Jewish customs, including a Jewish wedding. Tevye the milkman has five daughters, one of whom marries a gentile shortly before the whole family is expelled from their home by the Russian authorities, who also organized an attack on the Jews, burning their homes and assaulting their people. Finally, the family decides to go to America, as was indeed the case for 2.5 million Russian Jews between 1891 and 1924.

Without doubt, this musical was heavily influenced by religious custom and tradition. In 1952, two anthropologists, Mark Zbrowski and Elizabeth Herzog published *Life Is with People: The Culture of the Shtetl*, a detailed accounting of the daily life of the Eastern European Jews. This book greatly influenced the writers of Fiddler on the Roof.[150]

Hugo Weisgall (1912–1997) was an American Jewish composer who came from seven generations of synagogue cantors. In 1992, he wrote a song cycle,

"Psalm of the Distant Dove," which commemorated the 500th anniversary of the expulsion of the Jews from Spain. He also composed synagogue music, some of which[151] is sung in Hebrew. He also wrote "An Evening Prayer for Peace," commissioned by a New York synagogue, for tenor solo, chorus, and organ, and "Fortress, Rock of Our Salvation," sung in connection with the holy day of Chanukah (Dedication). In 1993, Weisgall composed an opera called "Esther." This opera is based on the story of Esther or Hadassah.[152]

In 1927, Warner Bros. produced the first feature-length motion picture with sound. It was called *The Jazz Singer* and featured the Jewish performer Al Jolson. This is the story of a traditional and devout Jewish family, the son of a synagogue cantor. The son leaves home and becomes a jazz singer in nightclubs. Yet, in the final scene he returns to his Jewish home and sings in the synagogue where he had been raised. This movie introduced the public to the Jewish religion, customs, and ceremonies. The movie was based on "The Day of Atonement," a short story by Sampson Rafaelson, which was later turned into a stage play *The Jazz Singer*. In 1980, a second version of *The Jazz Singer* was produced with Neil Diamond in the title role.[153]

Leonard Bernstein was without doubt one of America's principal composers, conductors, and performance artists. In addition to writing *West Side Story* and numerous other compositions, Bernstein also composed Jewish religious music as well as a Catholic mass. Included in his numerous Jewish compositions is his first symphony, subtitled *Jeremiah*. He also wrote synagogue music commissioned by New York's Park Avenue Synagogue. His third symphony, dedicated to the memory of President John F. Kennedy, includes "Trial by God's Law" and "Kaddish," which is the Hebrew prayer commemorating the dead. Another Jewish inspired composition by Bernstein is a *Lamentation*, which is sung in Hebrew. Finally, Bernstein wrote a mass in honor of John F. Kennedy, commissioned by Kennedy's widow Jacqueline Kennedy.[154]

Bernstein's *Mass* is part tradition and part popular culture. It interweaves the traditional Roman Catholic liturgy with swinging modern music. Included is an Agnus Dei (qui tolis peccata mundi) or "lamb of God, who takes away sins of the world." Bernstein included the Gregorian chant. The Gregorian chant has been part of Christian liturgy since the earliest days of the church.

Ancient Jewish worship significantly included ritual singing. Therefore some Hebrew words such as "Amen," meaning "so be it," and "halleluja" or "let us praise God," became part of the Gregorian chant. Moreover the threefold "sanctus" is derived from the threefold "kaddish" in the "Kedushah" included in the Jewish daily prayers.[155]

The Gregorian Chant

The Gregorian chant is named for Pope Gregory (540-604), a sixth-century pope. In later years, and particularly in the ninth century, French monasteries became the center of studies and practices of the Gregorian chant. More recently, in the 20th century, Benedictine monks developed a modern edition of the Gregorian chant. This was published in 1985. However, because Vatican II in 1965 stopped requiring the use of Latin as the official language in the liturgy of the Church, and the vernacular language of each country became the language of Catholic worship, the Gregorian chant was restricted to monasteries or admirers of the Gregorian word song.

Because Christianity originated in Judaism, it is not surprising that the oldest musical manifestation of Christian or Catholic music has its roots in the songs of the old synagogues since the first century. That ancient music relates to the Gregorian chant in that the first Christians, who were converted Jews, continued to sing the songs and songs of the Torah (Old Testament). When non-Jews became Christians as well, then Greek and Roman culture was introduced into Christianity. Therefore the Gregorian chant includes music from all the centuries from the first to the sixth, and its performance peaked in the ninth, 10[th,] and 11th centuries, which are generally viewed as the middle ages.

The principal characteristics of the Gregorian chant are that the melodies are sung in unison without soloists. The Chant is sung a cappella without any accompanying musical instrument. In 1994 the Gregorian chant was revived when it was recorded on a CD record selling 5 million copies. The Gregorian chant is, of course, also found on the internet.[156]

Contemporary Catholic Liturgical Music

Catholic music has been altered considerably since the Gregorian chant was first introduced. Yet, emphasis on musical expression among Catholics has been vital in promoting the Catholic message to the world.[157]

Because of cost and preference, fewer parishes use the traditional pipe organ. Instead, a good deal of new music has been written for chorus with piano, guitar and percussion instruments.[158]

The reforms of the Second Vatican Council led to a variety of styles of music being approved for Catholic liturgy. In the United States, the Gregorian chant was superseded by 1970s folk-based music, which has evolved into a matter of considerable importance to singing in the celebration of the Mass. Singing is emphasized for the celebrant and for the people, particularly on Sundays and on holy days. It is also recommended by Vatican II that

Catholics learn the order of the mass in Latin so that Catholics from different countries can sing together.[159]

Catholic music uses reciprocal or a responsive singing, in which the congregation sings only a short refrain between verses, which is sung by the Cantor and the choir.

Since the 1970s, an entire body of Protestant hymns and newly composed contemporary Catholic music was introduced to Catholic worship. A good part of contemporary Catholic liturgical music has been inspired by popular music of the day which used guitars and other instruments usually associated with full music. The most widespread of such music came from the St. Louis Jesuits.

In the 21st century, Catholic music has been greatly influenced by contemporary society. A good deal of the music played during Sunday Mass comes from contemporary American music, so that the Gregorian Chant has become rare in most American Catholic churches.

The Catholic University of America

Today, in the United States, these Catholic traditions are preserved and modernized by the Benjamin T. Rome School of Music of the Catholic University of America. This school trains men and women in performance composition and research concerning sacred music. The school offers both degree and non-degree study of music including a Master's and Doctor degree. The Institute includes in its curriculum chamber music, conducting, music education, musicology, theory and composition, and a Latin America center for graduate studies in music.

The Catholic University of America first began offering music courses in 1927. In 1950, a music department was established, which became the School of Music in 1965. It was named the Benjamin T. Rome School of Music in 1984. Today degrees are awarded by the school. These are Bachelor of Music, Master of Arts, Master of Music, Master of Music in Sacred Music, Doctor of Musical Arts, and Doctor of Philosophy.

The faculty teaches the use of numerous instruments, including bassoon, cello, clarinet, double bass, flute, guitar, harp, horn, oval, organ, piano, percussion, saxophone, trombone, trumpet, tuba, and viola. Also taught is voice, and vocal musical theater. Evidently, this is as comprehensive a music school curriculum as is found anywhere.[160]

It is significant that the school does not only require competence in music, but also demands that students enroll in several courses in English as well as Religious Studies. In addition, a number of academic electives are also required, as are other courses in the liberal arts in order that graduates of the school have a well-rounded education beyond music.

The school has produced more than 2000 music alumni who perform all over the world, including soprano Harolyn Blackwell and tenor John Aler.

The school has also sponsored benefit concerts, such as works by Gian Carlo Menotti and Mstislav Rostropovich. In 2003 the students and alumni performed Leonard Bernstein's *Mass*. The school accepts not only Catholics but members of all religions, ethnic backgrounds, nationalities, and races.[161]

The school schedules numerous concerts, recitals and special events throughout each academic year. Included in these productions have been *La Traviata* by Verdi, *Madame Butterfly* by Puccini, *The Magic Flute* by Mozart, as well as *Fiddler on the Roof*, *Hello Dolly*, and *West Side Story*.

Protestant Music

It has long been recognized that singing together helps create a sense of belonging together, thereby fulfilling one of the qualities of religion as recognized by the Roman author Marcus Cicero (106 BCE–43 BCE) in his book *De Natura Deorum* or *On the Nature of the Gods*. Cicero wrote that the word religion is derived from Res Ligare, or The Thing That Binds.

Protestant church music includes music derived from a number of ethnic geographical and ecclesiastical subdivisions. Some of this music is derived from original German sources music written by Martin Luther himself and translated into English. There is, however, also a good deal of Protestant music indigenous to the United States. That American Protestant music is divided by class divisions, including formal major hymns and music played in mostly white churches as well as spirituals derived principally from the black experience.[162]

Protestant music reflects the distinctions between Catholicism and the Protestant point of view. There are at least seven such differences. Protestants generally believe that salvation comes through faith alone, while Catholics view the seven sacraments of the church essential for gaining salvation.

Several of the hymns still used today, aside from those written by Luther, were also originally in German, such as "Let Us Ever Walk with Jesus," penned by Sigmund von Birken in 1653. There are also some Lutheran hymns which were originally written in Swedish. All of these were translated into English.

In 2017, Jason Bradley published a list of the ten top Lutheran hymns. The first of these is "Amazing Grace," written by John Newton, an Anglican priest, in 1772. This is undoubtedly the most popular Christian hymn in America and elsewhere.

John Calvin, the French Swiss theologian, was the founder of the Calvinist, Puritan and Presbyterian point of view which held that salvation is pre-determined by God prior to our birth. "Amazing Grace" reflects these beliefs. This is the second verse of that song: "'T'was grace that taught my heart to fear and grace my fears relieved: how precious did that grace appear the hour I first believed."

American Protestant church music is the outcome of a great deal of ethnic assimilation in the United States. Because America has total freedom of religion, contributions from all ethnic sources are included in American Christian music. In addition, Protestant music in particular has been greatly influenced by the westward movement of Americans since the days of the Revolution. As a result, American music, including Protestant music has been influenced by constant change. These changes are first changes in society, changes in communication, and therefore changes in music writing. These changes also include full hymns and spirituals which did not exist in the European tradition.

Jesus Christ Superstar is a rock opera. The music was written by Andrew Lloyd Webber, an Englishman and perhaps the least talented popular composer of show music, whose father was a composer and Methodist church organist. This musical depicts Jesus as a man without divinity. It has therefore been criticized by Christian believers as blasphemous (a Greek word meaning insulting). It is also been criticized because it repeats the anti-Jewish canards concerning the Christ killer accusation, which is undoubtedly the root of the Holocaust. Although this musical has played all over the world, it has not reached the level of popularity of such musicals as *Fiddler on the Roof, Oklahoma, The Sound of Music* or *Annie Get Your Gun*.

Other Popular Music

There are numerous American songs in the repertoire of popular and country-western singers and others which invoke the deity or are associated with Christmas. Irving Berlin notably wrote "Easter Parade" and "White Christmas," two songs dealing with Christian holy days but of a secular nature.[163] There are an unlimited number of other examples. Among these are the so-called "spirituals" which originated in the cotton fields of the American South centuries of slavery suffered by Africans who had been captured by the Arabs and sold to English slave traders in the American colonies and later the United States. The slaves had been deprived of their language their families and their culture. Consequently their descendants adopted the religion of their masters, Christianity. Because slaves were not taught to read, they could not read the Bible but they would memorize Biblical stories. These stories later became songs.[164]

These songs were transmitted orally from generation to generation and included "Sometimes I feel like a motherless child"; "Nobody Knows The Trouble I've Seen"; "Swing Low Sweet Chariot"; "Go down Moses "; "He's Got the Whole World in His Hand"; and numerous others.[165]

Over the years some composers have written spirituals for chorus and organized choral groups on college campuses and professional touring choirs. Hall Johnson started The Hall Johnson Negro choir in 1925 and thereby illuminated an art form which is unique in the world of music.[166]

It is hoped that spiritual solace sought with an understanding of the suffering of those slaves who created them. These unknown creators of American folk songs are no longer among us but theirs for freedom are expressed by those who sing them today and are emotionally charged.[167]

At the end of the 19th century and in the early part of the 20th century some African Americans form in their own Pentecostal churches which led to the development of gospel music. This music was performed for the first time with such instruments as the piano, drums and tambourines. Huge tents were set up for revival meetings where this gospel music flourished.[168]

Both spirituals and gospel music are expressions of a culture which developed in America over 300 years and which is unique as an art form derived from the Afro-American experience.

Christian Art

There are numerous American Christian artists who have produced modern art devoted to religion. Their works are found in many American museums and some of them are listed here. Evidently the influence of religion on art did not end with the Renaissance painters, but has continued to this day in the United States.

Makoto Fujimura is a great modern abstract Christian painter who combines abstract expressionism with the traditional Japanese art of Nihonga. Baptist preacher and artist Howard Finster creates Christian folk art paintings and mixed media work. Thomas Kinkade specializes in nostalgic landscapes. Jason Cianelli is an abstract artist. Christina Saj paints modern art icons. Lance Brown paints pictures of Jesus Christ before live audiences. Akiane Kramarik has been drawing and painting at a high level since her early youth. Justin Brown paints Bible parables. Edward Knippers paints Christian themes with a slightly abstract twist.

Other Christian themed artists include Daniel Jimick, Fred Baumbach, Daniel Arrendendo, Matthew Whitney, George Iannanou, Rosemarie Adcock, Michael Hanson, John Freeman, Chris Harber, Michael Dudash,

Bruce Herman, Fikos, Sandra Bowen, Kathleen Giles, Greek Orthodox priest Michael Courey, Grant Crawford, John Bell, Carlos Cazares, John August Swanson, Candis Kloverstrom, Jeffrey Baker, Laura Kranz, religious greeting card painter Mary Crittenden, Ron Dicianni, Catherine Andrews, Moldova native Ghenadie Sontu, graphic artist Joe Goode, Spencer Williams, Deborah Sokolove, Yisehak, Miska, Reima Hokasalo, cross makers Bruce and Kim Carey, Danny Hahlbohn, expressionist Cornelis Monsma, Kate Austin, and Stephen Sawyer.[169]

Both music and art are influenced by the Christian religion, exhibiting thereby that religion is embedded in American culture despite the decrease in church attendance and the increase of agnosticism.

CHAPTER 8: THE USE OF RELIGION TO JUSTIFY IMMORAL CONDUCT

We have seen that religion can be a positive force in society, in many ways. As Josh Stanton writes, the past, recounted in the Torah's [Old Testament] literal text, is one of religious violence, but the future is one of hope, made possible by exposure to and acceptance of other ethnic and cultural groups.[170] Stanton asserts that a careful reading of the foundations of today's religions point us in the direction of peace.

But religious teachings can be misused, and various stories or lessons can be taken out of context and distorted beyond recognition. Since religion is an emotional condition, it can be used to persuade people to do things that rationally they might consider unacceptable. We grant our leaders authority, and if they tell us certain things are permissible, we tend to believe them. Many people look up to their religious leaders with trust an d obedience. Further, religious loyalties, like national and racial loyalties, impel us to defend against — or even attack outright — perceived enemies.

Thus, religion has often been misused, or misunderstood, to condone harmful conduct and to instigate violence, causing much pain throughout history. The underlying motives usually are usually grounded in the fight for economic and political power, or sometimes social standing. At the same time, while religious identity can build a sense of unity, religious differences can fuel a sense of antagonism, fear, and a sense that the other is not fully human. Here are some of the consequences.

Slavery

In the 21st century, slavery is called a crime against humanity. However, slavery existed in the United States since the founding of the Republic in 1789. It was already established before the American Revolution. Prior to the Civil War (1861–1865), slavery was supported by the clergy in the United States. It was claimed by Baptists in particular that slavery is an institution of God. They arrived at this opinion by citing a number of verses from the Old Testament dealing with slavery. Of course, slavery was common practice in much of the ancient world, when these texts were written.

These biblical citations included Genesis 21:9-10 which tells us that Canaan, the son of Ham, was made a slave to his brothers. In Exodus 20:10-17, the commandment to remember the Sabbath includes the prohibition against working on that day, a prohibition which also concerns slaves. Slaves are mentioned again in Ephesians 6:5-8. Here Paul commands slaves to obey their masters, and in Philemon 12, Paul returns a runaway slave to his master.

The Christian clergy further argued in favor of slavery on the grounds that women were expected to play a subordinate role to men, and that slaves are stationed by God in their place. It was also argued that slavery is God's means of protecting and providing for an inferior race. Thus the clergy seemed to encourage slave owners and other supporters of slavery to believe that Christianity had in fact sanctioned this institution.

Therefore, men such as James Henry Hammond were elected to office in Southern states, which depended on slavery for their income. Hammond was a United States Representative, Governor of South Carolina, and a United States Senator. He sold more than 300 slaves on a large plantation, and on March 4, 1858, gave a speech in the U.S. Senate in which he said, in part, "In all social systems there must be a class to do the menial duties, to perform the drudgery of life... It constitutes the very mudsill of society." Hammond co-authored *The Pro-Slavery Argument* with several other authors who justified slavery on the grounds that slave owners were stewards of inferior beings.[171]

Hammond had sexual relations with two female slaves, one of whom was his own daughter. Such behavior was frequent among white men of power at the time. Mixed race children born into slavery remained there, and the situation was considered to be condoned by Christ. Hammond said on one occasion: "I firmly believe, that American slavery is not only not a sin, but especially commanded by God through Moses, and approved by Christ and his apostles."[172] Although Hammond was most prominent among 19th century slave owners, he was by no means unusual. His sentiments were shared by the slave-owning community and they were defended by asserting that it was condoned by religion.

Not only is slavery in itself now recognized as a crime, but in addition slaves became the victims of all kinds of brutality inflicted on them by slave owners. Physical violence against enslaved men and women was universal in plantations. Sexual violence against enslaved women was common. Even children were subjected to brutal punishments such as flogging, confinement in stocks, or house basements or jails. The amputation of limbs or part of the feet of runaway slaves, as well as beheadings, hangings, and both were used by slave owners. Some slave owners did not provide enough food for their slaves.[173]

Jewish colonials owned slaves, too. However, since they were more likely to live in cities than to own plantations, the numbers of slaves they owned were relatively small. However, as financiers, merchants and traders, Jews was active in the slave trade alongside Europeans and Americans, especially in the Caribbean colonies.

The Salem Witch Trials

In 1692 and 1693, twenty citizens of Salem Village in colonial Massachusetts were executed by hanging on the grounds of having been convicted of witchcraft. In retrospect, these judicial killings have been attributed to mass hysteria. The English settlers who had founded the Massachusetts Bay colony intended to live in a Bible-based society, largely concerned with the five books of Moses, which included the admonition: "Thou shalt not allow a witch to live" (Exodus 22:18).

Cotton Mather, the most prominent minister of the Puritan colony, believed in witchcraft and issued pamphlets about it. As hysteria concerning the presence of witches became widespread, a number of children claimed to have epileptic fits and a good deal of pain caused by witches. This led to a number of women and a few men being accused of witchcraft. Almost all those accused were people not liked by the community and regarded as outsiders for a number of reasons.

In June 1692, a court was assembled to hear accusations of witchcraft against a number of citizens, who were convicted and executed by hanging. In July 1692, five women were executed by hanging on the same charge, and in August 1692, four men and one woman were also executed by hanging on the grounds of witchcraft. More executions took place in September 1692 when some of the accused even pled guilty to the so-called crime of witchcraft.

In the 21st century, criminologists have shown that it is not rare for people to confess to crimes they did not commit.

Under the circumstances current in the Massachusetts Bay colony, some citizens concluded that their illnesses, or the loss or the death of a loved one, were caused by witchcraft. Those who believed this would accuse someone of witchcraft with the local magistrate. The accused would then be examined and, if found guilty, executed. Some of the accused were tortured in order to gain a confession. Sometimes the so-called witch was told to touch her accuser, who was having a fit. The fit stopped when the witch touched the accuser, which meant to the court that the accused was indeed a witch, and who was therefore hanged.

Accusations by children concerning witchcraft on the part of adults only came to an end when children began to accuse prominent citizens of the Bay Colony.

On the 300th anniversary of the witchcraft trials in 1992, a memorial park was dedicated in Salem, Massachusetts, including stone benches for each of those executed in 1692.

Some historians now attribute these 17th-century judicial murders to jealousy, a need for attention, and a means of revenging oneself as a result of dispute with the neighbor.[174]

Persecution of Mormons

In 1830, the prophet Joseph Smith published the Book of Mormon, which was an English translation of a book of golden plates to which he was directed by an angel sent by God. He then organized the Church of Jesus Christ of Latter-day Saints, which attracted a large number of followers who moved west from New York, where Smith had found the Book of Mormon. On reaching Kirtland, Ohio, where they established a temple, they were confronted by good deal of violence from local Christians who objected to the practice of polygamy by Smith and his followers. The Mormons left Ohio and by 1832 had settled in Jackson County, Missouri. Here, too, the native population resented the newcomers and feared that they would be outnumbered by the new religious motivated pilgrims from the East. As the Mormon population increased, the Mormons labeled non-Mormons Gentiles and predicted that these Gentiles will be cut off when the Kingdom was established in Jackson County. Mormons also engaged in business and were quite successful, particularly in Independence, Missouri, leading to conflict with the local population. Finally, the slavery issue drew denunciation of Mormons by so-called prominent citizens, who claimed that Mormons were abolitionists tampering with slaves and should be expelled from Missouri. Church newspapers agitated against the Mormons. Finally, mobs armed with rifles and clubs came searching for Mormon church leaders. The mob demanded that every man, woman, and child belonging to the Saints leave the county.[175]

More violence continued as Mormons were attacked physically. November 4, 1833, became known as "Bloody Day," as a mob fired on several Mormons, killing a number of them, as citizens collected arms and ammunition in preparation for a general massacre of the Saints the next day. Finally all Mormons were driven out of Jackson County and found temporary shelter in Clay County, Missouri.[176]

In the end, Mormons could no longer live anywhere in Missouri and thereupon moved to Nauvoo, Illinois, where Smith established himself as mayor and governed with an all-Mormon city council.[177]

When a local newspaper published by non-Mormons criticized him, he destroyed the newspaper. Smith was subsequently imprisoned in Carthage, Illinois, where a mob of Christians stormed the jail in which he and his brother were held and killed them both on June 27, 1844.[178]

Five defendants were tried for the murder of Smith and his brother. All five defendants were acquitted by a jury. The trial jury was composed exclusively of non-Mormons after the defense counsel convinced the judge to dismiss the initial jury, which included Mormons.[179]

After the death of Joseph Smith, 10,000 Mormons traveled west to the Great Salt Lake under the leadership of Brigham Young. There they established Salt Lake City, claiming to have found the Promised Land.

Mormon Violence: The Mountain Meadows Massacre

Members of the Church of Jesus Christ of Latter-Day Saints attacked and murdered a group of 120 men women and children known as the Fancher Party, most of them from Arkansas, as their wagon train was on their way to California.

On September 7, 1857, they were resting near Mountain Meadows in southern Utah. Unbeknownst to the travelers, a prominent Mormon, Parley Pratt, had recently taken the wife of a non-Mormon man — who then killed Pratt. Now the Mormons wanted revenge. At the same time, they were in a power struggle with President Buchanan over the status of Utah and there was word that a Federal army would be sent to restore order, adding to their state of alarm.

Thus the "Nauvoo Legion," a Utah territorial militia, descended upon the wagon train and began to shoot indiscriminately. The men who conducted these murders had disguised themselves as Native Americans, seeking to blame the so-called Indians for this crime. Having killed the men, the militia then murdered the women and children. The killers were intent on leaving no witnesses and left only a few children who were considered too young become later witnesses against them. The militia leaders believed that some emigrants had caught sight of white men and had discovered the identity of their attackers.

The perpetrators, following the massacre, burnt the victims and left their bodies to wild animals.

The United States Army investigated this atrocity after the Civil War. Only one man was ever convicted and executed for these murders.[180]

Violence Against Catholics

American violence against Catholics was the inevitable legacy of conflicts in the colonists' home countries in Europe, conflicts that began with Martin Luther (1483–1546) and were rooted in the Reformation. Luther called the Pope "the anti-Christ" and said the Catholic Church was the Whore of Babylon mentioned in the Book of Revelation.

Yet it was nativism and the secular variety of anti-Catholicism which became principally responsible for anti-Catholic sentiment in this country. This type of antagonism became most pronounced when waves of Catholic immigrants arrived in the United States from Ireland, Italy, Poland and other non-Northwestern European countries. Before these immigrations, the United States was 85% Protestant. This Protestant majority fueled theories that Catholics were seeking to dominate America and conduct all kinds of intrigues against the Protestant majority. The kind of Catholic-baiting produced by these beliefs has been called "the anti-Semitism of the liberals."[181] The historian John Higham described anti-Catholicism as "the most luxuriant and tenacious tradition of paranoiac agitation in American history."[182]

After the time of Henry VIII, English and Scottish identity was largely based on opposition to Catholicism, so that Robert Emmett Curran wrote, in his history spanning 1574–1783, "to be English was to be anti-Catholic." By this, he meant anti-papist, but the doctrines of the Church of England remained essentially Roman Catholic.[183]

Many of the British colonists in America, such as the Puritans and Congregationalists, were fleeing religious persecution by the Church of

England. In the late 17th century, a number of colonies prohibited Catholic settlers. These included Virginia, Rhode Island, and Maryland. John Jay, a member of the New York legislature, urged the legislature to require officeholders to renounce the Pope in all matters both ecclesiastical and civil.[184]

In the 19th century, anti-Catholicism reached its peak in the United States. The Rev. Lyman Beecher and the Rev. Horace Bushnell preached incitement against Catholics. They argued that the Church was not only theologically unsound but the enemy of Republican values. They claimed that the Catholic system is adverse to liberty, and the clergy to a great extent dependent on foreigners opposed to the principles of our government.[185]

In 1834, an anti-Catholic mob burned the Ursuline Convent in Charleston, near Boston. The crowd broke down doors and windows to enter the convent and ransacked the buildings. Around midnight, the rioters set fire to the building, burning it to the ground. Several arsonists were arrested and charged with arson, but all but one were acquitted by a jury. The governor then pardoned him in response to a petition signed by 5000 Bostonians.

The convent school educated primarily upper-class Protestant girls. This worried Protestants, who feared that Catholics would succeed in mass conversion of Protestants to the Catholic Church. It was rumored that the Ursuline sisters held some women against their will.[186]

In 1836, some Protestant clergy wrote a novel called *Awful Disclosures of the Hotel Dieu Nunnery in Montreal* by "Maria Monk." This fraud sold 300,000 copies. The book claimed that many of the nuns became pregnant and buried dead babies in the basements of convents. The ensuing agitation allowed numerous ex-priests and ex-nuns to go on the anti-Catholic lecture circuit with lurid tales, always evolving heterosexual contacts of adults.[187]

In 1844, a number of anti-Catholic riots occurred in Philadelphia between May 6 and July 7. These riots were stimulated by the growing population of Irish Catholic immigrants. Prior to these riots, nativists had spread a rumor that Catholics were trying to remove the Bible from public schools. At that time, in the 19th century, everything that was public was Protestant, and the Supreme Court had not yet ruled on the constitutionality of Bible reading in the public schools.

Students in Philadelphia schools began the day with reading the Protestant or King James Version of the Bible. This led the Roman Catholic Bishop Francis Kenrick to write a letter to the board of education asking that Catholic children be allowed to read the Douay version of the Bible used by Roman Catholics. When it became public that the bishop had written that letter, nativists claimed that the letter sought to attack the Bible used in

Protestant devotionals. And so, nativists rallied in the Kensington district of Philadelphia to protect Protestant worship from Catholic aggression.

The rally exploded into violence, leading to the destruction of two Catholic churches and numerous other buildings. In July, these riots continued after it was discovered that the principals of one of the Catholic churches had armed themselves for protection. When soldiers were sent to protect the church, fighting broke out the nativists and the soldiers, resulting in deaths and injuries. Several Catholic churches were burned, including St. Augustine's Church, St. Michael's Catholic Church, The Seminary of the Sisters of Charity, and a number of private homes. The rioters threw stones at Mayor John Scott when he pleaded for calm and cheered when one of the steeples of the burning churches fell.[188]

Later it was rumored that a Catholic school official, Hugh Clark, had visited a girl's school in Philadelphia and suggested that Bible readings not be conducted in the schools because it led to much confusion and animosity. This suggestion was twisted into a claim that Catholics, directed by the Pope, were trying to remove the Bible from all schools. This unjustified rumor led to another rally on the part of nativists, leading to fights between local Irish Catholics and the nativists. Consequently some nativists were shot by people in the windows of nearby buildings. Two nativists were killed. This led a mob of nativists to attack the Seminary of the Sisters of Charity and several Catholic homes. Before the night was over, numerous additional people were injured and several more nativists were killed.[189]

An indication of how widespread and popular anti-Catholicism was in the 19th century can be gathered from the comments made by Samuel Clemens, whose pen name was Mark Twain. He wrote a book in 1889 called a *Connecticut Yankee in King Arthur's Court*, including overt hostility to the Catholic Church. He let it be known that he had been educated to view everything Catholic with enmity.

In 1853, Pope Pius IX sent Archbishop Gaetano Bedini to the United States to report to him on the state of the Catholic Church in America. When Bedini arrived, some Protestants carried a sign which read "Down with Bedini," "No Popes, No Kings," and "Down with the Papacy." A crowd of demonstrators assembled before the residence of the Archbishop in Cincinnati. When the police attempted to turn back demonstrators, a fight developed in which one man was killed, 15 were wounded, and 63 were arrested. Most of the city's residents supported the protesters, blaming the police for brutality. Those who had been arrested were released and the charges dropped. As Bedini continued the tour of the United States, violence erupted in Cleveland, Louisville, Baltimore, and New York City.[190]

Anti-Catholic violence led to the murder of a priest in 1921. Father James Coyle, a priest in Birmingham, Alabama, converted a Protestant girl to Catholicism. Coyle then witnessed the girl's marriage. When her father found out about the clandestine wedding, he confronted Coyle and shot him. The father was a Protestant minister. Charged with the priest's murder, he was acquitted by a jury.[191]

A more recent murder related anti-Catholic teaching was the killing of Mary Stachowicz. She was the parish secretary of the Bishop of Springfield, Illinois. She was raped and murdered in 2002 because she confronted the killer about his gay lifestyle. Hardly any of the media reported this crime.[192]

Physical violence against Catholics in the 19th century was largely precipitated by a number of organizations devoted to an attack on the Catholic Church. The American and Foreign Christian Union announced its opposition to "corrupted Christianity," meaning Catholicism. The union also ran an anti-Catholic library in New York City. In addition, The Foreign Evangelical Society announced similar aims, as did other organizations across the country.[193]

There were in the 19th century many additional organizations, publications, and political parties devoted to anti-Catholicism. In the 20th century, the anti-Catholic movement was supported by the newly revived Ku Klux Klan, which had originally formed to intimidate Afro-Americans after the Civil War. In the 1920s, the Klan increased its membership immensely by denouncing Catholics and Jews, and gained a large Northern following, which also engaged in cross burning and some personal physical violence.[194]

In 1928, the Democrats nominated New York governor Al Smith as their presidential candidate. Smith lost the election by a landslide, having been denounced as a Catholic.[195]

The Second World War and subsequent election of the Catholic John Kennedy to the presidency has largely eliminated physical violence against Catholics in the United States. Nevertheless, there are even in the 21st century those who find it necessary to insult Catholics and their religion. For example, the off-Broadway show Late Night Catechism or Boxing Nun, like the movie Dogma and Stigmata, seek to insult and humiliate. In San Francisco, a gay parade included a so-called Sister Homo Fellatio, and a participant conducted a "condoms savior Mass" on the street. In New York City in 1989, a consecrated host was desecrated. This act is so religiously repugnant to Catholics that the Jewish Mayor Ed Koch publicly denounced this act of aggression.[196]

Some people claim that anti-Catholicism is still considered an acceptable prejudice in this country. Yet American democracy demands that no prejudice is acceptable, no matter who the target is.

Verbal and Physical Violence against American Jews

The Murder of Leo Frank

The American Jewish community is more secure and far more accepted than any European Jewish community during the 1,900 years since Emperor Constantine I issued the Edict of Milan, decriminalizing Christianity in the Roman Empire. However, since the Jews first came to New Amsterdam from Brazil in 1654, there have certainly been occasions over the years since in which physical assault occurred.[197] It may be seen that differences in race and religion can combine to be especially volatile.

Perhaps the most notorious anti-Jewish riot and murder of an innocent Jew took place in 1913 at an Atlanta, Georgia, pencil factory. Mary Phagan, a 13-year-old child laborer, was found strangled in the factory's basement. The murder was attributed Leo Frank, the Jewish factory superintendent. He was convicted of the crime, and then kidnapped from prison and lynched in 1915. Overwhelming evidence implicated Jim Conley, a black factory aide, in Phagan's murder. Instead, he was the prosecution's star witness against Frank. An all-white jury relied on his testimony to convict a Jewish industrialist. Thereafter, Conley was repeatedly sent to prison for violence against women. Frank was sentenced to death, but his sentence was commuted by the governor of Georgia, John Slaton, who deemed Frank innocent. Frank was sent to a prison farm from which he was abducted by a mob of Atlanta's social elites calling themselves the "Knights of Mary Phagan." They hanged Frank in an oak grove owned by the sheriff of Marietta, Georgia. This murder was well-planned. Some of the killers cut the prison's telephone lines and others drained the gas out of police cars so they couldn't give chase. Not one of the murderers of Frank ever stood trial.

In the wake of this crime, they convened on Stone Mountain and revived the Ku Klux Klan, while Jewish Americans formed The Anti-Defamation League, which seeks to defend Jews against anti-Jewish attacks.

One hundred years later, American Nazis continue to send messages around the Internet claiming that Frank was guilty and that Jews use the blood of Gentile children in sacrifice rituals.[198]

Al Sharpton's Role

Violence against American Jews reached pogrom proportions in 1991, when Al Sharpton, a black Baptist minister, and his followers attacked the Jewish community of Brooklyn, New York. This attack was fueled by an orchestrated series of anti-Jewish hate speeches delivered by black leaders Louis Farrakhan, Jesse Jackson, and Desmond Tutu. On July 20, 1991, a city college professor, Leonard Jeffries, held a two-hour long speech claiming that Jews were responsible for American slavery. When the Jewish community objected, the black leadership, including Sharpton and others, denounced all Jews. The African-American media fanned the flames of hatred and the desire for revenge.

In this atmosphere of religious bigotry, an auto accident became the catalyst for a massive attack against the entire Brooklyn Jewish community. A Jewish driver drove into two black children on the sidewalk; he immediately got out of his car and tried to help the children, but a crowd attacked him. A Jewish ambulance service arrived. The police arrived while the ambulance driver and his passengers were being assaulted and assisted the Jewish ambulance while the two children were driven to a hospital, where one of them died.

Thereupon Rev. Al Sharpton held a public meeting in which he claimed that the Jewish ambulance driver ignored the black children in favor of treating Jewish men. This falsehood was widely believed, and others were added, such as that the Jewish driver was drunk, that he didn't have a driver's license, that he went through a red light, and more. An agitator shouted, "the Jews are killing our children." This led young black men to throw rocks, bottles, and debris at residents and Jewish homes. More than 250 blacks went on a rampage while screaming "Jews."[199]

Three hours after the auto accident, a 29-year-old Jewish theology student, Yankel Rosenbaum, was attacked on the street by a gang of black teenagers. They stabbed him four times as he collapsed. The police intervened, and he was sent to a hospital, where he died during the night. He had identified Lemrick Nelson as one of the attackers who stabbed him. Nelson was tried for the murder of Rosenbaum but an all-minority jury found him not guilty.[200]

The next day Rev. Sharpton gave a speech which agitated the crowd as he shouted "Kill the Jews." The violence worsened as the police did nothing until Mayor David Dinkins intervened and deployed 2,000 police officers to suppress the riots. Dinkins visited the area personally; the rioters threw rocks at him. The attack against the Jewish community of Crown Heights lasted four days until the police finally restored order.

It then turned out that in addition to Yankel Rosenbaum, Anthony Graziosi was also murdered. He was dragged out of his car, brutally beaten, and stabbed to death because his full beard and dark clothing caused him to be mistaken for a Jew.

Sharpton continued to use the rage and resentment of the black community to gather followers and wreak havoc in Brooklyn, where there was a 180,000 strong black majority and a Jewish minority of 20,000 people.

The Rev. Al Sharpton orchestrated many more media-grabbing events over the years. In 1995, in one event, a Jewish-owned store was burned down and eight people were killed. Sharpton, as usual, refused to take any responsibility for the deaths that he had caused.[201]

During the Obama administration, Sharpton visited the White House 57 times.

Muslim and Jewish Violence

As repugnant as simple racial and religious hatred is, it can also blend with terrorism as a tactic of war. When President Donald Trump decided to recognize Jerusalem as Israel's capital in 2018, a senior Al-Qaeda leader called on Muslims to kill Jews and other Americans.

In the context of increased tension and the series of wars against Muslim countries in the Middle East, seen by many as being promoted by Israel, and with Israel continuing to extend its massive illegal housing settlements on Palestinian land, and its devastating blockade of the Gaza Strip, Muslim attacks on American Jews are going up. This is seen principally where there is an increase in the Muslim population, especially at colleges and universities with Muslim foreign students. University administrators have done next to nothing protect Jewish students who are Americans, while the antagonists are foreigners.[202]

Anti-Jewish and anti-Muslim hate crimes both went up from 2015 to 2016, as reported by the FBI Uniform Crime Reports; anti-Jewish crimes increased by fully one third. Jews were targets of 57% of all American hate crimes in 2016.

One such attack was waged on the Seattle Jewish Federation in 2006. At about 4 o'clock in the afternoon of July 28, Navedm Afzal Haq, shot six women, one fatally, at the offices of the Jewish Federation. This hate crime came about when Haq searched for something Jewish on the Internet. Haq legally purchased two semi-automatic handguns, and with them traveled from his hometown of Pasco, Washington, to Seattle for the express purpose of killing Jews. He entered the Jewish Federation building and at once shot Carol Goldman, an employee, in the knees. He then walked down a hallway, shooting at offices as he passed by. He shot three more women in the abdomen. He then fired at Dana Klein, who was five months pregnant. He shouted that he was a Muslim and then took several hostages. He finally surrendered to police, and was later convicted of homicide and sent to prison.[203]

Jewish students are also threatened physically. They are usually not allowed to speak at meetings, so that their opinions cannot be expressed. Even worse than the behavior of most students towards Jews is the threat which anti-Jewish faculty holds for Jewish students, who can be unfairly targeted in the classroom and whose grades are in jeopardy at the hands of religiously biased professors.[204]

A recent study has shown that expressions of anti-Jewish hate have risen dramatically on American college campuses between January and June of 2018. Anti-Jewish incidents and the suppression of Jewish students' freedom of speech has increased 45% during the same time period.

Of course, all other students have also had their freedom of expression curtailed, as any word or action questioning Israeli practices against Palestinians is disingenuously smeared as "anti-semitism." And ironically, in a country founded on the power of capital, the right to boycott Israel because of its war crimes has also been annulled.

Violence against Muslims in the United States

Since the attacks of September 11, 2001, were blamed on Muslims, violence and legal persecution directed against Muslims living in this country proliferated. Hate crimes against American Muslims have increased 78%. Attacks on people perceived as Arabs rose more. These attacks targeted mostly those wearing traditional Muslim clothes or appearing to be Middle Easterners.

These attacks were fueled by repeated terrorist attacks in Europe and the United States. Some of these attacks involved arson of Islamic institutions. While negative rhetoric against Muslims is in part responsible for this violence, Muslims themselves engage in negative rhetoric when their imams preach anti-Jewish hate at Friday prayers and shout at their congregation "kill all Jews."

It is fairly certain that there are far more hate crimes directed against minorities than is reported, because victims often do not report attacks for fear of inflaming community tension. When three Muslim students were killed in Chapel Hill, North Carolina, the authorities did not bring charges of hate crimes against the neighbor who was charged with murdering them but attributed it to a parking dispute.[205]

Another example of an anti-Islamic hate crime occurred when Ted Hakru, Jr., fired a high-powered rifle four times into a mosque next door to his Connecticut home. In Brooklyn, New York, two women out walking their children in strollers were attacked by a woman who screamed anti-Muslim obscenities and tried to rip off their traditional veils. And in Queens, a man was beaten by three strangers who shouted "ISIS." Also in Queens, an imam and his assistant were shot and killed execution-style on the sidewalk. In Minneapolis, Minnesota, men shouting obscenities about Islam shot Muslim men in traditional religious clothes. In St. Louis, a man was arrested after the police said he pointed a gun at a Muslim family.[206]

The Attack on Christianity in the United States

There are those who claim that Christianity is today (2018) the most persecuted religion in the world. Considering the manner in which Christians have been decapitated in Muslim countries solely because they're Christians and otherwise deprived of the most basic human rights in such countries, this claim may well be true. But even in the United States, reputedly a Christian country, attacks on Christian churches have become frequent and almost routine, even as anti-abortionists claimed that the Christian faith leads them to murder abortion doctors and their associates.

A number of examples of church shootings demonstrate the anti-Christian conduct of the shooters.

On June 17, 2015, Dylann Roof, then 20 years old, killed nine people during a prayer service at the Emmanuel African Episcopal Church in Charleston, South Carolina. Arrested the day after the killings, Roof admitted that he had committed these murders. One may speculate about the numerous motives that led Roof to commit this horrendous crime. Whatever these motives may be, the fact remains that murdering congregants during a church service is a direct attack on Christianity itself.

Roof had a history of drug addiction and had been arrested for number of misdemeanors on several occasions. He owned at least parts of an AR-15 semi-automatic rifle and had six unloaded magazines capable of holding 40 rounds each.[207]

On July 27, 2008, David Adkisson fired a shotgun at members of the Tennessee Valley Unitarian Universalist church in Knoxville, Tennessee. This shooting occurred as the church hosted a youth performance of *Annie*. An audience of 200 people was watching the performance by 25 children when Adkisson opened fire. Greg McKendry, 60 years old, deliberately stepped in front of the gunman to protect others and was killed on the scene.

A 61-year-old woman, Linda Kraeger, died from wounds suffered during the attack. The shooting stopped only when five members of the church seized and restrained him. Adkisson was a veteran of the US Army. Unable to find a job, he expected to be killed by police by shooting into the church congregation. Adkisson defended his murderous action on the grounds that the church members were too liberal.[208]

Early in the morning of December 9, 2007, Matthew Murray knocked on the door of the Youth with a Mission Center in Arvada, Colorado. Murray asked if he could stay at the center overnight. When he was refused, Murray opened fire, killing Tiffany Johnson, the director of hospitality, and Philip Crouse. He also wounded Dan Grebenow in the neck and Charles Blanche in the leg. Murray ran from the scene, but returned at 1 PM, when services had ended at the New Life Church. He opened fire in the church parking lot, injuring Judy Purcell. He then went to the church foyer, where he shot another member of the church until former Minneapolis Police Department officer Jeanne Assam, opened fire on Murray with her personally owned firearm and killed him.[209]

Anti-Abortionists and Pro-Life Agitators

Existence without the threat of violence is an essential prerequisite of democratic life. Among those who seek to suppress speech and actions not in accord with their opinion are those who call themselves anti-abortionists. Among them are some who have committed all kinds of crimes directed at institutions and people associated with abortion. Vandalism, stalking, assault, kidnapping, and murder have all been inflicted on people, while arson and bombing against property have also been used by some abortionists. The United States Department of Justice has considered these matters to be domestic terrorism. Among those who have committed such violence are Michael Griffin, James Kopp, Paul Jennings Hill, Scott Roeder, and Peter James Knight. These men and a number of others with similar beliefs claim commit these atrocities in the name of Christianity.[211]

There can be little doubt that the anti-abortionist violence is a political weapon against women's rights and that it is associated with violence towards women generally. It is further evident that anti-abortion violence is a form of Christian terrorism. The evidence for this is that at least eleven murders occurred in the United States since 1990 which were associated with anti-abortion sentiments. In addition, there have been 41 bombings and 173 arsons at abortion clinics. In 2008, there were 1793 abortion providers in the United States. The 11 people killed by anti-abortionists include four doctors, two clinic employees, and a number of others whom one might label innocent bystanders.[212]

On March 10, 1993, Dr. David Gunn of Pensacola, Florida was fatally shot during a protest. He had been the subject of wanted style posters distributed by Operation Rescue in the summer of 1992. Michael F. Griffin was found guilty of Gunn's murder and was sentenced to life in prison. The murder of Gunn was the first murder of an OB–GYN doctor whose killer sought to prevent the performing of abortions. Griffin, who was 31 years old at that time, waited outside of Gunn's clinics and shot him three times in the back and then yelled "don't kill any more babies." That killing led to the passage by congress of the Freedom of Access to Clinic Act.[213]

On July 29, 1994 Dr. John Britton and James Barnett, a clinic escort, were shot to death outside The Ladies' Center of Pensacola, Florida. Rev. Paul Jennings Hill was charged with the killings. He received a death sentence and was killed on September 3, 2003. Hill had a long history of using drugs and raising hell. After he was baptized in a muddy swimming pool, he found Jesus. At first Hill talked about using the weapon of the spirit against abortion doctors. Later he talked about using a pump action shotgun, as he began to advocate the murder of abortion doctors. He claimed that he himself could never murder. Yet on July 25, 1994, Hill came to The Ladies' Center at 7 AM where he had come before, protesting abortion for a year. When Dr. Britton arrived for regular duty at the clinic wearing a bullet proof vest, Hill raised his gun and shot Britton and Britton's escort James Barrett and Mrs. Barrett. Both John Britton and James Barrett died in the car. Mrs. Barrett survived, badly wounded. Hill had a wife and three children and had lived a comfortable life until he crossed the line from advocate of this cause to murder. The Pensacola clinic had been bombed in 1984 and in 2012.

On December 30[th,] 1994 receptionists Shannon Lowney and Lee Ann Nichols were killed in two clinic attacks in Brookline, Massachusetts. John Salvi was arrested and confessed to the killings. He died in prison; guards found his body under his bed with a plastic garbage bag tied around his head. Salvi had also confessed to a nonlethal attack in Norfolk, Virginia days before the Brookline killings. [214]

On January 29, 1998, Robert Sanderson, an off-duty police officer, was killed when the abortion clinic where he served as a security guard was bombed. The bomber was Eric Rudolph. He was convicted of this murder and received two life sentences. Likewise, on October 23, 1998, Dr. Bernard Slepian was shot to death by James Charles Kopp. Kopp used a high-powered rifle to kill Slepian in Amherst, a suburb of Buffalo, New York. Dr. Slepian was standing in the kitchen of his home when Kopp fired a single rifle shot from a nearby wooded area that entered the kitchen through a rear window. Slepian was a well-known obstetrician-gynecologist who performed abortions at a women's clinic in Buffalo, New York.

After the murder of Slepian, Kopp fled to Mexico under an assumed name. Later, he traveled to Ireland, and from there went to France, where he was arrested on March 29, 2001 while living in the town of Dinan. The French extradited Kopp to the United States upon receiving assurances from Attorney General Ashcroft that the death penalty would not be applied. The French will not extradite anyone who faces the death penalty. Consequently, Kopp was found guilty of second-degree murder by a jury and sentenced to a maximum of 25 years to life. There is a good possibility that the murder of Slepian was not Kopp's only crime. It is possible that, was also involved in the shooting of Ontario doctor Hugh Short.

Kopp had received help from sympathetic anti-abortion activists Loretta Marra and Dennis Malvasi. Both pled guilty to conspiracy and helping Kopp avoid capture. During his trial, Kopp argued that he was innocent of murder because "I have separated murderers from their weapons of mass destruction. I wish I could do 10 life sentences or 10 death penalties to save them," he said.[215]

On May 31, 2009, Dr. George Tiller was shot and killed by Scott Roeder. This was the second time Tiller was shot by an anti-abortion activist. The first time, in 1993, he was shot in both arms by Rochelle Shannon. Shannon was convicted of the shooting and was incarcerated. The second time, Dr. Tiller was shot during worship services at the Reform Lutheran Church in Wichita. Tiller was standing in the hall of the church speaking to a congregant when Scott Roeder approached him, put a gun to his head and fired. Roeder then fled in his car but was apprehended three hours after the shooting. He was charged with first-degree murder and aggravated assault.

On January 21, 2010, Scott Roeder was found guilty of murdering Dr. Tiller, and he was given a fifty-year sentence. Roeder was also known before the murder for vandalizing a women's clinic the week before and the day before killing Tiller. Roeder confessed that he had shot and killed Tiller and said that he felt no remorse.[216]

One of the most atrocious attacks on abortionists and abortion clinics was the murder of three people and the wounding of nine others, including five police officers, at a Planned Parenthood Center in Colorado Springs on November 27, 2015. That mass murder was perpetrated by Robert Dean, a man of questionable mental capacity.[217]

Anti-abortionists also invade abortion clinics and destroy equipment, pour paint all over the premises, and in many other ways vandalize the property of abortion providers. These providers have been greatly reduced the last several years because of the introduction of the French abortion pill, which makes physical abortions less necessary.

Chapter 9: The Influence of Religion on the Media

The Media and Popular Culture

The American media, and particularly television, reflect popular culture. Not all religions receive representation in the American media, nor are all those that are portrayed shown in the same light. Representation of religion on television and in the print media reflects ideologies which are in accord with popular opinion. This is necessary because the media depend for their income on advertisers, who need approval of consumers.[218]

The media, ever conscious of the advertising dollar, will portray members of the majority Christian religion in the far better light than they would portray an atheist, because atheism is most unpopular in the United States. Nevertheless, in recent years Christianity has taken a back seat to almost all other concerns of the media, as secularism seems to have gained more and more adherents in this country.

The fact is that opinions concerning religious groups on the part of media consumers are strengthened or weakened or altered by the manner in which they are portrayed in the media. Moreover, unfamiliar or remote religious rituals and religious behavior is generally omitted from media portrayal because they are unpopular.

The media stereotype religious events and religious persons. This means that in America the majority religion, Protestantism, is generally seen in a positive light, while atheism is generally viewed as abhorrent. It pays the media to portray religious characters in a manner which will conform or at least not disagree with common stereotypes. For example, Hollywood films represent all Muslims as Islamic fundamentalists.[219]

Because Christianity is divided into numerous denominations, television usually portrays Christians as nondenominational, so as to appeal to a large audience. This also allows non-Christians to see the character presently portrayed as a personification of Christianity in general.

Because religion is so emotional, it is important for broadcasting companies to portray any religious episodes in a manner that is approved by those who watch them. This leads to elimination of any representation that the public finds discomforting, so as to produce only episodes that get good ratings. All human beings make meanings of what they experience. Therefore, the media make sure that representations of race, ethnicity, class, and religion are in accord with prevailing stereotypes and acceptable norms. This means that the media give the audiences what they expect, including all kinds of piety and ceremony.[220]

This is particularly true of television, which is available to almost every American, even as reading has become less and less popular, so that fewer and fewer Americans know how to read or are interested in doing so. It takes little education or intellectual capacity to watch television, which even a two-year-old can do. From childhood on, the average American is taught by television how to think about just about everything, including religion. And religion is always presented as morally and ethically superior compared to atheism. At the same time, the media usually portray members of religious groups as happy people in general, despite the fact that religion is represented as inferior to science.

Unflattering depictions of Jews are common on television. The obnoxious and ridiculous lie that all Jews have large noses is continued in the media by assigning actors with large noses the role of Jews in television programs. These actors are usually descendants of Italian and other Mediterranean people who do in fact tend to be the beneficiaries of the so-called Roman nose. Since Judaism is a religion and a Jew somebody who believes that religion, it is impossible that adherence to a religious belief should somehow affect a person's nose. Yet the bigotry concerning the so-called Jewish nose has been perpetuated since the days of assigning such actors as Danny Thomas, a Catholic, the role of the Jew on television. In sum, religions other than Christianity are usually caricatures which reinforce cultural norms, stereotypes, and prejudices.[221]

One of the major changes that the media have been forced to recognize is that television is no longer insular but that it has gone global, so that American television programs can be sold all over the world — but only if all characters, including religious characters, are portrayed at the lowest common denominator. Culture is not produced locally any longer. Furthermore all media programs are now distributed worldwide. As a result, the media ignore any particularism or distinctions between religions, making an effort instead to label all religious people of all faiths as the same.

Different religions have different traditions, which are ignored by television. Religious beliefs guide many a television character's decisions concerning ethical conduct, depending on the principle of legitimacy, which holds that ethics or legitimacy differs from one culture to another. The media, however, give the public a watered down or stereotyped version of alternative lifestyles. In addition, the producers of these television products assume that the audience agrees with these ideas on religion, which may not be the case.[222]

The fact is that religion and the media affect each other. Because modern communication presents all Americans with the fact that there are numerous religions other than one's own, and even a good number of people without religion, the media help everyone to accept multifaith and interfaith relationships. People of all faiths share the same daily newspapers, the same national TV and radio, and the same websites. All of this affects the viewers as the consumers of the media as well as those who produce the media. The secular press exists in a society in which religion is common. This raises a problem for journalists who are expected to fact check the news and make certain that their stories reflect the truth. However, this can't be done with reference to religion, because religion is built on belief and not on objective scientific facts.[223]

In the last few years, the so-called social media networks have become major participants in the media world. About 1 billion users participate in Facebook and Twitter and they discuss religion together with many other topics. In fact 31% of Facebook users in the United States list religion in their profile, which is also true of 24% of users outside the United States. Facebook has installed a Jesus Daily Page which consists of a few quotes from Jesus each day produced by Dr. Aaron Tabor of North Carolina. Evidently it is much easier to find a Facebook site concerning your religion than to actually attend a synagogue or church service. For example, in 2008, congregation Beth Adam of Cincinnati, Ohio, launched an online congregation to reach Jews around the world who didn't have any connection to Judaism.

This effort has been very successful, as it reached soldiers in Afghanistan, old people who are homebound, and others who are isolated. Likewise, the Rev. Kenneth Lillard has written that "Facebook is the best chance for religious leaders to expand their congregations since the printing press helped Martin Luther usher in the Protestant Reformation." A good number of Facebook participants who offer daily prayers or spiritual teaching are not clergy; they are often laymen who invite like-minded people to share their thoughts and faith.[224]

Although there are religion writers in almost all major American newspapers, these writers are often incapable of dealing with the religious expressions of people of faith. This means that religion writers seldom believe what religious people say but presume that there is some other reason behind their actions or comments. Religion writers tend to defend the most radical deviations from the norm. For example, if someone argues that God ordained marriage as the union of man and a woman, most religion writers attribute such opinions to bigotry against homosexuals. A good number of religion reporters do not like Christianity and therefore cannot accept that some truly believe in the tenets of their faith.[225]

The same religion writers would excuse jihadist terror and support so-called liberal justification of that terror by claiming that jihadists resent colonialism or are angry over the Iraq war. However, this is another example of religion being misused to fuel a proxy war that is being carried out as part of the global competition for resources and influence. In fact, most sources say that traditional Islam abjures violence; jihadis frequently have been addicted to drugs and are not truly committed to a holy war.

This failure to understand religion leads many religion reporters to make some gross errors. For example, in 2013, when Roman Catholic Cardinals voted for the next pope, religion reporters asks a Catholic nun, Sr. Simone Campbell, which papal candidate she intended to vote for. This is a ridiculous question since women cannot possibly be priests and surely not cardinals, and so would not have a vote — as anyone except journalists seem to know.

The *New York Times* mischaracterized Easter and called the Jewish holiday of Chanukah (dedication) a festival of Spirit, although it is sometimes called a festival of light. The media also tends to characterize all followers as having the same opinions. For example, MSNBC leaned entirely on The Ethics and Public Policy Center concerning the overview of the papal selection without consulting representatives of most American Catholics. It needs to be understood, of course, that it is almost impossible to write a story that pleases all religious parties. For that reason, it is essential that religion writers familiarize themselves with the sociology of religion, which allows for objective and informed analysis of the functions of religion in general and of particular differences.[226]

Religion in American Television

Religion is not often portrayed in American television. Nevertheless, religion did enter into some television series in the 1990s. Earlier, there were always some radio programs which became television shows after television became more popular than radio. These included the National Council of Churches Programs, as well as programs by The United States Catholic Conference, The New York Board of Rabbis, and The Southern Baptist Convention.[227]

Somewhat later emerged what came to be called televangelism. The televangelists called themselves ministries and were almost entirely outside the mainstream of American religious institutions. These televangelists were fundamentalists or Pentecostals. They included Rex Humbard's *Cathedral of Tomorrow, Oral Roberts and You*, Pat Robertson's *700 Club*, and Jim and Tammy Bakker's *PTL Club*.[228]

Televangelists succeeded in developing their own universities, such as Liberty University, founded by Jerry Falwell, Oral Roberts University, and CBN University, founded by Pat Robertson and renamed Regent University.[229]

Over the years there have been a number of television situation comedies involving religious characters. These programs have not been very successful. They generally make religious characters as conventional as possible in order to avoid controversy.[230]

Televangelism

An evangelist is a "good messenger." Such evangelists have been preaching the gospel for centuries. However, in the electronic age, evangelists have made more progress than was ever possible before the advent of television. Almost all the evangelists appearing on American television seek to promote Christian conservatism as a political agenda. [231]

The fact is that television evangelists have gained considerable political influence because a number of religious leaders recognized that communications technology could be a means of spreading the faith to wider, more diverse audiences than was possible before the electronic age. The enormous financial potential of religious broadcasting led to such innovations as "The 700 Club," operated by the Rev. Pat Robertson on his Christian Broadcasting Network. Robertson's success was copied by a number of other broadcasters.[232] Robertson and his followers have been able to give the viewers a feeling that they are intimately related to an evangelist who speaks to them from his living room. The evangelists seem to be familiar to the viewer, and trustworthy, as the raise money for their cause from viewers glad to give it to them.

There are some Christians who claim that televangelists trivialize Christian rituals, practices, and beliefs. This has led some born-again Christians to develop family-friendly television services.[233]

Whatever the message or the method of conveying it, there are two constants involved in all of religious broadcasting. One of these is a perpetual request for money, which is labeled a "love gift." Some of these preachers stare directly into the camera and tell each viewer that "your miracle is on the way," followed by an appeal to give money. The other is a constant recital by preachers about the immorality of American society. Biblical prophecies of the last days features a review of a litany of physical, spiritual and social ills they intend to defeat by means of the contributions of the viewers.

The Pew Research Center has presented a study of *Participation in Electronic and Off-Line Religious Activities.* That study was conducted in May and June of 2014 and consulted 3,217 American adults. According to that study, 46% of American adults have participated in electronic religious activities online, while only 35% attend religious services once a week. In an average week, according to Pew Research, one in five Americans are involved with religion online, and another 20% listen to religious talk radio, or watch religious TV programs or listen to Christian rock music. This survey also discovered that young adults aged 18 to 29 are twice as likely as Americans age 50 and older to share their faith online. This study also shows that white evangelicals and black Protestants are far more likely than other US religious groups to watch a religious television program. Furthermore, 59% of religiously unaffiliated adults watch religious programs once a week. Among adults who attend religious services frequently, 31% share their faith online in any week, compared to just 8% of those who seldom or never attend religious services. Older adults are far more likely than younger adults to watch religious television in any one week.[234]

Televangelists

Because religion is the only defense that humans have against death, evangelists and other religion promoters have learned to use that human condition as a means of delivering their message. Indeed, sincere and believing women and men may well consider that they can alleviate much of the pain and many of the fears which beset all humans.

There are among those who are most successful in their efforts to convert the world to their religion a few who become nationally famous as the media and the politicians give them the platform promoting their prominence.

No better example of this development is that career of William "Billy" Graham, who reached celebrity status as an evangelist throughout the 20th century and into the 21st century. Ordained as a Baptist minister, he became well known for his Billy Graham Crusades beginning in 1947 and lasting until his retirement in 2005. Graham hosted a popular radio show called *Hour of Decision* and reputedly preached to 215 million people in more than 185 countries. As his popularity grew, it became evident to politicians that they could benefit by being associated with him. Therefore presidents Dwight D. Eisenhower, Lyndon B. Johnson, and Richard Nixon invited him to the White House for the benefit of both the host and the visitor.[235]

Although a registered Democrat, Graham not only supported the policies of Lyndon Johnson, but became advisor and regular visitor to the Republican Richard Nixon. Graham led Nixon's private worship services. Nixon in return attended Graham's East Tennessee revival and became the first president to speak from an evangelist's platform.

Some years after Nixon's resignation, "The Richard Nixon Tapes" were made public in which Graham called Jews "the synagogue of Satan" and further claimed that Jews control the American media.[236]

Graham operated a number of media and publishing outlets. These activities, together with his many broadcasts, allowed Graham to be selected as the most admired man on 60 Gallup polls.

Because of his humility and self-effacement, Billy Graham accumulated so many honors in the course of his life that a separate Who's Who for him alone would hardly hold all these adulations.[237]

Since the retirement of Billy Graham, a new televangelist superstar has become most popular among fundamentalist believers. Joel Osteen, the son of John Osteen, a Southern Baptist pastor, has become the senior pastor of a mega-church in Houston, Texas, the Lakewood Church, founded by his father.

Osteen's televised sermons are seen by over 7 million viewers weekly, and over 20 million monthly, in more than 100 countries. His sermons are broadcast 24 hours a day on Sirius XM radio. Osteen is also the author of seven *New York Times* bestselling books.[238]

Like many other mega-church pastors, Osteen has become exceptionally wealthy. His net worth has been reported between $40 and $60 million. He lives with his wife, Victoria (Iloff) and his family of two children in a 17,000-ft² mansion worth an estimated $10.5 million.[239]

According to the Bureau of Labor Statistics, the average salary of American clergy is $45,000. Mega-church pastors make a great deal more. According to The Leadership Network, an organization seeking to advance the Christian church, mega-church pastors earned an average of $147,000 annually, while some earned as much as $400,000. In addition, mega-church pastors usually receive a housing allowance and health insurance benefits, life insurance, and other benefits similar to what is paid business executives.[240]

Osteen memorizes his sermons, which focus on the goodness of God and living an obedient life rather than on sin. His messages are positive and avoid controversial issues. Osteen's sermons are seen in over 100 countries, which led Barbara Walters to select him as one of the 10 most fascinating people of 2006.[241]

One of the most spectacular televangelists to appear on American television is Jim Bakker, whose inventiveness is indeed unique. With his wife, Tammy Faye, Bakker was able to develop a Christian broadcasting empire which at one time reached 13 million viewers a day and brought in over $120 million in revenues. The Bakkers also built a 2500 acre Christian resort in South Carolina. This allowed the Bakkers to live in a $600,000 mansion Palm Springs, California. The Bakkers also bought a 55-foot houseboat, a Mercedes-Benz, and a Rolls-Royce. They bought diamonds and gold jewelry homes and apartments in various places in the South.[242]

The Bakkers also enjoyed numerous other luxuries. All of this came to a sudden end when it was discovered that Bakker had used $265,000 in church money to buy the silence of a church secretary with whom Bakker had an affair.[243]

In 1991, Bakker was handed a 45 year prison sentence for having cheated followers out of $158 million by selling them time in his vacation resort even though he knew that the space he sold was not available because he had sold it once before. His prison sentence was later reduced by an appeals court to five years, whereupon he reentered the televangelist enterprise and again earning a good deal of money by that means.[244]

Another evangelist who became involved in a sexual scandal is the Rev. Jimmy Swaggart. Swaggart is based in Baton Rouge, Louisiana. As early as 1986, Swaggart had revenues of $141 million annually. Swaggart was accused by a Louisiana television station of extravagant spending, exaggerated claims of financial need, and questionable contracts. He was also accused of spending little of the money raised for projects like a program to feed hungry children for the stated cause. Swaggart is also accused of extramarital sexual behavior, leading to an investigation by his denomination, the Assemblies of

God. According to that investigation, a woman testified that she had several sexual encounters with Jimmy Swaggart at a motel in New Orleans.[245]

With reference to his finances, Swaggart says that about one third of his total budget is spent on television and equipment costs. These expenses, says Swaggart, make him into a nearly full time fundraiser. As a member of the Assemblies of God, Swaggart's operation provides up to $48 million a year to the denomination's missionary activities. Swaggart's revenues come from contributions and sales of products ranging from a $40 leather-bound inspirational library to a $20 children's *Read and Grow* picture Bible. He also sells a $20 greatest hits album of his religious music. Since Mr. Swaggart's operation is a church, it does not have to report its income to the IRS.[246]

The foregoing examples clearly demonstrate the reasons for the decline of the so-called mainline churches in America. Such Protestant denominations as the Methodists, the Presbyterians, and the Episcopalians have lost considerable support in the decade ending in 2017, not only because of a general decline in an interest in Christian theology, but also because the nondenominational mega-churches are far more popular among Protestants than the established "mainline" denominations.

Religious Print Media

Roman Catholic Publications

It is unfortunate that there are some Americans who still persist in believing that all Roman Catholics hold the same views on all subjects and all issues as dictated by the Pope. Anyone who has ever read even one issue of *America*, a Jesuit magazine with a circulation of 45,000, will promptly recognize that this Jesuit publication is willing to discuss all kinds of controversial topics. For example, the October 2017 issue includes the following articles: "Are gun manufacturers and politicians complicit in the Las Vegas massacre?"; "Amoris Laetitia" " (The Joy of Love) deals with the preservation of the family; "The Florida Project" discusses American poverty; "Pope Francis commits the church to protect children from abuse etc."; and other issues. It would be hard to find a reasonable person who would object to a discussion of these topics which concern everyone and not only Catholics.

Most significant concerning *America* is the willingness of the editors to publish controversial articles. Undoubtedly, there are those who disagree with some of the views expressed in this magazine. Yet the writers of the various articles express opinions in accord with their beliefs without seeking to avoid possible criticism.

An excellent example is an article by Gerald Byer concerning the possible complicity of gun manufacturers and politicians in the Las Vegas massacre of October 1, 2017. Evidently the author agrees with criminologists that the responsibility for evil and criminal behavior is not only the responsibility of the perpetrator but is also that of social conditions that contribute to crime.

The Bishop of New York, Timothy Cardinal Dolan, has called failure to keep guns out of the hands of criminals "The Culture of Death."

This article is much longer than what can be reproduced here. It is important, however, because of the willingness of this magazine to confront the gun lobby and gun manufacturers.

In the same issue of *America*, Gerard O'Connell writes that the Pope objects to eliminating any difference between sexes. In view of the current American attitudes concerning this issue, such a discussion demonstrates again the willingness of *America* to confront differences of opinion.[247]

There are numerous other Catholic publications in the United States. Most of these are concerned with local events pertaining to the diocese, which supports a particular publication. In addition, there are national Catholic publications, including *The Catholic Digest*, *Magnificat*, and *The US Catholic Magazine*.

Protestant Publications

A Protestant Christian is a follower of Martin Luther or one of the Protestant denominations derived from the Lutheran Church. Therefore, neither Anglicans nor eastern Orthodox Christians are Protestants. Nevertheless, it has become customary for the American media to label all non-Catholics as Protestants. Included are numerous denominations that differ greatly among one another. Evangelical Christians publish *Christianity Today*, which the *Washington Post* has called evangelist's flagship magazine.[248]

Christianity Today has a circulation of approximately 118,000 with a readership of 260,000, of which 36,000 is free. The magazine publishes such articles as "The Jesus we'll never know."[249] This magazine was founded by Billy Graham as a counterpoint to *The Christian Century*, which is the predominant periodical of mainline Protestantism in the United States.

The Christian Century has a circulation of 36,000. The editors claim that they take a liberal editorial stance. Since the word liberal may mean almost anything, it may be better to look upon this magazine as progressive and reflecting mainline Christianity. The editors say that they seek to support what it means to believe and live out the Christian faith.[250]

In 1900, the erstwhile *Christian Oracle*, founded in 1884, was renamed the *Christian Century*, because the editors believed that the 20th century would be a Century of genuine Christian faith living alongside modern technology. Although heavily criticized by fundamentalists, the magazine promoted Christian activists, who became heavily involved in the civil rights movement. The magazine supported Martin Luther King and published such writers as Jane Addams, Reinhold Niebuhr, Richard Neuhaus, Albert Schweitzer, and Marilynne Robinson.[251]

Examples of the articles that appear in *The Christian Century* may be taken from the September 13, 2017 issue. These include "A God by Any Other Name: Truth and Difference in Other Religions" and "Counter Protesters Greet Free Speech Rally." There is another article dealing with the ordeal of a Canadian Christian pastor in prison for more than two years in North Korea. There is also a review of a book concerning science and its contributions to human knowledge and a review of a book concerning the history of English church music. Another article deals with an excavation in northern Israel of the city of Bethsaida. In another issue of the magazine there is a discussion of the international Fellowship of Christians and Jews and its founder Rabbi Yechiel Eckstein.

There can be no doubt that *The Christian Century* contributes a great deal to fellowship and inclusiveness concerning all Americans of whatever religion, ethnicity, or race.

Because the English were the earliest European settlers in North America, the Anglican or Episcopal Church is the oldest established Christian communion in the United States. Their magazine *The Living Church* includes the career of a retiring bishop, an article about a parish's 50th anniversary, an effort by the Episcopal Church to create new congregations, a communication from the Archbishop of Kenya, and a review of the response of Anglican Church leaders to Mexican earthquakes. The magazine features a number of pictures of clergy as well as congregants.

No doubt the largest Protestant denomination in America is the Baptists, who publish *Credo* magazine. A recent issue of *Credo* features an article called "The Reformation of the Family." The article refers to the 16th century Reformation and emphasizes that Martin Luther married a runaway nun, so that marriage was no longer off-limits to clergy. The issue of *Credo* deals with marriage as a holy institution ordained by God himself. The same issue contains articles called "The Best Compendium of My Life," "Uncommon Union," "The Reformation of Education," and others seeking to collect the believer to the fundamentalist view.[252]

There are numerous other Baptist publications, including *Baptist Bible Tribune, Baptist Standard, Biblical Recorder*, and *Cutting Edge*.

The Methodist Church in America publishes a good number of journals, books, and newspapers. Of particular interest is the journal *Methodist History*, which includes articles such as "The Making of a Modern Education," "Methodism in the American Forest," "Methodist Women Missionaries in Bulgaria and Italy," and "The Saddest Day: Jean Leggett and The Origins of the Incompatible Clause."

That clause refers to the declaration of the United Methodist Social Creed that homosexuality is "incompatible with Christian teaching."[253] Because of this ruling, a Methodist minister named Gene Leggett was dismissed because he openly admitted to being homosexual. The article discusses the issue of homosexuality at length. It is of course evident that all Christian and Jewish denominations have been faced with this development for the past 10 years or more.

The Methodist Church as well as the numerous other Protestant denominations issue magazines, books, and periodicals of all kinds. More recently, all churches of all denominations have also employed the Internet and such social networks as Facebook to distribute their message far and wide. Undoubtedly, the Christian community in America is faced with declining attendance and declining membership, which is also true of the Jewish community in face of the ever increasing number of agnostics in this country.

Jewish Publications

Although Jews officially represent only 1.8% of the American population, there are a large number of Jewish publications available in the United States. One of the most prominent of these publications is *Commentary*, published by The American Jewish Committee. The magazine has a monthly circulation of 33,000. This journal has published articles by such famous authors as Hannah Arendt, Daniel Bell, Sydney Hook, and Irving Howe.

This Jewish publication seeks to defend the Jewish people against bigotry and prejudices. An example of this effort is an article by Jonathan Tobin in the February 11, 2014, issue of *Commentary* entitled, "Presbyterians Declare War on the Jews." The article deals with the effort of Presbyterians and others to boycott Jewish-owned business and economically destroy Israel. The Presbyterian Church has published a 74-page illustrated booklet denouncing Israel. This was sent to all 2.5 million members of that church. The pamphlet even criticizes the Roman Catholic declaration "Nostre Aetate," which seeks to distance Christianity from the deicide myth that blames Jewish people as a whole for the execution of Jesus. According to the article, The Presbyterian Church openly advocates persecution and an almost medieval hatred of the Jewish people.[254]

On October 9, 2017, *Commentary* published an article entitled "The Commotion over Columbus Day," which points out some of the simplistic ideas that are used to discredit Columbus by denouncing him as a racist.

Another Jewish magazine is *The Forward*, which was at one time written in the Yiddish language but has been published in English for years now. The *Forward* has a circulation of about 28,000. It is published monthly in New York City. It was first issued on April 22, 1897, by a group of Yiddish speaking socialists. In modern times, the paper has distanced itself from socialism. It was published as a newspaper in separate English weekly and Yiddish biweekly additions, each with its own content. In 2015, the editor of *The Forward* was the first journalist from an American Jewish publication to be given an Iranian visa. For a few years there was also a Russian edition of *The Forward*, because at the end of the 1990s a good number of Russian Jewish immigrants came to the United States.[255]

Jewish Heritage features articles on Jewish culture by leaving Jewish scholars. *Jewish Magazine* Is a monthly publication dealing mainly with Israel, Zionism, mysticism, and Jewish humor. *Jewish Renaissance* discusses books, art, music, film, theater, and ideas. This also a journal called *Jewish Travel* as well as *The Jewish Week* and *Jewish World Review*, which deals mainly with practicing contemporary Judaism. *Kashrut Magazine* is limited to a discussion of kosher foods.

Moment Magazine has a circulation of 65,000. It was founded in 1975 by the Nobel prize laureate Elie Wiesel. The name of the magazine is the same as that of a Yiddish language newspaper published in Warsaw, Poland, until destroyed by the German invaders. The magazine gives grants to young journalists who write stories about anti-Judaism and other forms of prejudice. Some of the articles published are: "What Does It Mean to Be a Jew Today?"; "What Is Israel's Next Move in the New Middle East?"; "Can There Be Judaism without Belief in God?"; "The Origins of Jewish Creativity;" "Is There Such a Thing As Jewish Fiction?;" "Is There Such a Thing as the Jewish People?"; "What Is the Future of Religious Freedom in the United States?" and many more.

Reform Judaism reflects the concerns of the largest American Jewish denomination. It is the official magazine of the Union for Reform Judaism.

Tikkun magazine, although edited by a rabbi, seeks the destruction of Israel and consistently publishes anti-Jewish propaganda, generally derived from Arab sources.

The *World Jewish Digest* magazine deals with issues facing Israel and world Jewry, and includes articles by such well-known writers as Alan Dershowitz, Charles Krauthammer, and Nathan Sharansky.

There are so many Jewish publications in this country that one might guess from that outpouring of literature that the Jewish community is at least 10 times larger than its actual number. The reason for this considerable literacy lies in the history of the European and American Jews. Sometimes referred to as the People of the Book, Jewish authors also constitute a far greater proportion of all authors than their share of the American population. It is equally remarkable that 85% of all American Jews have at least some college education, compared to 32% of Americans generally.

Fourteen percent of American physicians are Jewish, and the number of Jewish Nobel Prize winners in science is disproportionately high.

Chapter 10: Religion and the Life Cycle

Americans, like all people, celebrate cycle events from birth to death. These events are influenced by religion even among the numerous agnostics. In 2011, two sociologists, Elaine Ecklund and Kirsten Lee, published a study describing the reasons why agnostics and atheists join religious groups, including churches and synagogues. These reasons include marriage to spouses who are religious, giving children a moral education, socializing with relatives and friends, and escaping criticism.

Agnostics and atheists often resort to the use of religious rituals in connection with the life cycle because their families do, and they do not wish to be excluded.[256] According to the Pew Research Center, about one in five Jews with no religious beliefs say they fast during all or part of the Yom Kippur observance, and 70% say they participate in the Passover meal, which has highly religious overtones.[257]

Weddings and the Jewish Tradition

Jewish wedding ceremonies include a marriage contract which is signed by two witnesses. The marriage contract usually has a Hebrew side and an English side. Jewish weddings are conducted under a wedding canopy with four staves supporting a roof symbolic of a Jewish home. While standing under that canopy, the groom gives the bride a ring followed by the breaking of a glass, such as a lightbulb, which lies on the floor and which the groom smashes with his foot.

Prior to the wedding ceremony, the face of the bride is covered with a veil. This ceremony is called by the German word "Bedecken," which means to cover. The purpose of this veil is to remind the Jewish people of how the patriarch Jacob was tricked to marry Leah before Rachel, as her face was covered.

Traditionally the bride walks around the groom seven times when she arrives at the canopy, known in Hebrew as a chupa. This ritual is derived from the biblical concept that seven denotes perfection.

Seven blessings are said at wedding ceremonies by seven guests or by the rabbi. Then the groom drinks a cup of wine and the bride drinks from the cup thereafter.

Most Jewish wedding ceremonies are followed by dancing and eating dinner, with relatives and friends who are invited with a view of contributing gifts to the newlyweds.[258]

According to The Pew Research Center, only one quarter of American Jews say that religion is important in their lives, and only one quarter attend religious services at least once a month. Nevertheless, seven in 10 Jews say they participate in the Passover rituals, and, as previously noted, one in five Jews of no religion say they fast on the Day of Atonement.

A similar result can be found with reference to marriage ceremonies.

Because the Jewish intermarriage rate with Christians is 58% during the first decade of the 21st century, and the overall Jewish intermarriage rate including older generations is about 48%, a good number are married to non-Jews in non-Jewish ceremonies. A Jewish wedding is highly symbolic.

Christian Weddings

The Catholic Tradition

Catholic weddings begin with the priest asking the bride and groom to state their intentions. They are further asked whether they have come of their own free will with the intention of bringing up children. Next they are asked whether they are willing to love and honor each other. Upon their consent, they join their right hands. The groom then declares that he is taking the bride as his wife and the bride makes a similar declaration concerning the bridegroom. Thereupon the priest asserts that what God has joined let no one put asunder. This is followed by the giving of rings. This ceremony concludes with the Universal Prayer.

A Catholic wedding may be conducted according to several options, depending in part on whether both woman and man are Roman Catholics. There is separate ceremony for a Roman Catholic and a Christian who is not Catholic, and yet another ceremony for a Catholic marrying a non-Christian.

As is customary among all Americans, the church ceremony is followed by a reception, which is a dinner dance involving relatives and friends, the taking of pictures, and other customs associated with marriage in this country.

The Lutheran Protestant Tradition

Although there are several branches of the Lutheran church in America who do not agree with one another, there are some essentials to which all Christians adhere concerning wedding services.

Because Lutherans were the first Protestants, the Lutheran Church is an excellent example of Protestant proceedings. Lutheran weddings usually begin with a prelude consisting of hymns played on musical instruments. This is followed by the wedding procession. There is considerable latitude concerning order for service and the words spoken, depending on different pastors in different churches. Usually the pastor greets the bridal party after the processional. Parental consent is given and an opening prayer is included. This is followed by scriptural readings, such as John 2:2–10, Song of Solomon 8:7, or Matthew 10:4-6.

The pastor then delivers a wedding ceremony sermon. The sermon usually deals with the couple's circumstances and life history. Thereafter the pastor blesses the rings and the couple exchanges them, reciting verses from the marriage service.

The service concludes with prayers, ending with the Lord's prayer, recited by the entire congregation. Then the pastor blesses the congregation and the couple before the recession. All of this is accompanied by music of a Christian nature. Non-Christian songs are generally not allowed.

Because there are numerous Protestant denominations, variety of wedding ceremonies exist among them. The Lutheran service is only one example of this variety.[259]

Birth

Because Christianity is the direct outgrowth of Judaism, it is reasonable to present Judaism first, despite the fact that the Jewish population of the United States is no more than 1.8% of the total population.

Traditionally Judaism prescribed that newborn boy babies shall be circumcised eight days after their birth. This tradition relies on the biblical command in Leviticus 12:2, which declares that "on the eighth day, the flesh of his foreskin shall be circumcised". According to tradition, circumcision is a symbol of the partnership of God with man, and will never be broken, as it has been etched into the flesh.

The circumcision ceremony is called brith, which is the Hebrew word for a covenant or an agreement which can never be forgotten. Although some circumcisions are conducted in hospitals, the vast majority are performed at home. The baby to be circumcised is handed by the mother to a female messenger, who in turn heads the child to a male messenger, who in turn carries the baby to where the circumcision will take place. That place is called the chair of Elijah, "The Angel of the Covenant." There the ritual circumciser is known as a mohel. The infant is lifted from the chair of Elijah by an honored participant. In turn, the father places the baby in the lap of his representative, who will hold it. The knife is extremely sharp and double-edged, to cause the least pain possible. The mohel recites, "Blessed are you, Lord our God, King of the universe, who has sanctified us with his commandments and commanded us to enter him into the covenant of Abraham our father."

After the foreskin has been removed, several blessings are recited over a cup of wine as the baby receives its name. Thereafter the community attends a festive meal in honor of the circumcision. After the meal, all are invited to give charity as the father presents a short talk about the significance of ritual circumcision. [260]

A majority of American families practice circumcision, less than 3% do so for religious reasons. The medical journal *Pediatrics* published an article called "Male Circumcision" to the effect that a task force on circumcision whose members are all medical doctors recommends circumcision for health reasons. Consequently, approximately 55% of all American men are circumcised.[261]

Although Orthodox Jews limit recognition of a girl baby to giving the child a Hebrew name and briefly recognizing the parents, Reform synagogues include a ceremony 30 days after a girl is born. These ceremonies seek to emphasize the egalitarian approach of Jewish tradition. This ceremony begins with the phrase: "Blessed be the child whom we now welcome." The child then receives a Hebrew name and both mother and father are honored at a reception called a kiddush, meeting sanctification. In addition, the parents are presented with a "welcome to the world certificate."

Birth and the Christian Tradition

American Christians introduce a new baby into Christianity by means of baptism, which is an age old Jewish custom. The word "baptize" means immersion, and is derived from the Greek word for "to dip." The practice of baptizing has continued in Judaism in that it is required for a convert to immerse himself in water. Jews also use a pool of water called a mikvah to cleanse themselves. This was practiced in the day of Jesus of Nazareth by a Jewish prophet called John the Baptist in the New Testament. He baptized Jesus by pouring water over his head.[262]

Consequently, the Roman Catholic baptism of a child consists of baptizing in water, by submersion, immersion or affusion, i.e., pouring water over the head.

Although the numerous Protestant denominations use immersion by water, i.e., baptize, the meaning and interpretation of that practice differs. Some denominations sprinkle water on the head, while others pour water over the head. Submersion is practiced by Orthodox Churches and several other Eastern Churches.[263]

Evidently all Christians view baptism as an essential aspect of membership in the Christian community.

Maturity

Bat and Bar Mitzvahs

Because life was much shorter in past centuries, adolescence as known today did not exist. Age 13 was viewed by Jews as an age at which religious responsibility could be imposed. Therefore Jewish boys are initiated into adult life at an age which commonly is viewed as the beginning of American adolescence. While orthodox Jews celebrate the coming of age of a girl, the majority of American Jews conduct a ritual for girls at age 12 called "Daughter of the Commandments" (Bat Mitzvah). A 13-year-old boy becomes "Son of the Commandments" (Bar Mitzvah).

In Europe and in 19th century America, Bat and Bar mitzvahs were conducted only in the synagogue. In that tradition, the child read a portion of Bible in Hebrew. The reading usually came from the prophets, although European congregations as well as immigrants to the United States had the child read from the Five Books of Moses.

In the United States, Bat and Bar Mitzvah celebrations usually include a dinner dance on the Saturday night or on the Sunday night after the synagogue ritual. In some instances these dinner dances have taken on rather gross dimensions. This means that an extraordinary amount of money is spent by the parents of the bar mitzvah child. Such ostentatious celebrations include the hiring of an orchestra which plays popular music. Some bat/bar mitzvahs include sports themes. Football players are invited to the 13 year old's party. Some parents indulge children by paying popular entertainers to sing or tell jokes. All kinds of devices are used in some of these celebrations, which lose any religious connotation.[264]

These excesses are generally avoided by rabbis, who view them negatively and as un-Jewish. Undoubtedly some people spend a great deal of money on these bar mitzvahs in order to exhibit their financial success.

It ought to be understood that the vast majority of American Jews restrict bar mitzvah celebrations to religious activities only.

Christian Confirmation

The Catholic Church considers confirmation one of three sacraments of initiation, baptism and communion being the other two. The sacrament of confirmation includes "laying on of hands" and the anointing (*annuere* = Latin, to smear) with oil. The Hebrew word Messiah, the Greek word "Christein," and the Latin word "annuere," all mean "smeared."

All Christians who have been baptized are eligible to be confirmed. The confirmand should also have participated in the sacrament of confession. The Catechism of the Catholic Church lists five effects of confirmation.[265]

It is a custom among American Christians to celebrate confirmation with a confirmation party.

An example of Protestant confirmation is the Lutheran tradition. Martin Luther continued the Roman Catholic form of confirmation on the grounds that confirmation is found in "The Acts of the Apostles." Young people are confirmed in public. Among Lutherans a minister can confirm, while among Catholics this is the privilege of the bishop.

Protestant confirmations vary somewhat between the numerous denominations.[266]

Funerals

Agnostics, atheists, and others cannot escape the lifecycle events that concern everyone. Evidently, everyone needs to confront the death of relatives and friends. Therefore all religious groups have developed ceremonies which seek to ease the pain of losing loved ones.

Among Jews, a blessing is said on learning of news of a person's passing. As soon as a death has been announced, a holy society, consisting of Jewish volunteers, prepares the deceased for Jewish burial. These burial societies are usually affiliated with a synagogue. The burial societies also study Jewish law concerning the treatment of the dead. Jewish law does not allow viewing of a body or opening the casket. From death until burial, some volunteers stay with the deceased and recite Psalms. Jewish law prohibits cremation as well as embalming. Flowers are also not allowed at a traditional Jewish funeral.

Jewish burials take place in a very short time after death, frequently occurring one to two days later. Usually, a rabbi recites a eulogy (good words) concerning the deceased.

After the burial mourners for seven days except on the Sabbath during the seven days mourners stay at home and receive visitors the visitors usually bring food so as to relieve the mourners of cooking. After the burial during a period of 30 days that mourners may not marry or attend any festival. Thereafter the mourner recites a prayer in memory of the deceased for 11 months. This "Kaddish" prayer is also recited on the anniversary of the deceased.

Among Orthodox Jews a good deal more is said and done.

Christian Funeral Traditions

Catholic funeral rites are divided into several parts. The first is called vigil or a wake and takes place during a period of visitation and viewing of the body of the deceased. Some people Include in the wake prayers and readings. Eulogies are also recited at the funeral and during visitations. Either a mass or a funeral liturgy is celebrated at the church or the funeral. At the graveside, the community speaks of all that the deceased will await upon the glory of the resurrection.[267]

Religious Influence on the Calendar

Genesis 2:2 tells us that God rested on the seventh day after creation, which lasted six days. Therefore, Jews have celebrated Saturday as the day of rest. Christians, in order to distinguish themselves from Jews, have designated Sunday as the Sabbath day, and Muslims make Friday the day of rest. In any event, the American working week consists of five days and two days called the weekend. This seven day week is directly derived from religious belief, but imposed on everyone, believer or not.

Likewise, Christmas Day is celebrated on 25 December to commemorate the birth of Jesus. Since the birth date of Jesus is not known, the early Christians, who were all Jews, celebrated the 25th of the Jewish month of Kislev as the birthday of Jesus. The 25th day of Kislev corresponds approximately with the 25th day of December, and is celebrated by Jews as the Festival Of Dedication (Chanukah). It appeared to the early Christians that conversion of Jews to Christianity would be more easily achieved by designating an already normal holy day as the birthday of Jesus.

Because Jewish boys are circumcised eight days after their birth the, Catholic Church designated the eighth day starting with December 25 as the feast of the circumcision. That date was also labeled the first of the year when Pope Gregory the 12th adopted a new calendar and 1582. This calendar superseded the Julian calendar, but kept the months intact according to their Latin names. As a result, September, October, November and December are called the ninth, tenth, eleventh, and twelfth months of the Gregorian calendar, although the Latin names of these months mean seventh, eighth, ninth, and tenth

And so all Americans, whatever they may believe or not believe, live by religious dogma, often without knowing it and without their approval.

It is yet to be seen whether science will put an end to the belief in the supernatural. One thing is certain, however. It is certain that religion is always with us, whether we believe in it or not.

Chapter 11: The Influence of Religion on American Social Movements

Prohibition of Alcohol

There is hardly an American who does not have at least a cursory acquaintance with Prohibition referring to the prohibition of manufacturing, importing, or drinking alcohol. It is well known that Prohibition was a failure. Nevertheless, as a social movement it was a great success in the sense that it grew from an organization representing the interests of a few citizens to inspiring a Constitutional amendment.

It is no exaggeration to say that the temperance movement was the most successful and oldest social movement in American history. At first, prohibition began as a defense effort by those who were adversely affected by the drinking of alcohol. Women were not allowed to drink alcohol, but were often married to men who drank to excess, using money badly needed by their families, losing their jobs for being absent, and, in many cases, becoming belligerent at home.[268]

Those who sought to eliminate alcohol from American life usually based their argument on Christian principles. The movement began in the late 19th century. It emphasized social reform and was at first almost entirely promoted by women who viewed themselves as the Army of God. These women demanded action on the part of the United States government, and did indeed succeed when on December 22, 1917, Congress passed the 18th amendment to the Constitution. That amendment was ratified by the states, so that one year later prohibition was the law. Article V of the Constitution of the United States provides for amending the Constitution either by a constitutional convention or by a two thirds majority vote in the House of Representatives and the Senate, and, in addition, agreement by two thirds of the state legislatures. It is therefore difficult to amend the Constitution. Consequently, those who had demanded this for some time thought they had won a great victory as the temperance crusaders turned from moral persuasion to legal coercion. Prior to the passage of this constitutional amendment, several states had already passed legislation prohibiting alcohol. The first of these was Maine, followed by 13 states that passed prohibition laws between 1846 and 1855.[269]

These moral crusaders formed a number of organizations, including The Prohibition Party, The Women's Christian Temperance Union, The Anti-Saloon League, and the Lincoln-Lee Legion. They also published a newspaper called *American Issue.* At first, the church was the principal voice of prohibition advocates. This was particularly true of the Methodists, who limited alcohol for their members as early as 1790. In 1808, The Union Temperance Society organized with a million members. When all these efforts failed to persuade the US government to prohibit alcohol, the opponents of alcohol founded the Prohibition Party. That party ran its first presidential candidate in 1872. The candidate, James Black of Pennsylvania, received no electoral votes and hardly any attention. Then the Women's Christian Temperance Union was organized in Ohio in 1874. This organization was more successful than the Prohibition Party. The members went from door to door and besieged saloons, singing, praying, and pleading with those inside. Some women stood in the streets and sang hymns, while others broke open kegs of liquor and let it run down the street. This led to the jailing of women who had demolished the property of saloonkeepers.[270]

In 1892, the WCTU claimed to have 150,000 members. These women were also participating in the women's suffrage movement, which did not succeed until 1920, when women finally voted in federal elections, although Wyoming allowed women to vote in 1890. The WCTU attempted to unite with the Prohibition Party, but was rejected because the male dominated membership of that party was opposed to women voting.[271]

In 1893, the Anti-Saloon League was founded in Oberlin, Ohio. This organization became most powerful. Their slogan was "The saloon must go." Motivated by Christian principles, they sought the end of alcohol distribution of any kind by influencing politicians to make liquor illegal. The Anti-Saloon League members announced that "The Spirit of the Lord came among us." With that, they pressured legislatures on a county, state, and federal level to enact anti-alcohol legislation.[272]

The Anti-Saloon League also provided a newspaper called *American Issue* and a six volume work called *The Standard Encyclopedia of the Alcohol Problem*.[273]

Although the 18th amendment to the Constitution appeared a great achievement by the anti-saloon forces, the unforeseen consequences of prohibiting alcohol led to a real disaster in America, as organized crime became the beneficiaries of that constitutional amendment.

Although historians do not agree as to the size of alcohol consumption during the prohibition years, it is a matter of indisputable fact that organized crime benefitted from that development. Shortly after the Volstead Act became effective, alcohol consumption fell about 30 percent. Then the Mafia and other organized criminal gangs made alcohol available to the public, so that consumption rose by 60 percent over pre-prohibition levels. Because numerous Americans produced alcohol privately, it is entirely possible that consumption was even greater.[274]

Because alcohol became more expensive than ever before and profits meeting the demand of the public exceeded by far pre-prohibition levels, so-called beer wars were fought out on the streets of major American cities. These "wars" were conducted by organized crime gangs of various ethnic origins. The murder rate before and after prohibition was repealed demonstrates the violence on American streets between 1920 and 1932. In 1920, the year in which the Volstead Act became effective, the murder rate in the United States was 6.8 per 100,000 inhabitants. The next year, 1921, saw an increase in the murder rate of 8.1 per 100,000. Murder continued at that level or more until after prohibition was repealed by means of the 21st amendment in 1932. The next year the murder rate returned to 6.1.[275]

Over the years, many of the major organized crime killers became culture heroes in the United States. Innumerable books, movies, and television programs have been devoted reciting the exploits of such criminals as Louis Buchhalter, Charles "Lucky" Luciano, Arthur Flegenheimer a.k.a. "Dutch Schulz," and Vito Genovese.[276]

It is no secret that prohibiting alcohol by legislation and even a constitutional amendment failed. In a democracy, laws which contradict popular opinion and the habits and wishes of the majority citizens must fail. The evidence for this is not only the failure of prohibition but also the inability of government to prevent the importation and widespread use of illegitimate drugs, as well as the considerable amount of gun violence to which the American people are subject continuously.

Religion and the Liberation of America Women

Nature has decreed that men living in caves and in jungles or in the world's deserts were physically better equipped to hunt, to fight enemies, and to provide for food and shelter for their families than was true of women. Because women bear children, the division of labor forced women to stay at home and be dependent for the necessities of life on men. This dependency oppressed women for centuries. This oppression was supported by religious beliefs of which the Hebrew Bible is only one example. In Genesis 3, the Bible tells the story of Adam, the Hebrew word for man, and Eve or Chava, the Hebrew word for life. This story tells the readers that Eve, the woman, conspired with the serpent and was therefore responsible for driving man out of the Garden of Eden. Consequently, Genesis 3:16 announces that "your husband will rule over you." Innumerable references to women in the five books of Moses and other books of the Bible confirmed the belief that women were untrustworthy and needed to be supervised by men. In the Greek New Testament, the apostle Paul wrote: "women shall keep quiet in church." Since Paul was a Jew, he transferred Jewish beliefs about women to Christianity, among whom these beliefs flourished from then on. The Muslim religion, Islam, continues these attitudes to the present, although they have gradually diminished among Americans. It is noteworthy that religion oppressed women for centuries, but is also responsible for the liberation of American women from that oppression.

It was during The Second Great Awakening at the end of the 19th century that the egalitarian views of its promoters allowed mixed prayer meetings and the association of women and men at their meetings. Women were allowed to speak at these mixed prayer meetings, although American culture continued to hold that women were to be segregated and that their nature suited them to stay out of active public work or politics.[277]

Despite these public pronouncements, a good number of women engaged in participating in the early women's rights movement, which protested the belief that women should stay out of the public sphere. At first, women who sought to escape these restrictions devoted themselves to religious or reform activities. They entered into the lay leadership of Protestant churches and founded organizations for women only. From the 1860s to the 1890s, women's foreign missionary societies were founded in 33 denominations.[278]

Missionary societies developed numerous missionary training schools, so that by 1916 there were over 60 religious training schools in America. The curriculum of the schools included religious studies, pedagogy, hygiene, citizenship, social and family relationships, as well as Bible, church history, and general history.[279]

During the Victorian age, women also left their homes in order to support The Women's Christian Temperance Union and women's suffrage.[280]

After considerable agitation on the part of women and some men demanding that women have the right to vote, Wyoming became the first state in the union to allow women to vote in 1890. In 1920, by means of the 19th Amendment, women were finally granted the right to vote in federal elections. At the same time, the 1920s saw the so-called higher criticism of biblical interpretation, which led to a reevaluation of women's status in the churches. Then, during the first several decades of the 20th century, Protestant women were allowed positions as professional lay workers in the churches. Furthermore, as early as 1853, a woman, Antoinette Brown, became the first woman to be fully ordained in the Christian ministry in an American denomination.[281]

As a result of Brown's ordination, women began to press for ordination in Protestant denominations, so that significant numbers of women were granted ordination beginning in the 1950s. Lutherans and the Episcopalians delayed such ordination until the 1970s.[282]

In the 21st century, the ordination of women is no longer unusual. Protestant seminaries have nearly as many women as men in programs leading to ordination, and at least one half of the students at the Jewish seminaries are women. Women in the clergy are known to have been more willing than men to involve the laity at significant levels of life. Women clergy have also succeeded in accessing leadership positions in several Protestant denominations. This ascendancy of women into high church appointments is best illustrated by the American Episcopal Church. In 2014 that church celebrated 40 years of women in the priesthood, whose presiding Bishop was Catherine Jefferts Schori. In recent decades, about one half of those ordained as Episcopal priests are women. A number of these women converted from Roman Catholicism because they wished to be priests, which the Catholic Church will not allow.[283]

The Episcopal Church in America has about 2 million members, making it one of the smaller denominations in this country, although the American Episcopal Church is affiliated with the Church of England. That Church became independent of the Roman Catholic Church in 1534 when the British Parliament revoked British allegiance to the Pope and appointed King Henry VIII head of the Church. To this day, the Queen of England, Elizabeth II, continues to hold that office.[284]

Although Catholic women have never been admitted to the priesthood, there were at one time more than 40,000 nuns in America. These Catholic sisters were occupied by teaching in the parochial schools and in nursing the ill. However, Catholicism demanded women's traditional role of wife and mother, a role which was also assigned to millions of Eastern European Jewish women who migrated to the United States between 1891 and 1924. These Orthodox Jewish women centered their lives on the home, and believed, as did men, that they were required to obey their fathers and husbands and to refrain from demanding any prominence for themselves. Reform Judaism introduced some radical departures from traditional Judaism concerning the position of women. Reform Jewish women participate fully in the Reform temple. Unlike Orthodox synagogues who force women to sit in balconies or in segregated parts of the synagogue, Reform Jewish women could sit with family as part of the quorum of 10 necessary for public prayer. The National Council of Jewish Women, a Reform organization, allows women to participate in religious, educational, and philanthropic activities.[285]

The conservative branch of Judaism is an American development. Conservatives did not want to accept the Reform position but nevertheless made numerous changes deviating from the Orthodox. As a result, Reform and Conservative Jewish women often work together in various organizations and on a number of causes. In 1972, Sally Priesand became the first Jewish woman to be ordained a Rabbi. Consequently Conservative and Reform feminism led to the full participation of women and girls in Jewish life, including public ceremonies and all positions and privileges at one time only reserved for men.[286]

The developments in religion inevitably led to extending these privileges to other spheres of life. Traditional female roles have therefore been rejected to some extent because of developments in technology. The time which was once spent in household maintenance was greatly reduced by the inventions of the industrial revolution.

An excellent example was the construction of the first successful American sewing machine by Elias Howe in 1848. Howe did not invent this machine alone. In fact, he relied on the work of Thomas Saint and William Wilson in England, and a French machine, none of which were very successful. The machine was improved later by the American Isaac Singer, who sold his machines all over the world.

The sewing machine relieved women of the continuous and unending effort to make shirts by hand at the rate of 35 stitches a minute. It took 20,620 stitches to make an average shirt by hand, so that a seamstress could produce a shirt in 10 to 14 hours. The poor women who were forced to do this dreadful labor were literal slaves to this continuing need to mend and produce clothing. Even wealthy women were engaged in this perpetual female task from generation to generation. For them, sewing became a social event, as women sewed in "sewing circles" in the company of their friends. Wealthy women sewed embroidery, which could take weeks and even months, and was regarded as a personal expression. Sewing was also used to raise funds for religious organizations and political parties. Of course, men did not sew.[287]

As the industrial revolution progressed and birth control became most efficient, women had smaller families and were able to take advantage of the numerous scientific discoveries and inventions which made household chores far easier and allowed women time to gain an education and challenge the patriarchy. Today, in 2018, female participation in the professions and in business is commonplace. Women now produce higher and higher incomes and achieve more higher education than men, as 60% of American college students are female. Male dominance over women has indeed come to an end in America. That dominance was first challenged by religion, the very institution which had for centuries relegated women to a second-class role.[288]

The Civil Rights Act and "Freedom Summer," 1964

One year after President John F. Kennedy asked Congress to consider his proposal to enact civil rights legislation, the Civil Rights Act of 1964 passed Congress. This important law was promoted vigorously by religious of all denominations in accord with the Social Gospel, which had already been applied to the crusade against alcohol and the effort of women to gain political rights. At the center of the church's efforts to support the civil rights act of 1964 was the National Council of Churches, a Protestant ecumenical body.[289]

In 1962, Eugene Carson Blake, the chief administrative officer of the Presbyterian Church, influenced The National Council of Churches to become active on behalf of James Meredith, a black applicant to the University of Mississippi, who was refused admission because he was black. Blake and others in the NCC became outspoken advocates of church activism in support of racial justice. Blake and other religious leaders were arrested on July 4, 1963, after participating in a sit-in at a segregated public facility in Baltimore, Maryland.[290]

In that same year, the Presbyterian Church General Assembly established a Commission on Religion and Race, with an initial budget of $500,000. It was at this time that Martin Luther King Jr. was beginning to make a major impact on the public by his outstanding speaking ability. King was interested in direct action, as he preached to white churches. By 1963, King had become the leading black interpreter of the civil rights movement to white people throughout the country.[291]

Also in 1963, a Commission on Religion and Race met in New York City and included Jewish and Roman Catholic representatives. That group met with President John Kennedy at the White House in June with a view to pressure Congress for the passage of The Civil Rights Act which they were then considering. In addition, The National Council of Churches organized a march on Washington in which 40,000 church people marched to the Lincoln Memorial in support of jobs and the vote for blacks.[292]

Thereafter, The National Council of Churches organized constant lobbying of both houses of Congress by clergy and others. There were some senators who launched a filibuster after the House approved legislation that came to the Senate for further action. The senators who undertook this filibuster hoped to talk legislation to death. This led a group of Jewish lawyers to visit Iowa Senator Bourke Hikkenlooper, to urge him to vote for the civil rights bill. Daily demonstrations were held in Washington for six weeks until Congress finally passed the Civil Rights Act in June 1964. This civil rights law included a breakthrough in affirmative action for women under title VII. [293]

A year later Congress also passed The Voting Rights Act of 1965.

Voting Rights and the Summer of 1964

The 15th amendment to the Constitution, ratified in 1870, clearly states that the right to vote cannot be denied because of race. Nevertheless, southern whites had disenfranchised almost all southern blacks by the late 1880s. Indeed, the House of Representatives did pass a number of poll tax bills in the 1940s, which the Senate rejected. During the Truman administration, the President's committee on civil rights recommended ending the poll tax. That recommendation had no consequences.[294]

In 1962, the 24th amendment, ratified in 1964, outlawed the poll tax in federal elections. This amendment did not deal with elections on a local basis. It therefore allowed southern whites to use all kinds of obstruction to prevent blacks from voting. It wasn't until 1965 that Congress passed the Voting Rights Act. This act established the registrar system, allowing the federal government to replace southern registrars. The laws suspended the use of literacy tests and other qualifications which had reduced black voting to less than 50%. The law affected mostly Alabama, Louisiana, and Mississippi.[295]

The immediate consequence of this law was the effort of white segregationists to use all methods including violence when it turned out that the traditional methods of keeping blacks "in their place" could no longer succeed. An example of such violence was the conduct of the sheriff in Selma, Alabama, who was accused of beating blackheads in the back of the jail for years.[296]

Despite the fact that this kind of cruelty had gone on for so long, the general population of the United States paid little attention to this behavior before 1964. In fact, less than 5% of the public mentioned civil rights as an important issue during the 1940s and 1950s. Even following the Emmett Till murder and the Montgomery bus boycott, few members of the public were concerned. It wasn't until the 1960s that public attention shifted to the civil rights issues, mainly at the instigation of religious bodies such as The National Council of Churches.[297]

Public attention to the civil rights struggle in Mississippi finally became most important and widespread because of the murders of Andrew Goodman, Michael Schwerner, and James Earl Cheney, who disappeared on June 21, 1964. That disappearance drew the attention of the news media, as hundreds of people searched Cody County in Mississippi even as public officials claimed that the disappearance was a hoax. Even after Cheney, who was black, and Schwerner and Goodman, who were Jewish, were found dead under 15 feet of earth, the killers were not convicted, as the jury composed of Ku Klux Klan members claimed that there was not enough evidence to convict the killers. It was this atrocity which aroused the American public, particularly on the part of Christians and Jews, whose religious sentiments supported the victims.[298]

It is therefore evident that Americans with religious convictions exerted a great deal of pressure on Congress to pass The Voting Rights Act. A good number of Afro-American clergy preached to their congregations as well as to the public concerning their hopes for a better future for black citizens. The most prominent among these preachers was Martin Luther King, Jr., the minister at the Ebenezer Baptist Church in Atlanta, Georgia. King gave several dramatic speeches to huge audiences, which made him the most prominent of the civil rights leaders of the day. Since his murder by James Ray on April 4, 1968, King has become a saint and an unassailable icon. His birthday has become a legal holiday and numerous statues of King have been erected around the country. King was unquestionably a great speaker by using the writings of others with great effect.

King had evidently earned a Ph.D. in theology from Boston University. To attain that degree, he had written a dissertation as is required. Therefore it became painful to his followers when several professors, under the leadership of Clayborne Carson, a Stanford University historian, discovered that King had copied a seminar paper by the French theologian Jacques Maritain.[299]

This came to light in 1984 when Coretta Scott King asked for the publication of her husband's papers. The committee of historians proceeded to review the work of King as a student. In June 1991, *The Journal of American History* devoted half of the issue to King's academic plagiarism.[300]

It is true that Martin Luther King was undoubtedly one of the greatest folk preachers of all time. His preaching ability attracted thousands of listeners and had a great influence on politicians, who were lobbied by King's followers. However, it was known for some time among King scholars that he had plagiarized his speeches by borrowing from such white preachers as Harold Bosley, Harry Emerson Fosdick, J. Wallace Hamilton, E. Stanley Jones, Gerald Kennedy, Halford Luccock, Robert McCracken, and Leslie Weatherhead.[301]

King also plagiarized his dissertation, which was affirmed by a committee of scholars at Boston University. The dissertation had been written in 1955. King's professors evidently did not recognize the plagiarism or did not want to do so. In any case, his doctor's degree was not revoked.[302] Newsweek magazine listed 10 high profile people whose degrees were revoked for similar offenses. Included in that list was Karl Theodor zu Gutenberg, the German defense minister, and nine others.[303]

There can be little doubt that King had a great deal of influence on the passage of the Voting Rights Act of 1965, which has since been amended several times. In 2006, the U.S. Senate voted 98-0 to approve a 25 year extension of the voting rights act. The new bill was signed by President George W. Bush during his visit to a convention of the National Association for the Advancement of Colored People. The House of Representatives had passed the bill one week earlier, including the provision which gives the Justice Department the authority to review changes in election procedures in several southern states and some others. The Justice Department is to ensure that any changes to voting requirements are not discriminatory.[304]

The passage of The Voting Rights Act is without doubt the most dramatic example of democracy in action, as the will of the American people became law in a country governed by laws, not by men.

The Influence of Evangelism and the Bible on American culture

The ancient Greeks imported palm trees from the city of Byblos in Lebanon. They dried the wide leaves of the palm and wrote books on them. The books were then rolled up in a scroll and kept in libraries. To this day, Jews throughout the world write the Five Books of Moses in Hebrew on scrolls and read from these scrolls every Sabbath in their synagogues.[305]

The New Testament is written in ancient Greek; all other books of the Bible are written in Hebrew, the language of Israel. Therefore, there are innumerable translations of the Bible depending upon the opinions of the translator concerning the meaning of the words and paragraphs he translates. There are Jewish, Catholic, and Protestant versions of the Bible. Not only do these differ in part but translations are undertaken over and over again, so that Bibles published a century ago or even a decade ago may not exactly correspond to Bibles published in the 21st century in English. The Bible has of course been translated into just about every language on earth, which causes even more variations. Furthermore, translators are likely to translate according to their beliefs, so that Protestants and Catholics, Christians and Jews do not always produce identical translations.

All told, about 100 million bibles are printed each year, of which about 20 million are sold in the United States alone. Since 1815, 2.6 billion Bibles have been printed worldwide. The Bible has a good deal of influence on American culture, not only because it is widely read, but also because it is used to support political opinions as well as personal conduct. For example, before the abolition of slavery in the United States, Baptist ministers quoted the Bible in support of slavery. Today, Christians quote the same Bible in opposition to slavery and other kinds of bigotry, as both Jews and Christians refer to the 10 Commandments as a guide to conduct and cite Leviticus 19:20 as a source promoting kindness and brotherhood. In the forefront of those who claim that the Bible is to be taken literally as the guide in determining all their actions are some 60 million evangelical (good message) Christians. These Christians believe that Jesus will return when the Jewish people are restored to their ancient land, leading to their conversion to Christianity. This belief in the restoration of Israel was preached by Puritan clergy such as Peter Bulkeley (1583–1659) and Increase Mather (1639–1723) in the 16th and 17th century.

"The Jews," wrote Mather," who have been trampled upon by all nations, shall shortly become the most glorious nation in the whole world, and all other nations shall have them in great esteem and honor."[306]

Bold English and American evangelists became convinced that their beliefs had become reality when Israel became an independent country in 1948. These evangelists established a Christian Embassy in Jerusalem and support the migration of Jews to Israel financially. As the number of Protestant and Catholic Christians has declined in the United States since 1970, evangelicals have held their own and have become politically influential, particularly because the Electoral College method of electing a president gives 60 million evangelicals a considerable amount of influence on the outcome of elections.[307]

Televangelism carries the message of the evangelists by means of television all over the country. Therefore evangelism is indeed a social movement with major influence on American culture.

Chapter 12: The Influence of Religion on Politics

The Constitution of the United States is a political document whose purpose is found in the preamble, which is a succinct statement of its principles. These principles are expressed by its initial paragraph. "We the people of the United States, in order to form a more perfect union, establish justice, insure domestic tranquility, provide for the common defense, promote the general welfare, and secure the blessings of liberty to ourselves and our posterity, do ordain and establish this Constitution of the United States of America."

Evidently, the founding fathers believed that the blessings of liberty were best secured by enshrining religious freedom at the head of the liberties listed in the First Amendment. It is therefore unfortunate that only about 4% of Americans asked about the contents of the First Amendment remember that it deals with religious freedom. This is true of the general American public as well its politicians in leadership positions and others, even including members of the clergy.[308]

According to several surveys conducted over a number of years, only 69% of Protestant ministers are aware that freedom of religion is respected in the Federal Constitution. Only 71% of academics know this. Among high school graduates, only 35% were informed concerning the guarantee of religious freedom, a number which shrank to 31% among college graduates. About one third of government officials and 40% of business leaders and 57% of rabbis were aware of the religion clause in the First Amendment. Fifty-five percent of Catholic priests included in these surveys were acquainted with the contents of the First Amendment.[309]

A study of public opinion in the United States concerning religion and politics revealed that three quarters of Americans think that religion is losing influence in American life. The majority also believe that religion plays a role in United States politics. The majority also believes that houses of worship should express their views on social and political issues. Even the belief that political leaders should express their religious faith has increased from 37% to 41% in the course of four years. Thirty-two percent of respondents to this Pew Research Center study think that churches should endorse candidates for political office, although most Americans oppose such direct involvement of religion in the electoral process.[310]

Because the number of Americans not affiliated with a religion has increased a good deal since 2010, those who continue to identify with religion have become more vocal in speaking out about political issues and the religious views of political leaders. These people believe that religion has a positive influence on society. Republicans are more likely than Democrats to favor religion in public life.

During the past few years, same-sex marriage has become an important political issue in the United States. Here, voters are equally divided concerning that practice, as 41% are opposed and 40% supportive. About half of all voters consider homosexuality a sin. These voters believed that caterers and florists should be allowed to reject same-sex couples as customers on the grounds of their religious beliefs.[311]

According to the Pew survey, the Democratic Party is favored by the vast majority of Afro-Americans, unaffiliated voters, and Jews. The Jewish affinity for the Democrats seems incongruous in view of the strong support Israel receives from Republicans but not from Democrats. Most Republicans are also opposed to illegal immigration. Democrats have no objection to illegal immigration and also favor so-called sanctuary cities.[312]

Some other issues which concern voters include the opinion by 34% of evangelical Christians and 20% of Catholics that in recent years it has become more difficult to be a member of their religious group. A considerable majority of American voters view the Republican Party as more friendly toward religion than the Democratic Party, and six out of 10 Americans say it is important for members of Congress to have strong religious beliefs.[313]

Religious Beliefs Among Members of Congress

The 115th Congress includes an overwhelming number of senators and representatives who are Christians. This is true of 91% of the membership. This constitutes a slight decrease of Christian membership from 95% in the 1960s. The share of Americans who view themselves as Christians has declined from over 80% to 71% in 2017. Among the general American population, those without a religion have grown a good deal. This, however, has not been true of politicians because the general public, including those without a religion, would prefer to vote for an elective representative who is religiously affiliated. When it comes to atheists, it appears that those who subscribe to that view have hardly a chance of being elected to anything. In short, being a nonbeliever is a political liability.[314]

About 13% of the 115th Congress affiliate with a non-Christian religion. Eight percent of the members of Congress are Jews. Since Jews are only 1.8% of the American population, they are more than four times overrepresented in Congress. 31.4% of members of Congress are Catholics, a minority religion, whose followers constitute 21% of the American population. Three Buddhists, two Muslims, and one Hindu are also members of Congress. Only one member of Congress, Representative Kristin Simena, is religiously unaffiliated.[315]

Religion and the Presidency

All but one of the forty four men who have been President of the United States have been Protestants. The exception was John F. Kennedy, a Catholic. In 1928, the Democrats nominated the governor of New York, Alfred E. "Al" Smith, as their candidate for the presidency. Smith lost when only eight states of the 48 states gave him 87 electoral votes. Herbert Hoover won 444 electoral votes in 40 states.

Over the years it has been assumed that Hoover won such a landslide victory because Smith was a Catholic. From then on, until the election of Kennedy in 1960, it was assumed by the media and all commentators that a Catholic could not be elected President. Yet, in later years, historians have challenged this popular opinion. In 1960, Richard Hofstadter wrote, "There was not a Democrat alive, Protestant or Catholic, who could have beaten Hoover in 1928."[316]

The historian Robert K. Murray wrote in 1956: "the Bible belt Republicans were not the only political species who sought the demise of the former employee of the Fulton Fish market."[317]

Those who have reviewed the election of 1928 speculated that it was not religion which defeated Smith, but his social class and his association with New York City, which rural and small town Americans viewed as obnoxious, un-American, and arrogant. Furthermore, Republicans in 1928 viewed Smith as an uneducated boor, not fit to sit in the White House. In addition, many

Americans in 1928 saw Smith as an opponent of prohibition who would defeat all the efforts of the Women's Christian Temperance Union and other enemies of the consumption of alcohol. It was rumored that Hoover was "sound on liquor" but that Smith was not.[318]

Undoubtedly, factors other than religion also influence of the outcome in 1928. Nevertheless, the anti-Catholic attitudes in the 1920s were such that the candidate's Catholicism played a major role in that election.

When John Kennedy was nominated as the Democrat candidate for the presidency in 1960, some voters had misgivings about his religion. Then, just as in 1928, there were Protestant preachers who doubted the loyalty of the candidate to the United States Constitution on the grounds that the Catholic would follow the dictates of the Italian Pope. Nevertheless, Kennedy was a wealthy aristocrat with a Harvard accent. Mrs. Kennedy, Jacqueline Bouvier, was a French-speaking educated woman who seemed to make a perfect First Lady. Furthermore, by 1959–60, the rural population of the United States had declined from 44% to 30% and the number of Catholics in America had increased substantially. Despite these advantages, Kennedy beat Nixon by a margin of only 0.17% of the popular vote, although the electoral vote favored Kennedy 303 to 219.[319]

In 2016, the Jewish Senator from Vermont, although an independent, ran in the Democratic Party presidential primary. Since Sanders was not a registered Democrat and was more than 70 years old, it was indeed surprising that he was able to attain the votes of over 13 million Americans, winning 1865 delegates from 23 states. That was certainly not enough to beat the front runner Hillary Clinton. It is nevertheless indicative of the willingness of the American people to consider a Jew for president of the United States.[320]

Local Politics and Religious Convictions: Homosexuality

"All politics is local," said former Speaker of the House Thomas "Tip" O'Neil. That insight applies to such controversial issues as same sex marriage, abortion, and the death penalty, all of which have religious implications.

The Bible rejects same sex marriage altogether, as may be found in Leviticus 18:22, which holds that: "you shall not lie with a male as one lies with a female; it is an abomination," and Leviticus 20:13 repeats this prohibition with the words, "if it is a man lies with a male as he lies with a woman, both of them have committed a detestable act; they shall surely be put to death. Their blood guilt is upon them."

These biblical prohibitions made their way into the laws of the United States as early as 1636, when the first known sodomy trial was conducted in

New York. The accused, Jan Creoli, was found guilty of sodomy, for which he was sentenced to death and "burned to ashes."[321]

These laws persisted into the 1980s, although penalties for sodomy gradually lessened and finally the sodomy laws were abolished in 2016 in all but 12 American states. Although the Supreme Court held sodomy laws unconstitutional, twelve states as of 2016 continued to maintain such laws. Except for Michigan and Vermont, the states all belong to the so-called Bible belt. The states are: Alabama, Florida, Idaho, Kansas, Louisiana, Mississippi, North Carolina, Oklahoma, South Carolina, and Tennessee. This abolition was precipitated by the events of June 27, 1969, when 13 people inside the Stonewall Inn in New York City were arrested by the police for homosexual activities. That police raid led to a six-day rebellion, involving the throwing of a firebomb into the bar, smashing windows, uprooting parking meters, throwing cobblestones, throwing beer bottles and repeated singing of "We Shall Overcome." The consequences of this uprising was a gradual recognition by the public that homosexuality cannot be suppressed by laws or by police action.[322]

Although strict Bible believers have lost their battle against homosexuality in the courts, their religious views have not changed, as almost all of them belong to congregations that view homosexuality as a sin.

Abortion

Not only homosexuality, but particularly abortion, has played a large role in fomenting disputes, in this instance between so-called pro-life anti-abortionists and those who believe that a woman has a right to choose whether or not to get an abortion.

This dispute has become an issue in America's political life, particularly in connection with presidential elections. Prior to the 20th century, abortion was not much of an issue, because women gave birth to large numbers of children, many of whom died before reaching maturity. Indeed, abortion was not favored by either Christians or Jews in the earlier years of the Republic. However, it received little consideration until the liberation of women from domestic slavery was gradually attained.

Until the Supreme Court of the United States decided in *Roe v. Wade* that Norma McCorvey had a constitutional right to abortion, the dispute between those favoring abortion and those who opposed it remained within the realm of political debate, as supporters of each side voted for candidates for public office whose opinions reflected their own.[323]

After *Roe v. Wade* had been decided, the anti-abortionists would no longer use the courts to gain their ends, so that some of those with strong religious convictions against abortion resorted to violence.

A horrible example of such violence was the murder of Dr. Barnett Slepian in Amherst, New York on October 24, 1998 by James Kopp. Kopp shot Slepian with a high-powered rifle from the dark backyard of Slepian's home as the doctor was standing in his lighted kitchen with his family. This atrocity was reported all over the world and in all American media. That murder was an example of how anti-abortionists tried to achieve their goals through violence rather than through the political process.[324]

For many years, the dispute about abortion was nonviolent. Before *Roe*, opponents of abortion relied almost entirely on legislative action without anti-abortion violence.

The first anti-abortion statute was passed in Connecticut in 1821. By 1828, New York, Missouri, and Illinois had passed similar laws.[325] The American Medical Association campaigned against abortion in the 1850s, labeled abortion the unwarrantable destruction of human life, and claimed that children are being murdered before they have seen the light of this world.[326]

Throughout the 19th century, legislators invented more and more abortion related laws. Public opinion at that time accepted legal abortion as more and more restrictions were placed on it without engendering any violence. Yet, after *Roe*, abortion opponents felt they had been deprived of their political power to effect democratic change.[327]

After the removal of abortion from the political process, anti-abortion violence began. The National Abortion Federation reported that from 1977 to 1983, 140 incidents of violence against abortion providers occurred, including eight bombings and 13 arsons. In 1984 there were 11 bombings and 14 arsons at abortion clinics, in 1985 there were 148 incidents, and 133 incidents in 1986. After 1987 violence decreased. By 1988 there were only 53 incidents, but thereafter violence increased again.[328]

In 1987 a group which called itself Operation Rescue was founded by Randall Terry. Terry attracted numerous Protestant fundamentalists to join his campaign of civil disobedience.[329] This tactic led to a major reduction in violence, as another 88 clinics were blockaded and more than 11,000 arrests resulted from this action. At the same time, more abortions were performed than ever before, so that the National Abortion Federation reported that in 1988 there had been 1,500,750 abortions.[330]

Operation Rescue did not succeed for long. Protesters were given jail terms and the New York office of Operation Rescue was fined $450,000 and had to close their offices when they could not pay the fine. Then clinic access laws were passed. The first such law was passed in Maryland. That law and subsequent laws and other states prohibited interference with entry or exit from a medical facility. Congress then passed the Freedom of Access to Clinic Entrances Act in 1994. This act led to a near end to these protests.[331]

In 1992, the Supreme Court decided in *Planned Parenthood v. Casey* that the right to an abortion would essentially remain the law. This decision was a great disappointment for the anti-abortionists, who resorted to violence again. In 1992 there were 196 acts of violence against abortion providers, and in 1993 these incidents reached 437 and the murder of Dr. David Gunn in Florida.[332]

Neither violence nor appeals to the courts could settle the dispute between those who call themselves pro-life and those who were labeled pro-choice. Instead, science ended the argument when in 1980 an abortion pill called RU486 was developed in France.

Although it took another decade before the pill was approved by the FDA, it became available to American women by traveling to France or by obtaining it on the black market or through friends and relatives. The pill made abortion private and eliminated surgical abortions. For politicians, this meant that they no longer had to side with opponents or supporters of abortion. Nevertheless, opponents of abortion now claimed that RU486 cheapens the value of human life, that RU486 means "better killing" through chemistry, and that RU486 means chemical warfare against children in the womb.[333] Most extreme was the contention that RU486 was used to do to children what the Nazis had done to the Jews.[334]

The Death Penalty

Because all members of the European Union have abolished the death penalty, the United States remains the only industrialized Western democracy which retains this barbarism in the 21st century. Twenty-seven states of the union and the federal government continue to keep the death penalty. This means that 23 states have either abolished the death penalty or it is subject to a gubernatorial moratorium, as is the case in Colorado, Pennsylvania, Washington, and Oregon.[335]

In 2004, the New York State Court of Appeals, New York's highest court, ruled that the capital punishment law violates the state constitution. This 4-3 ruling effectively ended the death penalty in New York. Since the last execution in New York had taken place in 1995 because juries would not impose capital punishment, it had been evident for some time that the death penalty was not popular in New York State. This unpopularity can be traced to the religious beliefs of New York citizens influenced in the main by Judaism and Christianity.[336]

Because the Five Books Of Moses prescribed over 30 reasons for applying the death penalty, those not acquainted with Judaism believe that modern Jews continue to support the death penalty in so many instances. Since Judaism has been based on the Talmud for centuries, much of what is found in the so-called Old Testament no longer applies.

The Talmud, a word meaning scholarship, consists of numerous volumes of lectures and debates by many rabbis over the centuries. This can be understood by considering that the Talmud is equivalent to the publication of all the lectures on all subjects taught at Harvard University since it began in 1636.

The rabbis found innumerable circumstances and reasons why the death penalty definitely should not be applied for any of the offenses mentioned in the Torah (five books of Moses), so that, in effect, the death penalty was no longer used and was abolished in Israel in 1956.[337]

Because the Jewish population of the United States is less than 2%, we must look to Christian opinion concerning the death penalty in this country. There are numerous Christian denominations in America, all of which make official statements concerning various social issues including capital punishment. Despite these pronouncements, there are a good number of Christians, as well as agnostics, who disagree with these official positions. Therefore, there are some states in the union where a candidate for public office can only be elected if he favors the death penalty. This is true of Alabama, Texas, Georgia, Louisiana, Florida, and California, and may well be true also of other states.

The Roman Catholic position concerning capital punishment has changed considerably over the years. Throughout its long history, the Catholic Church used capital punishment not only for violent crimes such as murder, but also in an effort to bring about religious conformity.[338]

The present American Catholic church no longer condones capital punishment. Pope John Paul II, Pope Francis, and the United States conference of Catholic Bishops have advocated for the outright abolition of the death penalty. The most recent edition of the Catechism of the Catholic Church rejects the death penalty on the grounds that it violates the dignity of the human person.[339]

Because American Protestantism includes many denominations, no one Protestant position is available. However, it appears that the various denominations are generally opposed to the death penalty. The Lambeth Conference of the Anglican and Episcopalian bishops condemned the death penalty in 1988. Likewise, 54 other American Protestant denominations reject capital punishment. There are, however, 26 Protestant denominations which affirm capital punishment. Included among those who support the death penalty is the Southern Baptist Convention, one of the largest Christian denominations in America.

The southern states which have a large Baptist following are therefore subject to the political aspects of this practice. A good number of Christians who belong to denominations that support the death penalty will not vote for a governor or other candidate for political office who does not support this ultimate penalty.

Religion in the Schools and the First Amendment

The influence of religion on politics has caused so much misery over the centuries that the Latin writer Lucretius (99-55 B.C.) wrote that famous sentence "*Tantum religio potuit suadere malorum,*" or "Religion has persuaded us to so much evil."[340]

That evil was well known to our third president Thomas Jefferson and to the founding fathers who inserted the First Amendment into the Constitution of the United States. That amendment prohibits the government dealing with religion, to the effect that Congress may make no law respecting an establishment of religion, or prohibiting the free exercise thereof. Despite this prohibition, religious bigotry and hatred led some Americans to commit atrocious violence between Protestants and Catholics in this country.

It 1844, on May 6 and May 8, so-called Bible riots occurred in Philadelphia, Pennsylvania, as Protestant nativists reacted to the rumor that Catholics were trying to remove the Bible from the public schools. This belief led to a deadly riot, resulting in the destruction of Catholic churches and many other buildings. Riots erupted again in July, as nativists and soldiers seeking to protect Catholic Churches shot at each other, leading to deaths and injuries.[341]

In 1844, the potato famine in Ireland led to the emigration of Irish Catholics to the United States. These Catholics sent their children to the local public schools. In Philadelphia, schoolchildren began the day reading the Protestant or the King James Version of the Bible in the morning. This led the Roman Catholic Bishop Francis Kenrick to write a letter to the Board of Education asking that Catholic students be allowed to read the Catholic or Douay version of the Bible (After Martin Luther translated the Bible from Hebrew and Greek into German, he wrote that all translations depend on the views of the translator, who has several options concerning the words he wishes to use. Therefore both the King James Version and the Douay Version are inaccurate).[342]

On learning about the letter from Kendrick, Protestants claimed that the Pope was trying to remove the Bible from all schools. Nativist speakers incited citizens to assault Irish Catholics, which led to fighting and killing of nativists. This in turn caused a bomb attack on the Seminary of the Sisters of Charity and several Catholic homes. The next day, May 7, 1844, speakers demanded that Americans defend themselves "from the bloodied hand of the Pope." This led the rioters to burn down St. Augustine Catholic church.[343]

In 1844, James Polk was elected the 11th president of the United States. The Philadelphia Bible riots became an issue in that election, as the Democratic Party damned the Native American party. The major outcome of the riots was the creation of Catholic schools.[344]

After the riots subsided, it turned out that at least 14 people had been killed, and an estimated 50 people were injured. 200 people fled their homes, and damages totaled $159,000, which was equivalent to $3.94 million in 2016.[345]

Some Supreme Court Decisions

It is remarkable that none of the courts including the Supreme Court of the United States intervened in 1844 to enforce the First Amendment's guarantees of religious liberty. It can be shown that courts were convinced that whatever was Protestant was also public. The fact remains that it wasn't until 1940 that the Supreme Court finally reviewed a Pennsylvania law requiring students in school to salute the flag of the United States. The court ruled that such a salute was legitimate and allowed by the Constitution (Minersville School District).[346]

In *Cantville v. Connecticut* in 1940, the court ruled that the state was entitled to require a permit to solicit religious or charitable purposes. The court supported these solicitations and held them legitimate.[347]

Perhaps the most important Supreme Court decision concerning religion and education was decided in 1947 case of *Everson v. Board of Education*. The court decided that a law allowing reimbursement to parents who sent their children on buses operated by the public transportation system for public and private schools, including parochial Catholic schools, was constitutional and allowed under the First Amendment.[348]

In *Engel v. Vitale*, the Supreme Court ruled in 1962 that a New York nondenominational prayer in school violates the Establishment clause of the First Amendment. Such a prayer was therefore ruled unconstitutional.[349]

In 1963, the Supreme Court ruled in *School District of Abington Township, Pennsylvania v. Schempp* that the public schools could not require students to participate in classroom exercises involving daily Bible verse readings. The law was struck down because it violated the First Amendment.[350]

An Arkansas law prohibiting the teaching of evolution was rejected by the Supreme Court in *Epperson v. Arkansas* (1968) because it violated the free-speech rights of teachers and the establishment clause of the First Amendment.[351]

Lemon v. Kurtzman (1974) dealt with a Pennsylvania law reimbursing religious schools with state funds for textbooks and teachers' salaries for nonpublic, non-secular schools. The court held that this violated the establishment clause of the First Amendment and that this law constituted an excessive government entanglement with religion.[352]

In *Stone v. Graham* (1980), a Kentucky law, mandating the display of the Ten Commandments in public school classrooms, violated the establishment clause of the First Amendment and was therefore prohibited by the Supreme Court.[353]

Likewise, in 1982, in *Mueller v. Allen*, the Supreme Court struck down a Minnesota state law allowing taxpayers to deduct from their state income tax expenses incurred in providing tuition, textbook, and transportation to parochial schools.[354]

In 1987, the Supreme Court held unconstitutional a Louisiana law that forbade the teaching of the theory of evolution in public schools unless accompanied by instruction in "creation science." The court held that the Louisiana statute violated the establishment clause and that the state sought to employ the symbolic and financial support of government to achieve a religious purpose.[355]

In 1992, in *Lee v. Weisman*, the court prohibited clergy led prayer at public school graduations in Providence, Rhode Island. Justice Anthony Kennedy wrote that clergy led graduation prayer created a state-sponsored and state-directed religious exercise in public schools and therefore violated the establishment clause of the First Amendment.[356]

In *Santa Fe Independent School District v. Doe* (2000) the court ruled that student led prayer at football games violates the establishment clause of the First Amendment. The court held that the policy failed for having no secular purpose and because it was implemented with the purpose of endorsing school prayer.[357]

It is evident from the foregoing that the Supreme Court of the United States has defended the religion clause of the First Amendment continuously throughout the 20th century and into the 21st century. Every effort to circumvent the First Amendment in this regard has been struck down. In view of this Supreme Court attitude as well as the relative decline of interest in religion in the United States, it is unlikely that the kind of religious violence occurring in Philadelphia in 1844 will be repeated in the future. It appears that religious bigotry is on the wane in the United States. This achievement may well be a welcome example showing that racism, sexism, and ageism may yet be overcome by the people of the United States by committing themselves to that great phrase that Thomas Jefferson inserted in the Declaration of Independence: "that all men are created equal."

Chapter 13: The Influence of Religion On Social Stratification

In 1904–1905, Max Weber, a German economist and sociologist, published a book which has been discussed and reprinted for 113 years.

Die Protestantische Ethik und der Geist des Kapitalismus or, *The Protestant Ethic and the Spirit of Capitalism*, is based on the relationship between the ethics of Protestant Chistianity and modern capitalism. Weber argues that the religious ideas of the Calvinists led to the creation of the capitalistic spirit. Weber observes considerable correlation between being Protestant and being involved in business. According to Weber, capitalists view profit as a virtue. This virtue is related to the concept of a "calling." Luther used the German term "Beruf," which means calling by God to one's occupation, no matter what it may be.

Weber shows that the Calvinists who founded the Massachusetts Bay Colony believed in predestination to the effect that God determines in advance who is and is not saved. Therefore these Calvinists thought that worldly success in business was a sign one had been saved in the next world. Weber did not claim that Protestantism caused capitalism, but that it was only one contributing factor.[358]

The difference between the Protestant view of eventual salvation and the Catholic teaching concerning salvation is considerable. Catholicism teaches *Ex Cathedra non Sallus est*", or, "Outside the Church there is no Salvation." Consequently, the Protestant inducements towards financial gain, such as the rejection of luxuries in favor of saving money, the investment in business to increased profits, the belief in hard work, and the view that the poor have only themselves to blame, are all absent from Catholicism.

In the 21st century, long after the Massachusetts Bay Colony has disappeared, Protestants and Jews have a household income exceeding Catholics. Of all Protestant denominations, Episcopalians have a household income exceeding all other Protestant denominations. According to the *Pew Religious Landscape Study*, 35% of Episcopalians have a household annual income of $100,000 or more, and 34% of have a household income of $50,000-$99,999. Only 19% of Episcopalians experience a household income of $30,000 or less.[359]

Episcopalians have therefore been called an American elite. Some have joked that God must be an Episcopalian from Boston. While that is unlikely, this small denomination of 3,100,000 members, or 2% of the country's population, has a greater economic impact on the United States than any other group. One reason for the ascendancy of the Episcopalians is that they have been in the United States since the settlement of Jamestown in 1607.

Because Episcopalians were some of the first European –Americans, they have disproportionately become America's social aristocracy. Their conduct and their mores and their religion are frequently adopted by non-Episcopalians. Episcopalians are considerably wealthier and better educated than other American Christians. Episcopalians are disproportionately represented in the upper regions of American business, law, and politics.

For example, while only 2% of Americans are Episcopalians, one in every seven members of Congress belongs to that church. Among cabinet members of several presidents before Trump, two of every 14 cabinet members have been Episcopalians. A study by Fortune Magazine found that one of every five of the country's largest businesses was run by an Episcopalian, and one in three of the country's largest banks was also run by an Episcopalian. A Gallup poll in 1981 showed that one of every two Episcopalians earned more than $20,000 a year, which at that time was true of one of every five Americans generally. About one half of all Episcopalians are either in business or in one of the professions, which is double the number among all other Americans.

Two thirds of the signers of the Declaration of Independence were Episcopalians. That is also true of such prominent families as the Vanderbilts, Astors, Morgans, and Whitneys.

Because of its power and wealth, the church has attracted numerous people who seem to join the Episcopalians because they wish to be upwardly mobile and not because of a religious commitment. Episcopalians are evidently very rigid and conservative. They belong to the same clubs, marry the same people, and inherit fortunes. Episcopalians seek out professions in the business world. They also make considerable contributions to libraries and universities as well as art museums. Everything that is true of Episcopalians is also true of American Jews.[360]

According to The Pew Research Center, American Jewish household income is the highest of all denominations in the United States. 44% of Jewish households have an income for one hundred thousand dollars a year or more, and 24% have an income of $50,090 to $99,999. 16% of Jews lived below the poverty line.[361]

Since Jews are a minority of only 1.8% of the American population, their exceptional income is highly correlated with the level of education. 59% of American Jews have a college degree, and only 3% have less than a high school education. Only Universalists and American Hindus exceed these numbers.

Since the Jewish population of the United States were not Puritans and did not come in the 17th century but, in the majority, at the end of the 19th century, it would seem that the Weber hypothesis concerning the Puritan religion and capitalism does not hold. However, the German sociologist Werner Sombart wrote in 1911 that sociologists identify Jews with Puritans as having the same attributes, such as frugality, sobriety, and a rational approach to business and to life in general.[362]

It is furthermore of considerable importance that the Puritans viewed themselves as the New Israel and structured their American colonies entirely based upon the Hebrew Bible. The Puritans believed that they had sailed to the new Israel in America. John Winthrop (1588–1649), the founder of Massachusetts Bay Colony, taught followers that it was their mission to establish in America a society modeled on the sacred Jewish Bible. The pilgrims regarded themselves the chosen people and the elect of God. They believe that the Hebrew prophets were speaking to them and they adopted a Mosaic form of government based on the Five Books of Moses. The Puritans used Hebrew names such as Daniel, Jonathan, Esther, Enoch, Rachel, and many others. They tried to live literally by Hebraic laws and made the Sabbath an obligatory day of rest. In short, Puritans were more Jewish than they were Christian, so that the affinity of Judaism and Christianity became secured early in American history.[363]

Because religion influences social class and vice versa, an explanation for the relative low income population among the 50 million American Baptists may be attributed to two historical factors.

American Baptists have a low household income; 32% of the Southern Baptist Convention have incomes of less than $30,000 a year. Fifty-three percent of American Baptist Churches, U.S.A., have a household income of less than $30,000, and 49% of The National Baptist Convention have a family income of less than $30,000.[364]

At least 20% of American Baptists are Afro-Americans. The median household wealth of America's black population in 2014 was $6,446, compared to the median household wealth of the white population, which was $91,425.[365]

This enormous discrepancy leads Afro-Americans to regard their poverty as the consequence of discrimination, while whites, and particularly evangelical Protestants and mainline Protestants, view this difference as caused by a lack of motivation.[366]

Religious Influence and Private Education

There are a number of private schools in the United States sponsored by religious communities. The largest of these are the Catholic schools. There are also a number of private Jewish schools in this country, and a few Protestant schools such as the Lutheran schools. In addition, the United States has a number of elite and very expensive boarding schools. These schools were mostly founded in the 19th century, although many are more recent. Among these is the Phillips Andover Academy located in Andover, Massachusetts. It was founded in 1778 by members of the Episcopal Church. It is today regarded as first among the 50 so-called "best boarding schools in the United States." This is a high school for the children of the rich and the superrich, although financial aid is available to some students. The tuition at that school is $53,271 for boarding students and $41,608 for day students. Books and supplies cost $900. In addition, students must pay for travel from and to home and furthermore need additional money for daily expenses of a private nature. Unlike public high schools, which have 30 students or more in each class, the Academy has only 11 to 16 students in each class. Phillips Exeter has an endowment of $1,150,000,000, which allows them to offer some students tuition reduction. This school teaches 417 courses, including the normal and usual English, mathematics, social studies, and science subjects. In addition, however, there are such courses as 20th century Russia, A Study of Human Sexuality, Absolutism and Revolution 1660–1800, Elementary Japanese, Advanced Astronomy Methods, Advanced Chinese, African Drumming, Algorism, and Public Policy.

The alumni of Phillips Exeter are generally of great wealth and influence in the United States. The 14th president of United States, Franklin Pierce, was a graduate of Phillips Exeter. His distant relative, Barbara Pierce Bush, was the first lady in the administration George H. W. Bush, the 41st president of the United States. That union was no accident, as George Bush visited girls' private schools with students from a financial background similar to his own in order to find a wife. The son of Prescott Bush, a wealthy Connecticut banker and Senator of the United States, George H. W. Bush attended Phillips Andover Academy. Biographers call the Bush family "devout Episcopalians."

Groton, Massachusetts, is the home of the Groton Academy. Its most famous graduate was Franklin Roosevelt, the 32nd president of the United States. The school has 381 students and a faculty ratio of 5 to 1, with an average class size of 11. About 80% of the faculty have graduate degrees. The endowment of the school is $360 million. Boarding students pay $56,500 for room and board, a technology fee of $600, and a health fee of $400.

The Episcopal High School in Alexandria, Virginia, charges $58,500 tuition. In addition, textbooks and academic materials cost about $700; private music instruction costs from $1,200 to $1,600 annually, and there is another $500 charge for participation in athletic teams and about $200 monthly charged for local transportation, laundry, and entertainment. The total expenses for studying at that school reach $60,000, not including transportation home, for those who come from out of town.

The Asheville School in Asheville, North Carolina, is a nondenominational Christian school. Its mission among others is to instill Christianity in its students, holding mandatory Sunday morning prayer services and engaging in other Christian practices. The school charges $54,900 for boarding students and $32,335 for day students. Textbooks and supplies cost another $600. The school was established in 1900. It has 267 students and 66 faculty. The curriculum includes a humanities program that integrates the study of literature, history, religion, art, music, architecture, film, and dance into a series of four-year long courses. Asheville School has an unusual mountaineering program. This includes backpacking, rock climbing, whitewater kayaking, snow skiing, caving, and mountain biking. The campus features a climbing wall, a swimming pool for kayak instruction, and 200 acres of forest with miles of trails for biking and exploring. The school offers off-campus trips to such places as Looking Glass Rock in the Pisgah National Forest, and the Tuckaseegee and French Broad rivers. All new students go to at least one overnight camping trip to become acquainted with the school's mountaineering program. All of these activities cost a great deal of money in excess of tuition and other fees. It is therefore not surprising that among the alumni are such billionaires as Edward Gaylord, owner of the Oklahoma Publishing Company, Gaylord Hotels, the Nashville Network TV channel, the Grand Ole Opry, and other investments. Other graduates of the

Asheville School are James Hormel, billionaire owner of Hormel Foods, and Samuel Curtis Johnson, Jr., who, according to Forbes, was the 24th richest man in the world during his lifetime. Several generations of the Firestone family, of the Firestone Tire and Rubber Company, were also graduates of the Asheville School.

Because Catholics have no denominations, wealthy Catholics cannot be identified by such church bodies as the Episcopalians or Methodists. However, the attendance at private, church related boarding schools by their children demonstrates that social class and religion complement each other even in the absence of denominational distinctions.

The Georgetown Preparatory School is located 5 miles from Washington, D.C. It was founded in 1789. Yearly tuition is $56,665 for boarding students and $33,665 for day students. The average class size is 16 students with a teacher ratio of 1:8. Georgetown graduates generally enter expensive colleges such as Notre Dame U., the University of Virginia, Princeton, Cornell, and Virginia. The list of "Notable Alumni" is indeed astonishing. It includes achievers from almost all important American professions, such as Supreme Court Justice Neil Gorsuch, John Dingell, Member of Congress, Jerome Powell, Governor of the Federal Reserve Board, Francis Rooney, U.S. Congressman and Ambassador to the Holy See.

Numerous business leaders are Georgetown Preparatory alumni. Included are Christopher Kennedy, son of Robert Kennedy and nephew of President John Kennedy, now President of Merchandise Mart of Chicago.

Other alumni have become leaders in medicine and science, in journalism, and in the arts.

There are at least 50 most recognized elitist private schools in this country, mainly concentrated in the east. In addition, there are also western private schools which are not as old as eastern schools but which serve the same purpose. Generally sponsored by religious communities, they segregate the wealthy and give them opportunities hardly available to the average American. Tuition alone exceeds the $49,000 a year, the average American income. Therefore, despite tuition reductions and scholarships available to some, graduates of these schools gain access to upper levels of American society and, in particular, to exceptional economic and political opportunities. Those who graduated from these private academies are almost certain to be accepted as students at Harvard, Yale, Princeton, and the U of Pennsylvania or Amherst College. These Ivy League universities claim that they accept only the best and the brightest students. This may be partially true. The fact is, however, that wealth and influence, family collections, and political power allowed numerous from wealthy families to graduate from these Ivy League colleges if they are only average students, as President George W. Bush readily admitted in a graduation speech at Southern Methodist University.

Wealth, power and influence are also the catalysts promoting the interests of the rich at the end of life. At a time when old age requires the assistance of others in meeting the needs of everyday living, Americans may turn to nursing homes for help, provided they can pay for these services. A sharp distinction is found among such facilities based on the religious sponsors of these facilities. Excluding the privately owned for-profit nursing homes, the cost of entering a Jewish or Presbyterian nursing home is staggering. Because both of these denominations are financially better off than the majority of the American population, these institutions charge $21,000 a month for a semi-private room housing two patients. A room occupied by one patient can cost $90,000 a month for those who can afford it.

It is obvious that end-of-life care is considerably better for those who can make use of Presbyterian or Jewish sponsored nursing homes. It needs to be emphasized that there is no religious discrimination associated with these expensive nursing homes. In fact, the Jewish homes usually house more Christians than Jews, because the Jewish population of the United States is only 1.8 percent.

Canterbury Woods is a Presbyterian nursing home located in a suburb of Buffalo, New York. It has a 62 acre campus described in a brochure with these words. "Light filters through the trees and gilds the landscaping that surrounds your choice of elegant apartments and graces patio homes. You'll join a warm, welcoming community of friends and neighbors for strolls around the pond, lunch in charming historic Williamsville (a suburb of Buffalo) and take trips to Buffalo for world class shopping and entertainment."[367]

The Weinberg Campus is a Jewish sponsored nursing facility in a suburb of Buffalo. Only twenty percent of the residents are Jewish. It is located in a 70 acre park. Some residents live independently, while others must take advantage of higher levels of care ranging from assisted living to skilled nursing and rehabilitation.

Medicare, a federal government sponsored insurance, does not ordinarily pay for assisted living costs, although some states make some limited payments through supplemental Social Security benefits. This means that the majority of Americans cannot afford assisted living.

This forces many home owners to agree to a "reverse mortgage" in which case a bank will make a loan and collect the debt from the eventual estate. Selling an existing life insurance is another way of gaining assets needed for nursing home care. In both events, the heirs of the wealthy will inherit the assets of the previous generation; the poor will not. Even in this way, those with upper class affiliations increase their wealth in every generation.[368]

We may compare the above-described facilities with some commercial nursing homes located in former motels on main thoroughfares in the city. There is no campus, no garden, and no pond, but only the sound of traffic and endless boredom. Here religion is associated with social stratification even into old age.

No better example of the relationship between religion and social stratification can be cited than the refusal of the Catholic Church to allow women to join the clergy.

As soon as Jorge Bergoglio became Pope Francis in 2013, he announced that women will never be priests in the Catholic Church. This announcement rested on the views of earlier Popes, and particularly John Paul II who proclaimed that "the church is not free" to ordain women. This view is contained in the Apostolic letter of May 22, 1994.

The letter presents the reasons for the exclusion of women from the priesthood. "Priestly ordination," writes the Pope, "entrusted by Christ to his Apostles ... has in the Catholic church from the beginning always been reserved to men alone." The Congregation for the doctrine of the Faith issued a declaration on this matter of women priests, which holds that the exclusion of women was not related to the culture of the time of Christ, but is assured because the Blessed Virgin Mary, the Mother of God, was not chosen to be a priest. This is considered evidence that failure to include women in the priesthood is not a form of discrimination but should be seen as "a plan to be ascribed to the wisdom of the Lord of the universe."[369]

The reaction of American Catholic women to this prohibition has not been favorable. In August 2006, 12 women were ordained priests of the Roman Catholic Church on a riverboat at Pittsburgh, Pennsylvania. Despite of the refusal of the Pittsburgh diocese to recognize these ordinations and despite the possibility of excommunication, a group calling themselves Roman Catholic Women Priests danced and sang *We Are Chosen* while holding hands with female bishops also ordained by women, or by a few male bishops who conduct such ceremonies in secret.

The leader of this defiance of church law was Patricia Fresen, who claimed to have been ordained by a European male bishop. She considered herself a bishop, and together with other female priests, administered the sacraments at weddings, confessions and the Eucharist (good gift). Baptisms were an exception, because even a non-Christian with the know-how could baptize.

Friesen was a Dominican nun for 45 years until she was expelled from the order upon challenging canon (rule) law. The Catholic hierarchy (holy rule) holds that true Catholics may disagree with doctrines but will act according to church teachings just the same. The church rejects the argument that women are not valued. Instead the church hierarchy claims that Jesus appointed only men as his apostles, and since bishops are the direct spiritual descendants of the apostles, only men can fill these positions. This view may be disputed by holding that Jesus was a Jewish carpenter and that therefore only Jewish carpenters may be priests.

This dispute was interrupted in 1982 when Professor Otranto published a study entitled "Notes on the Female Priesthood in Antiquity." This was written in Italian and concluded that there were indeed some women who administered the sacraments in the ancient world. According to Otranto, the history of Christianity indicates continuous debate and ongoing questions on the role of men and women in the church. Otranto showed that the reasons for the sharp division of views on this issue are that many of the contestants in this debate overlook or are not acquainted with "the testimony of early times." Otranto argued that the subjection of women in early Christianity is not certain and that it is not clear that women were always excluded from the priesthood. Otranto then presented a good deal of evidence for this view. He relied on the writings of a ninth century bishop of Vercelli named Atto, who was asked by a priest how the words *presbytera* and *diacona* should be understood. His response leaves no room for doubt. He begins by declaring that since, in the ancient church, "many were the crops and few the laborers," women too received sacred orders. " *Commende vobis Phoebem sorarem meam quae est in ministerio Ecclesiae quae est Cenchorare,*" or, "I commend you to my sister Phoebe, who is in the ministry of the church which is in Cencharae." In addition, Bishop Atto reputedly claimed that, in the ancient Christian church, "not only men but also women were ordained and were the leaders of the community." They were called *presbytariae* or elders and they assumed the duties of directing, preaching, and teaching, which are the three roles defining the status of priest.

It appears that the argument concerning the ordination of women can be supported by both sides of the dispute, as best seen by the demands of American Catholics who have been most vociferous in promoting a feminist agenda.[370]

This example of the influence of religion on social stratification based on gender is not unique to Catholicism. Jews also have faced this dispute, although their numerous denominations have allowed those on both sides of the argument to view themselves as justified in their position.

The Jewish version of the role of women rests on the refusal of Orthodox, or Torah true Jews, to allow women congregants a role in the rituals. While men are called to bless the seven parts of the Torah (Bible) read in Hebrew by the rabbi or cantor (assistant), women are not called to do so in Orthodox congregations. In fact, women are excluded from all participation in the conduct of public rituals and are confined to segregated areas of the synagogue (assembly: Greek) by a wall or curtains. The Orthodox clergy claim that it is not women but men who are segregated, because men cannot be trusted to pay attention to prayer and ritual if women are visible. Conservative and Reform Jews reject that argument and allow women and men to sit together in the pews, and they not only call women to participate in the rituals but ordain women as rabbis.

Muslim women in the United States are gradually changing some of the traditional status roles imposed on them by male dominance. Islam has been used in Muslim countries to entrench inequality between the genders. Riffat Hassan, professor of Islamic studies at the University of Louisville, wrote: "The way Islam has been practiced ... has left millions of women with battered bodies."

According to traditional Islam, men can have four wives, but women only one husband. The legal age for marriage for girls in Muslim countries is nine. Muslim men can obtain a divorce by simply saying three times, "I divorce you." Women can also get a divorce, but it is very difficult. In cases of divorce, fathers, not mothers, usually win custody of children. The Koran, the Holy scripture of Islam, states in Sura 4:23 that men are "pre-eminent" and "oversee women." Even beating a disobedient wife is permitted by the Koran. Women are expected to wear a veil outside the home and never to walk outside without the company of a man related to them. Women are segregated by sitting in balconies in mosques.

In the United States and England, a growing number of Muslim women seek to change these traditions, particularly the use of female circumcision, which is illegal in America. Some America Muslim parents send their young daughters to a Muslim country to have such operations performed.[371]

Ayan Hirsi Ali, a Muslim woman born in Somalia in 1969, has been most vocal concerning her intimate knowledge of women's role in Islam. She came to America at age twenty-two. She calls "Sharia law" a law that kills women for having sex before marriage, a law in which homosexuals are beaten and apostates are killed. Ali has written a book called *Infidel and Nomad* in which she describes how her grandmother gave birth to a daughter in the desert, cut her own umbilical cord, and "raged at herself for producing too many girls," whom she then had circumcised. In all her writings, Ali calls for reform of Islam, which gradual assimilation to the American ethos and values may well accomplish, as it has for so many other immigrants over the past 233 years.[372]

Religion has undoubtedly contributed much to the gender stratification in Jewish, Christian, and Muslim societies. These three examples are not distinct but related, as Christianity was literally produced by Jews and Islam inherited much from both Judaism and Christianity.

We have seen that secularism is growing in America. No doubt, part of this trend lies in the effort of American women to gain full equality with men in light of the disabilities so long imposed on women by religious tradition. We conclude once more with Lucretius: "Tantum religio potuit, suadere malorum."

Chapter 14: The Influence of Religion on the Military

Combat and Its Aftermath

There is a common proverb that "there are no atheists in foxholes." This belief, like so many others, may be popular but is not true. A survey of Second World War veterans who saw the worst horrors of war found this to be true for those who had a religious commitment, but it is not true for agnostics and atheists. Although badly shaken by the experience of violent combat, the unbelievers continued in their opinions. Nevertheless, veterans of the worst slaughters reported years later that soldiers who were reported praying in frightening conditions rose from 42% to 72%. Evidently, the twenty-eight percent who were agnostics and atheists continued in their attitudes toward religion.

In 2000, researchers analyzed a random national survey of 1,122 veterans to discover whether the propensity to pray in horrific conditions had a long term effect throughout their lives. The outcome of that survey is indeed surprising. Those who saw no combat attended services three times a month. Veterans who viewed their military experience positively had different reactions to those with a negative experience. Among the "positives," those who experienced light combat attended church 2.7 times a month and those who saw heavy combat attended 2.3 times a month. Evidently, among "positives," church attendance is reduced as combat experiences are remembered as most horrifying.

Veterans who had a "negative" experience in the armed forces reported that as their combat experiences increased, their church attendance also increased. Veterans who saw no combat attended church 2.3 times a month, light combat 2.4 times a month, and heavy combat 2.8 times a month. Questions concerning membership in a religious congregation had similar results.[373]

This demonstrates that the combat–religion relationship depends on how a veteran views his military experience. Those who associate military service with glory and victory have a below average interest in religion, while those who view military service as an experience in misery are more often relating to religion. It needs to be remembered that Second World War veterans belong to a generation which favored the need to be a member of some religion. Therefore there is a good chance that a number of veterans who are church members are also agnostics. This is common in any event among all Americans.

Terrifying and horrible experiences lead some people to increase their faith, while others lose their faith. A similar result can be found among holocaust survivors.[374]

America's Wars

The United States has been involved in war almost continuously since the American Revolution of 1775–1783. Of the 217,000 men who served in the revolutionary army, 4,435 became casualties. The War of 1812 lasted until 1815 and resulted in 2,260 American casualties. The Mexican War of 1846–1848 resulted in 1,783 battle deaths and 11,500 other deaths, with a total casualty list of 13,283. Then came the Civil War of 1861–1865. This was America's costliest war. It resulted in 140,414 deaths among the Union soldiers and another 74,524 among the Confederate forces. The Spanish–American War of 1898 led to 385 battle deaths and 2,061 related deaths. In World War One, 1917–1918, the US had 116,708 casualties, including. 53,402 battle deaths and 63,114 other deaths. In the Second World War, 1941–1945, the US had 291,557 battle deaths and 113,347 related deaths. The Korean War of 1950–1953 caused 33,741 battle deaths and 106,117 related deaths. The first American casualty in the war in Vietnam was in 1956 and the war ended in 1975. It cost 47,424 battle deaths and 42,785 related deaths. The Persian Gulf War, from 1990–1991, ended with 147 battle deaths and 1,825 related deaths. Finally, the War on Terror began in October 2001 after 3,000 civilians and military died as a result of attacks on the United States.[375]

Casualties endured through these wars also include the wounded, the maimed, and the crippled. Those who lost a limb, an eye, or other body parts have never recovered and must suffer their entire lives. Therefore, religion becomes an important and generally the only means of mental/emotional defense against death. Members of the armed forces know, of course, that they are in danger of dying or losing their health while deployed in a battle. In fact, new recruits are told over and over that they need to pay attention to what is taught in basic training and later because knowledge of strategy and personal commitment to the other men in one's unit may save one's life.

Few American service personnel would not have heard of the invasion of Normandy by American and allied forces on "D" day, June 6, 1944. Because the battle plans were poorly developed, the slaughter of so many young boys and men at the invasion beaches was extraordinarily severe. The historian Stephen Ambrose has described the horrors of that day. Men who had left the landing crafts and were walking though deep water to reach the beach before them would drown if they fell, as their equipment was so heavy they could not recover and stand up. Other soldiers, about to reach the beach, waded through the corpses of their comrades even as the Germans on top of the cliff behind the beach machine gunned them. Numerous soldiers were killed and wounded indiscriminately as their bellies were shot open and their intestines jumped out. Heads, arms, and torsos were hit and blood flowed among the screaming of the wounded and the dying.[376]

A number of veterans of that day have published their experiences.

These veterans were between eighty and ninety years old in the 21st century. The knowledge of the horrors of D day and other such events become part of the new recruits' expectations. The result is fear and apprehension, which is in part alleviated by religion, a powerful tool used to alleviate anxiety and promote courage. Religion is therefore personified in the form of the clergy who are designated chaplains in the armed forces of the United States.

The Military Chaplains

Although the First Amendment to the U.S. constitution prohibits the government to become "entangled" with religion, no court has ever challenged the right of the armed forces to employ clergy as chaplains.

The U.S. government spends about $85 million on the chaplains associated with the armed forces. The military chaplaincy is designed to encourage religion. This encouragement is in part promoted by the recognition that religion can function to insure a sense of unity and belonging to the troops whose life may well depend on the "thing that binds," as Cicero called it. Marcus Tullius Cicero (106–43 B.C.E.) wrote the book *De Natura Deorum* in which he shows that the word *Religio* is derived from *Res Ligare* or *The Thing that Binds.377*

Religion in the military is expected to be pluralistic, ecumenical, and patriotic by minimizing the distinctive forms of the religion in favor of reducing any tensions between denominations. [378]

Military chaplains must have a college degree and three years of seminary training. These requirements automatically exclude numerous clergy who have been "called" but did not receive any formal education.[379] Chaplains are uniformed, ranked officers but may not exercise command. They are responsible to the Chief of Chaplains.[380]

Because there are frequent shortages of chaplains, commanders can employ civilian auxiliary chaplains.

Some religious groups feel that the free exercise of their religion is somewhat constricted by the military. The United Presbyterian Church has announced that the conflict between state and church led the military to dominate their chaplains, leading to the conclusion that the military threatens the loyalty of chaplains to their churches.[381]

Because the U.S. Government supports the military chaplaincy, the Establishment Clause of the first amendment to the U.S. Constitution is affected. The 1st Amendment prohibits the excessive government entanglement with religion and demands that government be neutral with respect to religion. This means that the courts apply the three part *Lemon Test* to any dispute concerning government and religion. This test holds that government action must have a secular purpose, that government may neither advance nor inhibit religion, and that there be no "excessive" entanglement between government and religion.

Role Conflict

All individuals play many roles in their lifetimes. A role is the sum of our obligations and a status is the sum of our rights and privileges. Therefore, sociologists speak of status-roles in the sense that one's status can only be fulfilled if we meet the requirements of the role supporting it. We assume the role of mother and father even as we are also an employer or employee. We play a number of roles at different times or simultaneously. That can lead to role conflict, as is the case with many chaplains who must represent their religious institutions and act as officers of the U.S. armed forces. Such a requirement can create emotional conflict and confusion among those who deal with military chaplains on a daily basis. Chaplains therefore need to resolve the conflict between the demands of their churches and the demands of the military. It becomes evident at once that the Judeo-Christian ethic rests on such admonitions as "you shall love your neighbor as yourself" (Leviticus 19:20) and "turning the other cheek." The military is of course determined to kill the enemy and to revenge itself on any aggression.

The ensuing conflict leaves the military chaplain with the need to reconcile these conflicting issues. Therefore he can abandon one of his roles; reconcile the conflicting demands or rationalize that the conflict does not exist.[382]

If these techniques of neutralization fail, the individual displays symptoms psychologists call "neurotic". Hence chaplains face the dilemma of the Christian or Jew or Muslim in wartime. Religious ideology rejects force, violence and killing. Military ideology demands it.

A study by Burchard concluded that 25% of military chaplains were influenced primarily by patriotic motives and sided with military assumptions, while only 10% were mainly motivated by their religious ideology.[383]

A good number of military chaplains also reported that they enjoyed the freedom the military provided them. This would seem strange to any enlisted personnel, whose status in the U.S. military resembles that of a prisoner. Officers are far less subject to the degradations enlisted personnel must endure.

Some chaplains, and other military men, feel free in the military because they need not worry about finances, the pressure of wives and children, and the controls exercised by congregations who burden the clergy with their constant demands. According to these chaplains, freedom was the most enjoyable aspect of their military life. Chaplains also questioned the need for their services in time of peace.

Drinking alcohol is so important among U.S. enlisted men and officers that it is no exaggeration to maintain that promotion as well as acceptance by fellow soldiers depends on the willingness of any man to drink with his fellows. Failure to drink alcohol is regarded as an insult. This requirement runs counter to the teachings of some churches that prohibit the use of alcohol. Some Methodists, Mormons, and Muslims are forbidden by religious strictures to consume alcohol. Even those who face no such obstacles will be conflicted as to the amount of drinking they can justify.

Chaplains are also confronted with a conflict concerning discipline in the armed services. The military codes of conduct are rather harsh and penalties are far less lenient than in civilian life. The clergy-chaplain is therefore frequently asked by a defendant in military criminal cases to help the accused and speak for him. This places the chaplain into another dilemma, as he needs to conform to the wishes of his commanding officer, who is unlikely to welcome the opinions of the clergy. Consequently, chaplains tend to identify with the officers with respect to a disciplinary hearing. Here again, the chaplain faces conflict, since he cannot very well be effective with the enlisted men if he follows the dictum that officers may not fraternize with enlisted men. It seems almost impossible to be a spiritual advisor and a distant officer at the same time. It has been suggested that chaplains be enlisted men. That, however, cannot succeed, because officers view enlisted men as less than human, and, in that case, would not accede to the wishes of chaplains.

Clergy who wish to become chaplains need to be recommended by their denomination. This can create a dilemma, because various passages in the Bible forbid the use of violence. Most denominations, whether Jewish or Christian, ignore such demands. The few who take such admonitions seriously create yet another role conflict for their chaplains. The majority of chaplains believe that the individual soldier has an obligation to serve the country and therefore need not worry about this or that Bible passage. The Commandment "You shall not murder" is interpreted to mean that killing in wartime is not included in that commandment. The Department of Defense has issued a "Character Guidance Program" which assures chaplains and military personnel that their relationship to God will not suffer because they kill in wartime.[384]

Religious Discrimination in the Military

Chaplains are not alone in dealing with role conflict in the military. Seeking to promote Protestant Christianity, a number of Air Force Academy staff have resorted to "insensitive" methods of introducing their religious beliefs at every occasion without regard to the minority who believe otherwise.

Lt. General Roger A. Brady of the Air Force led a 16 member team seeking to define the boundary between acceptable and unacceptable religious expression in view of the requirements of the First Amendment to the Constitution.[385]

The zealots among the Air Force staff screened the movie "The Passion of Christ" at every seat in the dining hall and included a message in the base newspaper signed by 250 people that "Jesus Christ is the only real hope in the world." The same Air Force staff prohibited an atheist student from organizing a "Freethinkers" club.[386]

The Air Force Academy has 19 clubs promoting a religion. Most of these clubs invite clergy from Colorado Springs to lecture at the Academy, with the result that many of the outsiders violate the Air Force standards of religious respect. One such incident concerned a Pentecostal minister told the audience that they need to accept Christ of "burn in hell."[387]

General Johnny A. Weida, commandant of cadets, sent a campus wide message announcing the Day of Prayer, including an instruction that all cadets were "accountable to God." He also demanded that cadets chant together, "Jesus rocks".

The Air Force Academy football coach, Fisher DeBerry, prayed with the team in the locker room and posted a "Team Jesus" banner.[388]

Americans United for the Separation of Church and State gave the Secretary of Defense a report that demonstrated religious coercion at the Air Force Academy. The Superintendent of the Academy, General John Rosa, told an audience that over ninety percent of Christians at the Academy found the religious situation acceptable but that only 50% of non-Christians agreed.

The Air Force Academy has 4,400 18 to 24 year old cadets. Eighty five percent are Christians, two percent were atheists, 2 percent were Jewish, 0.3 percent were Hindu, and 0.3 percent were Muslims, from 2003-2018. 9.3% called themselves "other" and gave no information about their religious views. Because only 1.8% of Americans are Jewish, the Jewish contingent at the Air Force Academy is quite small. Nevertheless, General Norton Schwartz and General David Goldfein, two Jewish Air Force Academy graduates, have been commanding generals of the U.S. Air Force in recent years. This demonstrates that the Department of Defense is committed to religious neutrality.

In response to the assault on the First Amendment at the Air Force Academy, a 1977 Honor Graduate of the Air Force Academy, Michael Weinstein, founded The Military Religious Freedom Foundation. This foundation seeks to insure religious neutrality in the armed services by means of law and by reaching out to public opinion.

The Four Chaplains

There are occasions in the life of the nation (the U.S.A.) which are so dramatic that every history contains these events and their protagonists can never be forgotten. That is true for Lieutenant George A. Fox, a Methodist chaplain, Lieutenant Alexander D. Goode, a Jewish chaplain, Lieutenant George A. Washington, a Catholic chaplain, and Lieutenant Clark A. Poling, a Dutch Reformed chaplain. Their story enhances all Americans and tells us that self-sacrifice and heroism are not dead.

On February 2, 1943, amidst the horrors of the 2nd World War, the U.S.S. Dorchester, a troop ship, was carrying 902 sailors, merchant marines, and civilians across the Atlantic en route from Newfoundland to an American army base in Greenland. The Dorchester was one of three ships in a convoy escorted by three Coast Guard cutters. It was late in the war and the Germans knew that they were losing. Therefore Hitler ordered "unrestricted warfare" by submarine against all allied shipping. Admiral Karl Dönitz was the commander of the U (Untersee) boat fleet. Dönitz became Hitler's successor after the "Führer" killed himself.

At 12:55 a.m. on that February night, the German submarine U223 sighted the Dorchester. The German captain gave orders to fire three torpedoes at the Dorchester. One of these torpedoes hit the ship below the water line. The Dorchester immediately took on large amounts of icy water through a gaping hole. The ship was sinking fast as those crew members who had been below deck swarmed to the top deck to gain access to lifeboats and life jackets. The boats were soon overcrowded, leaving the desperate sailors on deck searching for life jackets. The four chaplains found a storage room with life jackets, which they distributed to the men. Keeping calm amidst the chaos, the chaplains spread out in the ship and gave out the jackets. But then, the storage room had no more jackets, and the ship was sinking fast.

Then, the survivors witnessed an event which one survivor called "the finest thing I have seen this side of heaven." It was then that the four chaplains removed their own life jackets and handed them to four sailors. The four chaplains, the Reverends Poling and Fox, Rabbi Goode, and Father Washington locked arms and prayed together as the Dorchester took them to an icy grave.

Only 230 of the 902 men aboard survived to tell the story of the four chaplains. Congress authorized a special medal for heroism delivered to the chaplains' families. Several books, a movie, and a number of monuments have kept their heroic deed alive. Yet too few people are familiar with these great men, who showed us all what patriotism, faith and humanity really mean.[389]

There are today numerous Four Chaplains memorials in the United States. A documentary called "Sacrifice at Sea" was produced by 60 Minutes in 2004. Three books have been written and published concerning these events. There are a number of artistic displays in the country commemorating the Four Chaplains, and several memorial parks bear their names. The U.S. Government has issued a stamp in honor of the Four Chaplains.

POSTSCRIPT: THE SOCIOLOGY OF RELIGION

This book is a contribution to the sociology of religion, an undertaking which began with the book *The Elementary Forms Of The Religious Life* by Emile Durkheim, a French sociologist.[390] The German sociologist Max Weber continued this study of the sociology of religion with *The Protestant Ethic and the Spirit of Capitalism*.[391] Weber also wrote works concerning ancient Judaism and the Chinese religions.

The sociology of religion was continued in the English language in the United States and in the United Kingdom. Peter Berger, Brian Wilson, Ernest Gellner, and, more recently, the French Michel Foucault have continued these studies. There are numerous other scholars contributing to the sociology of religion.

From the sociological point of view, there's only one religion. This means that despite the numerous churches and denominations which seem to teach different beliefs, all appear to conduct the same sociological functions. A function in sociology is an anticipated consequence. Therefore we recognize that all religions separate the sacred from the profane. For example, the Hebrew Torah is a scroll treated with reverence and respect. This is also true of the New Testament and of the Koran and so many other sacred books. Buildings, such as churches, temples, mosques, and synagogues, are viewed as sacred spaces, and the clergy is generally respected as being representatives of the sacred.

All religions are concerned with such existential questions as: "Is there life after death?" "What is the purpose of all life on earth?" "What is right and what is wrong?" and many other existential issues.

All religions use ritual to make the unseen visible. Because supernatural beings are not visible to the believers, such practices as Catholic mass, the baptism ceremony, bar mitzvahs and funerals serve to ensure the believer that the deities are with him.

Another function of religion is communion of the believers with one another. People who belong to different religious denominations feel at home with others of the same faith. Praying together, singing together, and celebrating the same holy days together leads to a sense of belonging. This means that members of the same religious group support one another and distinguish the in group from the out group. Such distinctions may be achieved by eating only certain food and avoiding other foods which are eaten by the unbelievers. Examples are kosher foods, which Jews are allowed to eat, or forbidden food, a practice also used by Muslims to distinguish themselves from the infidels.

Using the word church as a designation for all religious establishments, the sociology of religion recognizes that organization may differ somewhat between the denominations. Some, like the Roman Catholic, are hierarchies (Holy rule). Others are governed by congregational dominance, as is true in Judaism, and yet others elect elders, as is done by Presbyterians and Mormons.

The sociology of religion also distinguishes between sects and cults. Sects are newly formed religious groups that protest elements of the parent religion. Thus, Christians were once a Jewish sect and Protestants were once a Roman Catholic sect. Both religions had a founder and a second founder.

The sociology of religion has developed several theories. These are called "structural functionalism." This view teaches that religions worship human society, including social cohesion, social control, and the meaning and purpose in life.

Social conflict theory argues that religion seeks to maintain the control of the poor by the wealthy by promising rewards in the afterlife but not in this life. Conflict theorists, like Karl Marx, usually wish to eliminate religion altogether.

Many religious issues cannot be discussed scientifically because science is based on probability, while all religions know the absolute truth. The sociology of religion is also interested in the status-role of women and men, race relations, class differences, and the avoidance of the horrors of war, criminal behavior, philanthropy, and education.

ENDNOTES

1 No author, "America's Changing Religious Landscape," New York: *Pew Research Center* (May 12, 2015), p. 1.

2 Ibid., p. 9.

3 Ibid., p. 11.

4 Ibid., p. 62.

5 H. Floris Cohen, *The Scientific Revolution*, Chicago: The University of Chicago Press (1994), pp.35-39.

6 A.M. McKinnon, "Reading Opium of the People," *Critical Sociology* (vol.31, no.1-2), pp.15-38.

7 Emile Durkheim, *The Elementary Forms of Religious Life*, New York: Free Press (1954), p.355.

8 Anthony J. Carroll, *Protestant Modernity, Weber, Secularization and Protestantism*. Scranton, Pa. The University of Scranton Press (2007), p.86.

9 Peter Berger, *The Sacred Canopy*, Garden City, NY, Doubleday & Co. (1967).

10 Rodney Stark, "Secularization, R.I.P." *Sociology of Religion*, vol.60, no.3 (Autumn 1999), pp.249-273.

11 Sam Harris, *The End of Faith*, New York, W.W. Norton & Co. (2004).

12 Brian Thomas, "Physics, Not God Explains the Universe?" Dallas, Texas, The Institute for Creation Research (June 9, 2012).

13 Russell Chandler, "Women's Role in Clergy Bleak," *Los Angeles Times* (March 2, 1978), p. B3.

---

14   Globe Spotlight Team, "Church Allowed Abuse by Priests for Years," *The Boston Globe* (January 6, 2002), p. 1.

15   Robert Wothnow, Albert Bergeson & Mark Warr, "A Crisis in the Moral Order: The Effect of Watergate on Confidence in Social Institutions," IN: *The Religious Dimension*, pp. 278-301.

16   John Wilson, *Religion in American Society: The Effective Presence*, Englewood Cliffs, N.J. Prentice-Hall (1978).

17   Berger, *The Sacred Canopy*.

18   Max Jammer, *Einstein and Religion: Physics and Theology*, Princeton, N.J. Princeton University Press (2002), p.65.

19   Ernest Cassirer, *Philosophy and the Enlightenment* (Boston: Beacon Press, 1951), p.181.

20   Vitaly L. Ginzburg, *The Physics of a Lifetime: Reflections on the Problems and Personalities of 20th Century Physics.* Berlin: Springe (2001), pp. 3-200.

21   Emile Durkheim, *The Elementary Forms of the Religious Life*, New York: The Free Press (1912, 1995). *See also* Richard Petts and Chris Knoester, Parents' Religious Heterogamy and Children's Well-being," (2007) *Journal for the Scientific Study of Religion*, vol.46, no.3 (373-389).

22   Christopher Ellison, "Conservative Protestantism and the Parental Use of Corporal Punishment," 1995, *Social Forces, 74 (3)*:1003-28.

23   Annette Mahoney, "Religion in the Home in the 1980s and 1990s," *Journal of Family Psychology, 2001* vol.15 (4) :559-596.

24   Lee M. Williams, "Religious Heterogeneity and Religiosity," *Journal for the Scientific Study of Religion*, 2001 vol.40, no.3

25   James H.S. Bossard, *Ritual in Family Living*, Philadelphia, University of Pennsylvania Press (1990):81.

26   Michael Lipka, "Muslims and Islam: Key Findings in the U.S. and Around the World," *Pew Research Center* (February 27, 2017).

27   Kate Shekknut, "Be Fruitful and Multiply: Muslim Births Will Outnumber Christian Births by 2035." *Christianity Today* (April 5, 2017):1.

28   Jehamot 62.6 and Kiddushin 41a.

29   Shabbat 10b and Semahot 2:6.

30   Christopher G. Ellison and Darren Sherkat, "Obedience and Authority: Religion and Parental Values Reconsidered," *Journal for the Scientific Study of Religion*, vol.32 (1993):313-329.

31   2014 Religious Landscape Study. Pew Research (May 6, 2015).

32   Pew Charitable Trusts and The Lilly Endowment, Inc. 2015.

33 Ibid.

34 Stephanie Hanes, "Interfaith America: 'Being both' is a rising trend in the US." *The Christian Science Monitor* (November 23, 2014):1.

35 Philip Zuckerman, "How Secular Family Values Stack Up," *The Los Angeles Times* (January 14 2015).

36 National Center for the Family and Marriage Research, Bowling Green, Ohio (2015).

37 Catechism of the Catholic Church, 2nd Edition, Washington DC: United States Conference of Catholic Bishops (2016).

38 Michael Paulson, "As Vatican Rejects Divorce, Many Catholics Long for Acceptance." *The New York Times* (November 23, 2015).

39 Chabad Center, Brooklyn, New York (2016).

40 J.D. Teachman, "Stability Across Cohorts in Divorce Risk Factors," *Demography*, vol. 36 (1999):415-420. *See also*: Mason, W.M. and Wolfinge, N.H., "Cohort Analysis" In: N.J. Smelser & P.B. Baites, Eds., *International Encyclopedia of the Social and Behavioral Sciences,*(2001):2189-2194.

41 Jay Teachman, "Premarital Sex: Pre-marital Co-habitation and the Risk of Marital Dissolution Among Women," *Journal of Marriage and the Family, vol.65* (2003):444-455.

42 K. Kiernan "The Rise of Cohabitation and Child Bearing," *International Journal of Law, Policy and the Family*, vol.15 (2001): 1-21.

43 No author, My Jewish Learning," Jewish Views on Homosexuality," http:// www.myjewishlearning.com.

44 Catechism of the Catholic Church: The Vocation to Chastity. http:// www.vatican.va/archive/ENG0015/_P85.HTM

45 Catechism of the Catholic Church 2396: "Among the sins gravely contrary to chastity are masturbation, fornication, pornography, and homosexual practices."

46 Richard Vara, "Carey Says Anglican Communion is in Crisis," *The Houston Chronicle* (January 11, 2008):1.

47 Ibid.:1.

48 Laura R. Olson, Wendy Cadge and James T. Harrison, "Religion and Public Opinion About Same Sex Marriage," *Social Science Quarterly*, vol.87 (2006):340-360.

49 Dr. Ursula Falk, Interview May 2, 2017.

50 Ross W. Beals, Jr. "Studying Literacy At the Community Level: a Research Note," *Journal of Interdisciplinary History*, v. 9 (1979): 93-102.

51   Raoul N. Smith, "Interest in Language and Languages in Colonial and Federal America," *Proceedings of the American Philosophical Society*, Philadelphia (1979) v.123:36-38.

52   Nila Banton Smith, *American Reading Instructions*, Newark, DE, International Reading Association (1965):17-18.

53   William R. Hart, *The English Schoolmaster*, Lansing, MI, The University of Michigan Press (1963):3.

54   James Axtell, *The School Upon a Hill*, New Haven: The Yale University Press (1974):174-175.

55   Walter H. Small, "Girls in Colonial Schools," *Education*, vol. 27 (1902):534.

56   Abraham Kafsh, *The Biblical Heritage of American Democracy* (New York: KTAV Publishing Co., 1977), Chapters 3 and 5.

57   Charles Angoff, *A Literary History of the American People* (New York: A.A. Knopf, 1931):64.

58   George H. Martin, *Evolution of the Massachusetts School System.* (New York: Nahu Press, 2010):75.

59   Thomas J. Wertenbaker, *The First Americans.* (New York : Macmillan, 1927):246.

60   Robert Middlekauff, *Ancients and Axioms: Secondary Education in Eighteenth Century New England* (New Haven, CT: Yale University Press, 1963):8-9.

61   No author, "New England's First Fruits," in: *The Annals of America* (Chicago: The Encyclopedia Britannica*, 1976)1:176.

62   Max Weber, *The Protestant Ethic and the Spirit of Capitalism* (New York: Penguin Books, 2002).

63   Elliott Essman, "The Protestants," *Life in the USA Magazine*,2014.:1-5.

64   Deuteronomy 6:7.

65   Proverbs 1:8.

66   Simon M. Dubnow, *History of the Jews in Russia and Poland* (Philadelphia: Jewish Publication Society, 1910):60.

67   William Helmreich, *The World of the Yeshiva* (New Haven, CT: Yale University Press, 1982).

68   Eli Touger, "A Child's Entry into Cheder," http://www.chabad.org/library/article_cdo/aid/81572/jewish/Areinfirinish-A-Childs-Entry-Into-Cheder.htm (accessed 1/24/18).

69   Jacob Neusner, *The Blackwell Reader in Judaism* (New York: Blackwell Publishers):422.

70 No author, *Religion and Education Around the World*," Washington, D.C. *Pew Research Center* (December 13, 2016).

71 No author, *Philadelphia Bible Riots of 1844*, Unlearned History http://unlearnedhistory.blogspot.com/2015/09/philadelphia-bible-riots-of-1844.html, accessed 1/24/18.

72 *Helen Marks, "Perspectives on Catholic Schools," in: Mark Berend, Handbook ofResearch on School Choice* (New York: Taylor and Francis, 2009).

73 Timothy M. Dolan, "The Catholic Schools We Need," *America* vol. 9, September 30, 2010:1.

74 David Gibson, "Declining Numbers of U.S. Nuns, Even Among Traditional Orders, Charted in New Study, *Religion News Service* (October 13, 2014), http://religionnews.com/2014/10/13/declining-number-u-s-nuns-even-among-traditional-orders-charted-new-study/, accessed January 24, 2018.

75 United States Department of the Treasury, "History of "In God We Trust" (June 18, 2017).

76 Adam Liptak, "Supreme Court Rejects Contraceptives Mandate for Some Corporations," *The New York Times* (July 1, 2014):A1.

77 Public Law 103–141 103rd Congress (November 16, 1993).

78 Little Sisters of the Poor v. Sebelius (6 F.Supp. 3d 1225 (D. Colo. 2013)).

79 Bob Jones University v. United States (1983); Texas Monthly. Bullock (1989); Town of Greece v. Galloway (2014).

80 Thornton v. Caldor (1985).

81 Board of Education of Kiryas Joel Village School v. Grumet (1994).

82 Dwight H. Sullivan, "The Congressional Response to Goldman v. Weinberger," *Military Law Review*, vol. 121 (1988):125-152.

83 Good News Club v. Milford Central School, 533 U.S. 98 (2001).

84 Hosanna – Tabor Evangelical Lutheran Church And School v. Equal Employment Opportunity Commission, 565 U.S. 171 (2012),

85 Carolyn Thompson "Supreme Court Playground Ruling Feeds School Voucher Debate," *Associated Press* (June 27, 2017).

86 Benjamin Liu, "Turner v. Suffley *and* O'Lone v. Estate of Shabbaz," *UCLA Law Review, v.51 (4) (1987)*.

87 Naomi Zevelof, "Not Just Jews eat Kosher food in Prison," *The Forward* (April 20, 2012) :1.

88 U.S.D.C. (S.D. Fla) Case No.1:12cv-22958.

89   Albert I. Slomovitz, *The Fighting Rabbis*, New York : New York University Press (1999):59-61.

90   Military Chapels of the United States.

91   David R. Segal and Mady W. Siegal, "America's Military Population," Washington: *Population Reference Bureau*, Vol.59, no.4 (December 2004).

92   Headquarters, United States Air Force. The Report of the Headquarters Review Group Concerning the Religious Climate at the US Air Force Academy (June22, 2005).

93   Lori Goldstein, "Air Force Chaplain Tells of Academy Proselytizing," *The New York Times* (May 12, 2005): Education.

94   Hall v. Welborn No.08-2008 (Kan. March 5, 2008).

95   Headquarters United States Air Force. "The Report Of the Headquarters Review Group concerning the Religious climate At the US Air Force Academy (June 22, 2005).

96   Ibid.

97   Michael L. Weinstein, *With God on Our Side*, New York :St. Martin's Press, 2006.

98   United States Department of Labor, Washington DC, Bureau of Labor Statistics, *Clergy*.

99   Ibid.

100 Genesis 12:1.

101 Tiferes Stam, "Buying a Sefer Torah," Brooklyn, N.Y. (2017), http://www.tiferes.com/index.php?route=information/information&information_id=8, accessed 1/30/18.

102 Gerhard Falk, *The Jew in Christian Theology*, Jefferson, N.C. (McFarland, Publishers, 1992):277-280.

103 David Breitenstein, "U.S. Catholics Face Shortage of Priests," *USA Today News Press* (May 24, 2014):1.

104 Bryan Pearson, "Holiday Spending to Exceed $1 trillion," *Forbes* (December 21, 2016):1.

105 Ibid.:20.

106 Ed Stetzer, "What Is Church Attendance Like During Christmas?" *Christianity Today* (December 4, 2015):1.

107 https://cathedral.org/about the cathedral/mission and vision, accessed 1/30/18.

108 No author. "Temple Emanuel," *New York Architectural Images*," http://nyc-architecture.com/UES/UES039.htm, accessed 1/30/18.

109 Daniel Radosh, "The Good Book Business," *The New Yorker* (December 18, 2006).

110 Jennifer G. Hickey, "Museum of the Bible Extended Fly-Through," *The New York Post* (May 4, 2007): Living.

111 Washington, DC, U.S. Department of Labor, Bureau of Labor Statistics, 2016.

112 Leonard Ross, "The Bernstein Files," *The New Yorker* (August 10, 2009).

113 Scott Thompson, "The Pay Scale for Jewish Cantors," http://work.chron.com/pay-scale-jewish-cantors-17855.html, accessed 1/30/18.

114 Jaweed Kaleem, "Best Paid Pastors Make Hundreds of Thousands to Millions of Dollars, Annually," *Huffpost.* (January 19,2012) https://www.huffingtonpost.com/2012/01/19/best-paid-pastors_n_1214043.html, accessed 1/30/18.

115 Richard Ostling, "The Day of Reckoning Delayed," *Time* (September 4, 1989):30-31.

116 "Joel Osteen Biography," Editors@The Famous People.com (September 30, 2014.), https://www.thefamouspeople.com/profiles/joel-osteen-3903.php, accessed 1/30/18.

117 Max Weber, *The Protestant Ethic and the Spirit of Capitalism*, New York: Penguin Books (2002).

118 Exodus 20 and Deutoronomy 5.

119 A.M. McKinnon, "Elective affinities of the Protestant Ethic." *Sociological Theory, vol.28 (2010)*:108-126.

120 Reinhard Bendix, *Max Weber: An Intellectual Portrait*, Berkeley, The University of California Press, 1977.

121 Nina Martin, "The Growth of Catholic Hospitals, By the Numbers," *Pro Publica* (December 18, 2017):1.

122 Ibid.:4.

123 Ibid.:5.

124 Joanna Corman, "Hospitals Revamped Chapels Interfaith Meditation Rooms," *Religious News Service* (May 25, 2011).

125 Washington, DC, U.S. Department of Labor, Bureau of Labor Statistics, "Hospital Chaplain," 21-2011.

126 No Author, The Salvation Army International, http://www.salvationarmy.org

127 U.S. Conference of Mayors: Hunger and Homelessness Survey, A 25 City Survey (December 2014).

128 Ralph da Costa Nunez, *Homelessness*, Citylimits.org(March 2012).

129 Salvation Army USA: Hunger Relief http://salvationarmysouth.org/ways-we-help/hunger-relief/, accessed 2/2/18.

130 Herbert H. Stroup, *Social Welfare Pioneers*, Lanham, MD, Rowman and Littlefield (1985):185.

131 Anndee Hochman, "Empty Plates in the Land of Plenty," *Broadstreet Review*,(March 7, 2017).

132 No author, *Statistic Brain, Poverty Statistics https://www.statisticbrain.com/homelessness-stats/, accessed 2/2/18.*

133 Gerhard Falk, *Stigma*, Buffalo NY, Prometheus Books (2001):46.

134 Sheila Rule, "Three Synagogues to Aid City's Homeless," *The New York Times*,(January 21, 1983):Region 3.

135 Catholic Charities of New York, "What We Do," No date, no author, https://catholiccharitiesny.org/what-we-do, accessed 2/2/18.

136 WGN Desk "Chicago Jewish Community Joins Efforts to Help Syrian Refugees," (December 16, 2016), http://wgntv.com/2016/12/16/chicagos-jewish-community-joins-effort-to-help-syrian-refugees/, accessed 2/2/18.

137 Michael d. Shear and Abby Goodnough, "Trump Plans to Declare Opioid Epidemic a National Emergency, *The New York Times* (August 10, 2017):A13..

138 Lisa Girion, "Rate of Heroin Use in the U.S. has Climbed 63% in the Last Decade," *The Los Angeles Times* (July 7 2015):A1.

139 William W. White and Alexander Lauder, "Spirituality, Science, and Addiction Counseling," *Counseling Magazine*, v.71 (2006) no.1, :56-59.

140 J.F. Corrington, "Spirituality and Recovery: Relationships Between Levels of Spirituality, Contentment and Stress During Recovery from Alcoholism in AA." *Alcoholism Treatment Quarterly*, vol.6 (1989):151-165.

141 Ibid.:59.

142 https://www.eliterehabplacement.com/christian-rehab-enters, accessed 2/2/18.

143 https:// rehab. com/Catholic- charities- substance- abuse- and- mental-health, accessed 2/2/18.

144 Ibid.:5.

145 Ibid.:6.

146 Bruce Ritter, *Sometimes God Has a Kid'sFace*, New York, Doubleday (1987).

147 Jewish Drug and Alcohol Rehab Centers, http://www.rehabcenter.net/types-of-addiction-treatment-programs/, accessed 2/2/18.

148 Jamie Katz, Smithsonian.com (October 6. 2009).

149 Robert Brusten, "Fiddle Shtick," *the New York Review of Books* (December 18, 2014), vol.61, no.20:82-83.

150 Mark Zbrowski and Elizabeth Herzog, *Life Is with People: The Culture of the Shtetl* (New York: Schocken Books, 1952).

151 Allen Hughes, "Hugo Weisgall Conducts Own Works," *The New York Times* (December 10, 1970):59.

152 Martin Bernheimer, "Opera: Hugo Weisgall's Grandiose 'Esther' Justifies a Festival," *The Los Angeles Times* (October 11, 1993).

153 Mordaunt Hall, "Al Jolson and the Vitaphone," *The New York Times* (October 7, 1927): Movies.

154 Rodney Greenberg, "The Jewish Leonard Bernstein," *Jewish Quarterly* (No.208, Winter 2007).

155 David Hiley, "Chant" In: *Performance Practice*, Howard M. Brown, Ed. (New York: WW Norton &Co., 1990):37.

156 David Hiley, "Chant" 32.There are numerous source concerning the Gregorian chant in all European languages.

157 Zachary Wolfe, "Liturgy and a Tale: Revival and Sprawling as Ever," *The New York Times* (November 4,2014):C5.

158 The American Guild of Organists, https://www.agohq.org/, accessed 2/5/18 .

159 Jim McDermott, "Sing a New Song," *America* (May 30, 2005):1.

160 The Catholic University of America, Announcements, Benjamin D. Rome School of Music (2010-2011).:3.

161 Ibid.:11.

162 Kyle C. Sessions, "Protestant Church Music," *Church History*, vol.45, no. 3 (September 1976):400-401.

163 Eileen Reynolds, "God Bless America" Forward (July 17, 2013).

164 Velma M. Thomas, *No Man Can Hinder Me: The Journey From Slavery to Emancipation Through Song* (New York: Crown Publishers, 2003):14.

165 William F. Allen, *Slave Songs of the United States* (New York: A. Simpson–Applewood, 1995):4-5.

166 Hall Johnson, "Notes on the Negro Spiritual," In: *Readings n Black American Music.* (New York: W.W. Norton 1983): 277.

167 Ruby Elzy, "The Spirit of th Spirituals," *Etude*. Vol.61, no. 8 (August 1943):495.

168 J. Jefferson Cleveland, *Songs of Zion*. (Nashville, TN: Abington, 1981):172.

169 No author. "Christian Modern Art," *The Best Christian Art in the Universe*, http://christianmodernart.com/, accessed 2/5/18.

170 *Rabbis Without Borders*, July 19, 2017, at https://www.myjewishlearning.com/rabbis-without-borders/what-do-we-do-about-violence-in-the-torah/

171 William Harper, et.al. *"The Proslavery Argument*," Philadelphia, Lippincott, Grambo & Co. (1853): 35

172 Ibid.36.

173 John W. Blessingame, *The Slave Community*, New York: Oxford University Press (1972).

174 Margo Burns and Bernard Rosenthal, "Examination of the records of the Salem witch trials," *William and Mary Quarterly*, vol.65, no.3, (2008):401-422).

175 Susan Easton, "City of Refuge," *Mormon Historical Studies*, vol.2 No.1 (2001):82-94.

176 No author, *Church History: In the Fullness of Time.*(2003):193-210.

177 Eugene Campbell, *Establishing Zion: The Mormon Church in the American West*, Salt Lake City: Signature Books (1988).

178 Marvin S. Hill, "Carthage Conspiracy Reconsidered: a Second Look at the Murder of Joseph and Hyrum Smith," *Journal of the Illinois State Historical Society,*(Summer 2005):207.

179 Dallin H. Oaks and Marvin S. Hill, "Carthage Conspiracy: The Trial of the Accused Assassins of Joseph Smith": *Journal of the Illinois Historical Society* (Summer 2004).

180 Shannon Novak, "Remembering Mountain Meadows collective violence." *Journal of Anthropological Research.* Vol.62, no.1, (2006):1-25.

181 Will Herberg, "Religion in a Secularized Society: Some Aspects of America's Three Religion Pluralism." *Review of Religious Research*, vol.4, no.1 (Autumn 1962):37.

182 Philip Jenkins, *The New Anti-Catholicism: The Last Acceptable Prejudice.* New York: Oxford University Press (2004).

183 John Tracy Ellis, *American Catholicism.* Chicago: University Of Chicago Press (1969):37.

184 Ibid.38.

185 Lyman Beecher, *A Plea for the West*, Cincinnati: Truman and Smith (1835):61.

186 Mark Twain, *The Innocents Abroad*, New York: Velvet Element.

187 Robert E. Curran, *Papist Devils: Catholics in British America. 1574-1783.* Washington DC, The Catholic University of America Press (2014):201-202.

188 Jennifer Coval and Kathryn Wilson, "City of Unbrotherly Love: Violence in 19th Century Philadelphia," *Exploring Diversity in Philadelphia History*, Philadelphia: The Historical Society of Philadelphia (2008).

189 Margaret E. Fitzgerald, "The Philadelphia Nativist Riots," Irish Cultural Society of the Garden City Area, 1992.

190 Ellis, American Catholicism:37.

191 Paul F. Boller, "George Washington and Religious Liberty," *William and Mary Quarterly* (1960): 486-506.

192 Ron Dreher, "Hate is Hate is Hate," *The Washington Times*, December 4, 2002:1.

193 Ryan Smith, "The Cross: Symbol and Contest in 19th Century America," *Church History*, vol.70 (December 2001):716-717.

194 John Higham, *Strangers in the Land: Patterns of American Nativism 1850–1925*, New Brunswick: Rutgers University Press (1958):298-299.

195 Michael Williams, *The Shadow of the Pope* (New York: Whittlesey House, 1932):170-172.

196 Ed Koch, "The St. Patrick Cathedral Event," *The New York Post* (December 12, 1989).

197 No author, "Brazil," *The New Standard Jewish Encyclopedia*, New York (1992):172.

198 Jacob Bogage, "Leo Frank was Lynched for a Murder He Didn't Commit. Now Neo-Nazis are Trying to Rewrite History," *The Washington Post* (May 22, 2017):22.

199 David Stout, "The Case that Rocked Crown Heights," *The New York Times* (August 12, 1996):1.

200 Ibid.:11.

201 John Kifner, "Death on 125th St.: The Overview; Gunmen and Seven Others Die in Blaze at Harlem Store," The New York Times (December 9, 1995):Region 1.

202 Leah Speyer, "Campus Watchdog; Jewish Students Single Largest Target of Systematic Suppression of Civil Rights at American Universities." *Algemeiner* (July 26, 2016):1.

203 Levi Pulkinnen, "Jury finds Haq guilty In Jewish Federation Center Shooting," *Seattle Post-Intelligencer* (December 15, 2009):1.

204 No author: "Why Are Student Leaders and Jewish Bruins Under Attack at UCLA?" *The Tower*, Issue 14, June 2014.

205 Eric Lichtblau, "Hate Crimes Against American Muslims Most since Post 9/11 Era" *The New York Times* (September 18. 2016):A13.

206 Ibid. A13.

207 Frances Robles, "Dylan Roof Had AR-15 Parts During Police Stop IN MRH," *The New York Times* (June 26, 2015)A:1.

208 Mark Hutsether, "Hate Crime Update," *Religion Dispatches* (July 27, 2008):1.

209 John Holusha, "Gunmen Kill 2 Missionary Ctr." The New York Times (September 3, 2015):1.

210 No author, "Three Leaders of a Missouri Church," *The New York Times* (August 14, 2007):1.

211 Michelle Wilson and John Lynxwiler, "Abortion Clinic Violence As Terrorism," Studies *in Conflict and Terrorism*, vol.11, no.4 1988):263-273.

212 National Abortion Federation, Washington DC, *Violence and Description Statistics* (2015).

213 Harvey Kushner, *Encyclopedia of Terrorism*: Ann Arbor: University of Michigan Press (2003):154.

214 Alesha E. Doan, Opposition and Intimidation: the Abortion Wars and Strategies of Political Harassment (Ann Arbor: The University Of Michigan Press):23.

215 Juan Ignacio Blanco, *Murderpedia: The Free Online Encyclopedia Dictionary Of Murder.* (July 26, 2016), http://murderpedia.org (accessed 2/5/18).

216 Judy L Thomas, "Suspect Until His Death Supported Killing Abortion Providers, Friends Say," Kansas City Star,(June 4, 2009).

217 No author, "Three Killed, Nine Wounded in an Attack on Planned Parenthood," Midland Daily News (November 17, 2015):1.

218 Wendy Griswold, *Cultures and Societies in a Changing World.* Los Angeles: Pine Forest. (2008):16.

219 Rubina Ramji, Representation of Islam in American News and Film: Becoming the Other," *Mediating Religion: Conversations in Media, Religion and Culture.* London: T. & T. Clark (2003):65.

220 Daniel Stout and Judith Mitchell Buddenbaum, *Religion and Popular Culture.* Ames, Iowa: Iowa State University Press (2001):45.

221 Ibid.:40.

222 George Gertner and Larry Gross, "Living in Television: the Violence Profile," *Journal of Communications*, vol.26 (1976):172.

223 T.K. Barger, "Religion, Media Affect each Other." *The Blade* (July 20, 2013).

224 Jason Miller, "Social Media and Religion," *Huffington Post* (November 19, 2011).

225 David French, "Religion and America Media: Why is Religion Reporting so Dumb? " *National Review* (December 14, 2016).

226 Jack Jenkins, "The American Media Needs to Take a Theology Class," *Think Progress*,(May 13, 2014), https://thinkprogress.org/viewpoint-the-american-media-needs-to-take-a-theology-class-or-three-4b1a3aa4d6ca/, accessed 2/6/18.

227 J. Harold Ellens, *Models of Religious Broadcasting*, Grand Rapids, MI: Erdman's,(1974).

228 Hal Erickson, *Religious Radio and Television in the United States, 1921 – 1991*. Jefferson, NC: McFarland (1992).

229 Richard Flory, "Revisiting the Legacy of Jerry Falwell, Sr." University of Southern California, Center for Religion and Civic Culture (July 17, 2017).

230 Thomas Skill, "The Portrayal of Religion and Spirituality on Fictional Network Television." *Review of Religious Research* (1994).

231 John F. Persinos, "Has the Christian Right Taken Over The Republican Party?" *Campaigns and Elections*, vol. 15, no. 2, 1994:20-25.

232 George Parsons, "Foreign Focus: Be Careful How You Pray," *Religious Broadcasting* (February 1995):109.

233 Cynthia Littleton, "God is my TV Pilot," *Variety*, vol. 9 (February 1999):1. God is my TV

234 Pew Research Center, "Sharing Religious Faith Online," *Religion and Electronic Media* (November 2014), http://www.pewforum.org/2014/11/06/religion-and-electronic-media/, accessed 2/6/18.

235 William Martin, "The Riptide of Revival," *Christian History and Biography*, No. 92 (2006):24-29.

236 Cathy Lynn Grossman, "In Nixon Tapes, Billy Graham Refers to Synagogue of Satan," *USA Today* (June 24, 2009):1.

237 Grant Wacker, "Billy Graham's America," *Church History*, vol.78, No.3:489-511.

238 Ralph Blumenthal, "Joel Osteen's Credo: Eliminate the Negative, Accentuate Prosperity," *The New York Times* (March 30, 2006).

239 No author, "Osteen Net Worth 2017; How Rich is the 54 Year Old Evangelist?" *Christian Post*, 197347.

240 Elise Wile, "The Average Income of a Pastor of a Mega-Church," *The Houston Chronicle* (October 6, 2017):1.

241 Barbara Walters, "The Most Fascinating People of 2006," 20/20 ABC 12/12/2006.

242 William E. Schmidt, "For Jim and Tammy Bakker, Excess Wiped Out a Rapid Climb to Success," The New York Times, (May 16.1987).

243 Hanna Rosin, "Televangelist Jim Bakker's Road to Redemption" The *Washington Post* (August 11, 1999):C1.

244 Ibid: C1.

245 Peter Applebaum, "Scandal Spurs Interest in Swaggart Finances," *The New York Times*, February 26, 1988):3.

246 Ibid.:8.

247 Michelle Boorstein, "America, a Popular Intellectual Catholic Magazine, Bars Terms 'Liberal' and 'Conservative'," *The Washington Post* (June 23, 2013):1.

248 Jacob Lupfer, "Why a Yes to Gays is Often a No to Evangelism," *The Washington Post*, (June 10, 2015).

249 No Author, "Christianity Today Advertising - Connecting You with Christian Audiences," (November 10, 2016), http://www.christianitytodayads.com/, accessed 2/6/18.

250 Gary B. Bullert, "Reinhold Niebuhr and the Christian Century." *Journal of Church and State*, vol.44 (2002):271-290.

251 Martin E. Marty, Modern American Religion: Under God, Indivisible. *University of Chicago Press* (1999):189.

252 Michelle De Rusha, "A Sixteenth Century Scandal," *Credo*, v.7, no.3 (2017).

253 Robert W. Sledge, "The Saddest Day: Gene Leggett and the Origins of the Incompatible Cause," *Methodist History*, vol. 55, no.3 (April 2017):145-179.

254 Jonathan S. Tobin, "Presbyterians Declare War on the Jews," *Commentary* (February 11, 2014).

255 Avi Y. Decter, "The Other Promised Land" *Jewish Museum of Maryland* (2005):104.

256 Elaine H. Ecklund and Kristen S. Lee, "Atheists and Agnostics Negotiate Religion and Family," *Journal for the Scientific Study of Religion*, vol. 51, no.1 (March 5, 2012).

257 The Pew Research Center, "Religious Beliefs and Practices of Jewish Americans," October 1, 2013, http://www.pewforum.org/2013/10/01/chapter-4-religious-beliefs-and-practices/, accessed 2/6/18.

258 Aryeh Kaplan, *Made in Heaven: A Jewish Wedding Guide.* (New York: Mozaim Publishing Co. 1983), Chapter 17.

259 Amy Hoover, "Lutheran Denominational Wedding Service," *The Lutheran Church* (No date).

260 The Chabad Staff, "The Circumcision Ceremony in a Nutshell," Chabad *(No date).*

261 No Author, "Male Circumcision" *Pediatrics,* v. 30, :756 *(August,27,2012).*

262 John 1:19-29

263 Everett Ferguson, *Baptism in the Early Church.* Grand Rapids, MI: Eerdmans (2009):860.

264 Stefanie Cohen, "$1 Million Parties – Have NYC Bar Mitzvahs Gone Too Far?" *New York Post,* April 18, 2010, https://nypost.com/2010/04/18/1-million-parties-have-nyc-bar-mitzvahs-gone-too-far/, accessed 2/6/18.

265 Scott P. Richert, "The Sacrament of Confirmation in the Catholic Church," *Thought* (May 1, 2017):1.

266 An Explanation of Luther's Small Catechism, Concordia Publishing House (2017):241.

267 United States Conference of Catholic Bishops. "An Overview of Catholic Funeral Rites." (No date), http://www.usccb.org/prayer-and-worship/bereavement-and-funerals/overview-of-catholic-funeral-rites.cfm, accessed 2/6/18.

268 David E. Williams, "The Drive for Prohibition: A Transition from Social Reform to Legislative Reform," *Southern Communication Journal,* v.3 (1996):185.

269 John A. Krout, "Prohibition," *Dictionary of American History,* New York: Charles Scribner' Sons (1940 ed.).

270 Anna A. Gordon, *The Beautiful Life of Frances A. Willard, Chicago,* The Women's Temperance Publishing Association. (1998):98.

271 Williams, "The Drive for Prohibition,":186.

272 Gordon, "Beautiful Life,":111.

273 Ernest H. Cherrington, *The Standard Encyclopedia of the Alcohol Problem.* Westerville, Ohio. American Issue Publishing Company. (1925).

274 Jeffrey A. Miron and Jeffrey Zwiebel, "Alcohol Consumption During Prohibition," *AEA Papers and Proceedings,* vol.87, no.2 (May 1991):242.

275 Howard Abadinsky, *Organized Crime*, Chicago: Nelson Hall (1991).

276 Ibid. Chapter Three and Four.

277 Nancy Hardesty et.al. "Women in the Holiness Movement," In: *Women of Spirit*, Rosemary Reuther, Ed. (New York: Simon and Schuster, 1979).

278 Rosemary Skinner Keller, "Lay Women in the Protestant Tradition," In: *Women in Religion in America.*(New York: Harper and Row. (1981): 342-392.

279 Janet W. James, "Statistics About Women's Training Schools," In: *Women of Spirit*, Philadelphia: University of Pennsylvania Press,):1980):178.

280 Latin: *Suffragium* means prayer or request.

281 Rosemary R. Reuther, *Sexism and God Talk* (Boston: Beacon Press, 1987):199.

282 Jackson Carroll, et.al. *Women of the Cloth* (New York: Harper &Row, 1983):102.

283 Bill Tammeus, "Episcopal Church Celebrates 40 years of Women in the Priesthood," *National Catholic Reporter* (July 23, 2014):1-15.

284 Arthur Kinney, *Tudor England* (New York: Routledge, 2000):132.

285 Naomi P. Pratt, "Transitions in Judaism" In Pratt, *Women in American Religions* (New York: James Books):226.

286 Ibid.:226.

287 Gerhard Falk, *Twelve Inventions Which Changed America*, Lanham, MD, *Hamilton Books* (2013):58.

288 Gerhard Falk, *End of the Patriarchy* (New York: University Press of America, 2016).

289 Samuel M. Cavert, *The American Churches in the Ecumenical Movement*, New York: Association Press: (1968).

290 No author, *New York Times* (July 5, 1963)1:44.

291 Martin Luther King, Jr. "Letter from Birmingham Jail," *Christian Century* (June 12, 1963):762-763.

292 No author, "March on Washington", *The New York Times* (August 28, 1963):1.

293 R.J. Tresolion, "Congress Makes a Law: The Civil Rights Act of 1964," in: *Cases in American National Government and Politics*, Englewood Cliffs, N.J., Prentice Hall (1966):97.

294 Steven Lawson, *Black Ballots*, New York, Columbia University Press (1976).

295 Neil McMillen, "Black Enfranchisement in Mississippi," *Journal of Southern History*, VOL.43, NO.3 (1977):351-372.

296 James H.. Laue, "Power, Conflict And Social Change." In: *Riots And Rebellions*, Don Bowen and Louis Massotti, Eds. Santa Barbara, Cal. Sage Publications (1968)pp85-96.

297 Tom W Smith," America's Most Important Problem-a Trend Analysis, *Public Opinion Quarterly*,vol.44, no.2 (1980):164-180.

298 Shaila Dewan, "Former Klansman Guilty of Manslaughter in 1964 Deaths," *The New York Times* (June 21, 2005):A1.

299 Clayborne Carson, et.al. *The Papers of Martin Luther King*, Berkeley, The University of California Press (1992):436-439.

300 David J. Garrow, "King's Plagiarism: Imitation, Insecurity and Transformation, *Journal of American History*, vol.76 (June 1991):86-92. "Plagion" is Greek for kidnapping or robbery.

301 Keith D. Miller, "The Roots of the Dream," *New York Times Book Review* (March 15, 1992):13-14.

302 Ellen K. Coughlin, "Plagiarism by Martin Luther King, Jr." *Chronicle of Higher Education*,(October 16, 1991):A:21.

303 Menachem Wecker, "10 High Profile People Whose Degrees were Revoked," *Newsweek*, (May 2,2012).

304 Carl Hulse, "By a Vote of 98-Zero, Senate Approves 25 Year Extension of Voting Rights Act," *The New York Times*,(July 21, 2006):A1.

305 Synagogue is Greek and means assembly.

306 Increase Mather, *The Mystery of Israel's* Salvation.(London, John Allen publisher, 1669):1-11.

307 Pew Research Center, Washington, D.C. "America's changing religious landscape,"(May 22, 2015).

308 U.S. Constitution. Amendment i.

309 Hans Linde, "First Things First: Rediscovering the Bill Of Rights," 9 UBalt L Rev 379 (1980).

310 No author. "Public Sees Religious Influence Waning," Washington DC, *Pew Research Center*,(September 27, 2014):1.

311 Ibid.:2.

312 Ibid.:4.

313 Ibid.:5.

314 Emily McFarla Miller, "Religious Makeup of the New Congress Overwhelmingly Christian." *Religion News Service* (January 3, 2017):1.

315 Ibid. 4.

316 Richard Hofstadter, "Could a Protestant have beaten Hoover in 1928?" *The Reporter*, vol.22 (March 17, 1960):31.

317 Robert K Murray, "A Catholic Runs for President," *The Mississippi Valley Historical Review*, vol. 43 ((December 1956):516.

318 Edward A. Moore, "A Catholic runs for President,"

319 Scott Bomboy, "The drama behind President Kennedy's 1960 election win," *Constitution Daily* (November 17, 2017):1.

320 Jonathan Zimmerman, "A Jewish Candidate Won a United States Primary for President for the First Time and America Yawned." *Los Angeles Times*, February 11, 2016):1.

321 E.B. O'Callaghan, *Calendar of Historical Manuscripts in the Office of the Secretary of State*. Albany, Weed, Parsons &Co.(1865).

322 Garance Franke Ruta, "An Amazing 1969 Account Of the Stonewall Uprising," *The Atlantic* (January 24, 2013): Politics.

323 Roe v. Wade, 410 U. 113. (January 23, 1973.)

324 Editorial, "One More Terrorist Act," *The Los Angeles Times* (October 27, 1998):A16.

325 James C. Mohr, *Abortion in America* (Oxford University Press) 100-1900 p.28.

326 James Risen and Judy L. Thomas, *Wrath of Angels: The American Abortion War*, New York: Basic Books (1998).

327 No author, "Statement by Two Cardinals," *The New York Times* (January 23, 1973):20.

328 Carl Weiser," Anti-abortion Violence Increased" *USA Today* (January 16, 1998):7A.

329 Ibid. 181.

330 Allan Gutmacher Institute, "Facts in Brief"(1998).

331 Deborah Epstein and Barbara Weiss, "Will Violence RND Patience Access to Abortion?" *Medical Economics*, vol.76 (1999):51.

332 Felicity Barringer, "Abortion Clinics Prepare for More Violence," *New York Times* (March 12, 1993)A1..

333 Robert Mahoney, "RU4it? Z *Magazine* vol.3, no.5 (1990):40-42.

334 S. Greenhouse, "A New Pill: a Fierce Battle." *New York Times Magazine* (February 12, 1989):23-28.

335 Death Penalty Information Center, "The States With and Without the Death Penalty" *Death Penalty Information Center* (November 9, 2016):1.

336 William Glaberson, "4-3 Ruling Effectively Holds Death Penalty in New York," *The New York Times* (June 25, 2004):1-5..

337 Ben Ziopn Bokser, "Statement on Capital Punishment." *Proceedings of the Committee on Jewish Law.* Vol. 3 (1 (1970) pp.1537-1538.1

338 Edward C. Brugger, *Capital Punishment and Roman Catholic and Roman Catholic Moral Tradition,* South Bend, IN, University of Notre Dame Press,(2003):104.

339 Laura Iraci, "Pope Francis Calls the Death Penalty Unacceptable." *National Catholic Reporter,*(July 3, 2016):1.

340 Titus Lucretius Carus, *De Rerum Naura. On the Nature of Things.* Cambridge: university of Cambridge Press (2013).

341 Jennifer Coval, *"City of Unbrotherly Love"* Philadelphia: The Historical Society of Pennsylvania (2008):5-8.

342 Works of Martin Luther, "On Translating," Weimar: Harman Boelaus. Vol.30, Pat II, pp. 632-640.

343 Dennis Clark, *The Irish in Philadelphia,* Philadelphia: Temple University Press (1973):2.

344 Archdiocese of Philadelphia; Office of Catholic Education History. Philadelphia (May 9, 2008).

345 Federal Reserve Bank, "Consumer Price Index" ((January 2, 2018):2,

346 310 U.S. 624.

347 310 U.S. 296.

348 330 U.S. 1

349 370 U.S. 42.

350 374 U.S. 203

351 303 U.S. 97.

352 403 U.S. 602

353 429 U.S. 39

354 463 U.S. 388

355 482 U.S. 578

356 505 U.S. 577

357 530 U.S. 290

358 Max Weber, *The Protestant Ethic and the Spirit of Capitalism,* New York: Penguin (2002).

359 David Masci, "How Income Varies among US Religious Groups," Pew Research Center,(January 30, 2009)..

360 B. Drummond Ayres, Jr. "The Episcopalians: an American Elite with Roots Going Back to Jamestown," *The New York Times* (April 28, 1981).

361 David Maci, How Income Varies etc."

362 Colin Loader, "Puritans and Jews: Weber, Sombart and the Trans-Valuators of Modern Society, *The Canadian Journal of Sociology,* (vol.26, no.4 (2001):635-653.

363 H.B. Alexander, "The Hebrew Contribution the Americanism of the Future," *The Menorah Journal,* vol.4, no.2 (1920):65-66.

364 David Masci, "How Income Varies among US Religious Groups." Pew Research Center, Washington, D.C. (2016):2.

365 Tami Libby, "5 Disturbing Stats." *Money* (August 22, 2014):1.

366 Victor Hinolosa and Jerry Z. Park "Religion and the paradox of racial inequality attitudes'" Journal for the Scientific Study of Religion,vol.43, no.2 (2004):230.

367 Welcome to Canterbury Woods, Williamsville.

368 http://www.Top rated senior facilities.

369 John Paul II, "Ordinatio Sacerdatolis" Women for Faith and family http:www.wff.or/ OrdSac.html. p.5.

370 Mary Ann Rossi, "Priesthood, Precedent and Prejudice: On Recovering the Women Priests of Early Christianity" *Journal of Feminist Studies in Religion,* vol.7, no.3 (Spring 1991):71-94.

371 Tammy Gaber, "Eve's Apple and the Mosque: Transmitted and Layered Additions to the Mosque Pertaining to the Space for Women," *Study of Traditional Environment, http:www.//jstor.org./stable4195842.*

372 "Ayaan Hirsi Ali, A Critic of Islam. Dark Secrets." *The Economist,* Vol. 382 no. 8516 (2007A): February 10-16.

373 Brian Wansink and Craig Wansink, ""Are there atheists in foxholes," *Journal and Religion and Health,* vol.52, no.3 (2013):768-769.

374 Ibid.: 760.

375 U.S. Department of Defense, Washington, D.C. *Office of Veterans Affairs* (September, 2010).

376 Stephen Ambrose, *D Day: June 6, 1944,* New York: Simon and Schuster (1995).

377 Marcus Tullius Cicero, *De Natura Deorum,* New York: Loeb Classical Library (1933).

378 Army Rc. 165-20 Paragraph 2-2b(1976).

379 36 U. S. Congress, 311-313(1982) *Patriotic Societies and Observances*", Military Chaplains Association of the United States of America.

380 Army Rec.165-20(1976).

381 United Presbyterian Church in the USA, 187th General Assembly (1975).

382 Jackson Toby, "Role, Role Conflict and Effectiveness," *The American Sociological Review*, vol.19 (April 1954):164-175.

383 Waldo W. Burchard, "Role Conflict of Military Chaplains," *American Sociological Review*, vol.19, no.5. (October 1954):530.

384 Ibid.:535.

385 Laurie Goldstein, "Air Force Academy Staff Found Promoting Religion," (June 23, 2005):1 (Politics).

386 Ibid. :2 (Politics).

387 Ibid.

388 Ibid.:4.

389 Philip Gourevitch, "Former Enemies Meet in Memory of Four Martyrs," *The New Yorker* (February 21 and 28, 2002).

390 Emile Durkheim, *The Elementary Forms of the Religious Life*, Oxford, England: Oxford World Classics, Oxford University Press (no year).

391 Max Weber, *The Protestant Ethic and the Spirit of Capitalism*. Oxford, England: The Oxford University Press (2010). Die Protestantische Ethik und der Geist des Kapitalismus.

BIBLIOGRAPHY

Abadinsky, H. (1991). *Organized Crime.* Chicago: Nelson Hall.

Abington School District v. Schempp, 374 U.S. 203 (Supreme Court of the United States 1963).

Aguila, Sheanne. "Osteen Net Worth 2017: How Rich is the 54 Year Old Evangelist." *Christian Post.* August 31, 2017. https://www.christianpost.com/news/joel-osteen-net-worth-2017-how-rich-is-the-54-year-old-evangelist-197347/ (accessed February 22, 2018).

Alexander, H. B. (1920). The Hebrew Contribution to the Americanism of the Future. *The Menorah Journal,* 65-66.

Allan Gutmacher Institute. (1998). Facts in Brief.

Allen, William F. *Slave Songs of the United States.* New York: A. Simpson - Applewood, 1995.

Ambrose, S. (1995). *D Day: June 6, 1944.* New York: Simon and Schuster.

The American Guild of Organists. n.d. https://www.agohq.org/ (accessed February 5, 2018).

Angoff, Charles. *A Literary History of the American People.* New York: A. A. Knopf, 1931.

Applebaum, Peter. "Scandal Spurs Interest in Swaggart Finances." *The New York Times,* February 26, 1988: 3.

Ayres Jr., B. D. (1981, April 28). The Episcopalians: An American Elite with Roots Going Back to Jamestown. *The New York Times.*

Barger, T. K. "Religion, Media Affect Each Other." *The Blade,* July 20, 2013.

Barringer, F. (1993, March 12). Abortion Clinics Prepare for More Violence. *The New York Times*, p. A1.

Beals, Ross W. Jr. "Studying Literacy At the Community Level: a Research Note." *Journal of Interdisciplinary History*, 1979: 93-102.

Beecher, Lyman. *A Plea for the West*. Cincinnati: Truman and Smith, 1835.

Bendix, Richard. *Max Weber: An Intellectual Portrait*. Berkeley: The University of California Press, 1977.

Berger, Peter. *The Sacred Canopy*. Garden City, NY: Doubleday & Co., 1967.

—. *The Sacred Canopy*. Garden City, NY: Pew Charitable Trusts and the Lilly Endowment, Inc., 1967.

Bernheimer, Martin. "Opera: Hugo Weisgall's Grandiose 'Esther' Justifies a Festival." *The Los Angeles Times*, October 11, 1993.

Blanco, Juan Ignacio. *Murderpedia: The Free Online Encyclopedia Dictionary Of Murder*. July 26, 2016. http://murderpedia.org (accessed February 5, 2018).

Blessingame, John W. *The Slave Community*. New York: Oxford University Press, 1972.

Blumenthal, Ralph. "Joel Osteen's Credo: Eliminate the Negative, Accentuate Prosperity." *The New York Times*, March 30, 2006.

Board of Education of Kiryas Joel Village School v. Grumet. 512 U.S. 687 (U.S. Supreme Court, 1994).

Bob Jones University v. United States. 461 U.S. 574 (U.S. Supreme Court, May 24, 1983).

Bogage, Jacob. "Leo Frank was Lynched for a Murder He Didn't Commit. Now Neo-Nazis are Trying to Rewrite History." *The Washington Post*, May 22, 2017: 22.

Bokser, B. Z. (1970). Statement on Capital Punishment. *Proceedings of the Committee on Jewish Law*, (pp. 1537-1538).

Boller, Paul F. "George Washington and Religious Liberty." *William and Mary Quarterly*, 1960: 486-506.

Bomboy, S. (2017, November 17). The Drama Behind President Kennedy's 1960 Election Win. *Constitution Daily*.

Boorstein, Michelle. "America, a Popular Intellectual Catholic Magazine, Bars Terms 'Liberal' and 'Conservative'." *The Washington Post*, June 23, 2013: 1.

Bossard, James H. S. *Ritual in Family Living*. Philadelphia: University of Pennsylvania Press, 1990.

Bossard, James H.S. *Ritual in Family Living.* Philadelphia: University of Pennsylvania Press, 1990.

"Brazil." In *The New Standard Jewish Encylopedia,* by Geoffrey Wigoder. New York: Checkmark Books, 1992.

Breitenstein, David. "U.S. Catholics Face Shortage of Priests." *USA Today News Press,* May 24, 2014: 1.

Brugger, E. C. (2003). *Capital Punishment and Roman Catholic and Roman Catholic Moral Tradition.* South Bend, IN: University of Notre Dame Press.

Brusten, Robert. "Fiddle Shtick." *The New York Review of Books ,* December 18, 2014: 82-83.

Bullert, Gary B. "Reinhold Niebuhr and the Christian Century." *Journal of Church and State,* 2002: 271-290.

Burchard, W. W. (1954). Role Conflict of Military Chaplains. *The American Sociological Review,* 530.

Bureau of Labor Statistics. *Clergy.* Washington, DC: United States Department of Labor, n.d.

Bureau of Labor Statistics. *Hospital Chaplain.* Washington, DC: U.S. Department of Labor, 2011.

Cadge, Wendy, and James T. Harrison. "Religion and Public Opinion About Same Sex Marriage." *Social Science Quarterly,* 2006: 340-360.

Calvert, S. M. (1968). *The American Churches in the Ecumenical Movement.* New York: Association Press.

Campbell, Eugene. *Establishing Zion: The Mormon Church in the American West.* Salt Lake City, UT: Signature Books, 1988.

Cantville v. Connecticut , 310 U.S. 296 (Supreme Court of the United States 1940).

Carroll, Anthony J. *Protestant Modernity, Weber, Secularization, and Pretestantism.* Scranton, PA: The University of Scranton Press, 2007.

Carroll, J. (1983). *Women of the Cloth.* New York: Harper & Row.

Carson, C. E. (1992). *The Papers of Martin Luther King.* Berkeley, CA: The University of California Press.

Cassirer, Ernest. *Philosophy and the Enlightenment.* Boston: Beacon Press, 1951.

Catholic University of America. "Announcements, Benjamin D. Rome School of Music." 2010-2011.

Chabad Staff. "The Circumcision Ceremony in a Nutshell." Chabad, n.d.

Chandler, Russell. "Women's Role in Clergy Bleak." *Los Angeles Times*, March 2, 1978: B3.

Cherrington, E. H. (1925). *The Standard Encyclopedia of the Alcohol Problem.* Westerville, OH: American Issue Publishing Company.

"Christian ModernArt." *The Best Christian Art in the Universe.* n.d. http://christianmodernart.com/ (accessed February 5, 2018).

"Christianity Today Advertising - Connecting You with Christian Audiences." *Christianity Today.* November 10, 2016. http://www.christianitytodayads.com/ (accessed February 6, 2018).

Church History: In the Fullness of Time. Salt Lake City, UT: Church of Jesus Christ of Latter Day Saints, 2003.

Cicero, M. T. (1933). *De Natura Deorum.* New York: Loeb Classical Library.

Clark, D. (1973). *The Irish in Philadelphia.* Philadelphia: Temple University Press.

Cleveland, J. Jefferson. *Songs of Zion.* Nashville, TN: Abington, 1981.

Cohen, H. Floris. *The Scientific Revolution.* Chicago: The University of Chicago Press, 1994.

Cohen, Stefanie. "$1 Million Parties - Have NYC Bar Mitzvahs Gone Too Far?" *New York Post.* April 18, 2010. https://nypost.com/2010/04/18/1-million-parties-have-nyc-bar-mitzvahs-gone-too-far/ (accessed February 6, 2018).

Constitution of the United States. (n.d.).

Corman, Joanna. "Hospitals Revamped Chapels Interfaith Meditation Rooms." *Religious News Service*, May 25, 2011.

Corrington, J. F. "Spirituality and Recovery: Relationships Between Levels of Spirituality, Contentment and Stress During Recovery from Alcoholism in AA." *Alcoholism Treatment Quarterly*, 1989: 151-165.

Coughlin, E. K. (1991). Plagiarism by Martin Luther King, Jr. *Chronicle of Higher Education*, A21.

Coval, Jennifer, and Kathryn Wilson. "City of Unbrotherly Love: Violence in 19th Century Philadelphia." In *Exploring Diversity in Philadelphia History.* Philadelphia: The Historical Society of Philadelphia, 2008.

A Critic of Islam: Dark Secrets. (2007, February 10-16). *The Economist.*

Curran, Robert E. *Papist Devils: Catholics in British America, 1574-1783.* Washington, DC: The Catholic University of America Press, 2014.

De Rusha, Michelle. "A Sixteenth Century Scandal." *Credo*, 2017.

Death Penalty Information Center. (2016, November 9). The States With and Without the Death Penalty. Death Penalty Information Center.

Decter, Avi Y., and Melissa Martens. *The Other Promised Land*. Baltimore: Jewish Museum of Maryland, 2005.

Deuteronomy. n.d.

Deuteronomy. n.d.

Dewan, S. (2005, June 21). Former Klansman Guilty of Manslaughter in 1964 Deaths. *The New York Times*, p. A1.

Doan, Alesha E. *Opposition and Intimidation: the Abortion Wars and Strategies of Political Harassment*. Ann Arbor: University of Michigan Press, 2007.

Dolan, Timothy M. "The Catholic Schools We Need." *America*, September 30, 2010: 1.

Durkheim, Emile. *The Elementary Forms of Religious Life*. New York: Free Press, 1954.

Easton, Susan. "City of Refuge." *Mormon Historical Studies*, 2001: 82-94.

Ecklund, Elaine H., and Kristen S. Lee. "Atheists and Agnostics Negotiate Religion and Family." *Journal for the Scientific Study of Religion*, 2012.

Editors@The Famous People.com. "Joel Osteen Biography." *TheFamousPeople. com*. September 30, 2014. https://www.thefamouspeople.com/profiles/joel-osteen-3903.php (accessed January 30, 2018).

Edwards v. Aguillard, 482 U.S. 578 (Supreme Court of the United States 1987).

Ellens, J. Harold. *Models of Religious Broadcasting*. Grand Rapids, MI: Erdman's, 1974.

Ellis, John Tracy. *American Catholicism*. Chicago: University of Chicago Press, 1969.

Ellison, Christopher. "Conservative Protestantism and the Parental Use of Corporal Punishment." *Social Forces*, 1995: 1003-1028.

Ellison, Christopher G., and Darren Sherkat. "Obedience and Authority: Religion and Parental Values Reconsidered." *Journal for the Scientific Study of Religion*, 1993: 313-329.

Elzy, Ruby. "The Spirit of the Spirituals." *Etude*, 1943: 495.

Engel v. Vitale, 370 U.S. 421 (Supreme Court of the United States 1962).

Epperson v. Arkansas, 393 U.S. 97 (Supreme Court of the United States 1968).

Epstein, D. A. (1999). Will Violence End Patients' Access to Abortion? *Medical Economics*, 51.

Erickson, Hal. *Religious Radio and Television in the United States, 1921 – 1991.*. Jefferson, NC: McFarland, 1992.

Essman, Elliott. "The Protestants." *Life in the USA Magazine*, 2014: 1-5.

Estate of Thornton v. Caldor, Inc. 472 U.S. 703 (U.S. Supreme Court, June 26, 1985).

Everson v. Board of Education, 330 U.S. 1 (Supreme Court of the United States 1947).

Exodus. n.d.

An Explanation of Luther's Small Catechism. St. Louis, MO: Concordia Publishing House, 2017.

Falk, G. (2016). *End of the Patriarchy.* New York: University Press of America.

—. *The Jew in Christian Theology.* Jefferson, NC: McFarland, 1992.

Falk, Gerhard. *Stigma.* Buffalo, NY: Prometheus Books, 2001.

Falk, G. (2013). *Twelve Inventions Which Changed America.* Lanham, MD: Hamilton Books.

Federal Reserve Bank. (2018). *Consumer Price Index.*

Ferguson, Everett. *Baptism in the Early Church.* Grand Rapids, MI: Eerdmans, 2009.

Fitzgerald, Margaret E. *The Philadelphia Nativist Riots.* Irish Cultural Society of the Garden City Area, 1992.

Flory, Richard. "Revisiting the Legacy of Jerry Falwell, Sr. in Trump's America." *University of Souther California Center for Religion and Civic Culture.* July 17, 2017. https://crcc.usc.edu/revisiting-the-legacy-of-jerry-falwell-sr-in-trumps-america/ (accessed February 22, 2018).

Gaber, T. (2012). Eve's Apple and the Mosque: Transmuted and Layered Additions to the Mosque Pertaining to the Space of Women. *Traditional Dwellings and Settlements Review.*

Garrow, D. J. (1991). King's Plagiarism: Imitation, Insecurity and Transformation. *Journal of American History*, 86-92.

Gerard, Jeremy. "Winfrey Show Evokes Protests." *The New York Times*, May 6, 1989.

Gertner, George, and Larry Gross. "Living in Television: the Violence Profile." *Journal of Communications*, 1976: 172.

Gibson, David. "Declining Numbers of U.S. Nuns, Even Among Traditional Orders, Charted in New Study." *Religion News Service.* October 13, 2014. http://religionnews.com/2014/10/13/declining-number-u-s-nuns-even-among-traditional-orders-charted-new-study/ (accessed January 24, 2018).

Ginzburg, Vitaly L. *The Physics of a Lifetime: Reflections on the Problems and Personalities of 20th Century Physics.* Berlin: Springer, 2001.

Girion, Lisa. "Rate of Heroin Use in the U.S. has Climbed 63% in the Last Decade." *The Los Angeles Times*, July 7, 2015: A1.

Glaberson, W. (2004). 4-3 Ruling Effectively Holds Death Penalty in New York. *The New York Times*, 1-5.

Globe Spotlight Team. "Church Allowed Abuse by Priests for Years." *The Boston Globe*, January 6, 2002: 1.

Goldstein, L. (2005, June 23). "Air Force Academy Staff Found Promoting Religion." *The New York Times*, p. 1 (Politics).

Goldstein, Lori. "Air Force Chaplain Tells of Academy Proselytizing." *The New York Times*, May 12, 2005.

Good News Club v. Milford Sternal School. 533 U.S. 98 (U.S. Supreme Court, 2001).

Gordon, A. A. (1998). *The Beautiful Life of Frances A. Willard.* Chicago: The Women's Temperance Publishing Association.

Gourevitch, P. (2002, February 21 & 28). Former Enemies Meet in Memory of Four Martyrs. *The New Yorker.*

Greenberg, Rodney. "The Jewish Leonard Bernstein." *Jewish Quarterly*, 2007.

Greenhouse, S. (1989, February 12). A New Pill: A Fierce Battle. *New York Times Magazine*, pp. 23-28.

Griswold, Wendy. *Cultures and Societies in a Changing World.* Los Angeles: Pine Forest, 2008.

Grossman, Cathy Lynn. "In Nixon Tapes, Billy Graham Refers to Synagogue of Satan." *USA Today*, June 24, 2009: 1.

Hall v. Welborn. 08-2008 (n.d.).

Hall v. Welborn. 08-2008 (District Court, D.Kansas, 2008).

Hall, Mordaunt. "Al Jolson and the Vitaphone." *The New York times*, October 7, 1927.

Hanes, Stephanie. "Interfaith America:'Being Both' is a Rising Trend in the US." *The Christian Science Montor*, November 23, 2014: 1.

Hardesty, N. E. (1979). Women in the Holiness Movement. In R. E. Reuther, *Women of Spirit.* New York: Simon and Schuster.

Harper, William, James H. Hammond, and William G. Simms. *The Pro-Slavery Argument*. Philadelphia: Lippincott, Grambo & Co., 1853.

Harris, Sam. *The End of Faith*. New York: W. W. Norton & Co., 2004.

Hart, William R. *The English Schoolmaster*. Lansing, MI: The University of Michigan Press, 1963.

Headquarters, United States Air Force. *The Report of the Headquarters Review Group Concerning the Religious Climate at the US Air Force Academy*. United States Air Force, 2005.

Herberg, Will. "Religion in a Secularized Society: Some Aspects of America's Three Religion Pluralism." *Review of Religious Research*, 1962: 37.

Hickey, Jennifer G. "Museum of the Bible Extended Fly-though." *The New York Post*, May 4, 2007.

Higham, John. *Strangers in the Land: Patterns of American Nativism 1850 – 1925*. New Brunswick, NJ: Rutgers University Press, 1850-1925.

Hinolosa, V. a. (2004). Religion and the Paradox of Racial Inequality Attitudes'. *Journal for the Scientific Study of Religion*, 230.

Hiley, David. "Chant." In *Performance Practice*, by Howard M. Brown, 37. New York: W. W. Norton & Co., 1990.

Hill, Marvin S. "Carthage Conspiracy Reconsidered: a Second Look at the Murder of Joseph and Hyrum Smith." *Journal of the Illinois State Historical Society*, 2005: 207.

Hochman, Anndee. "Empty Plates in the Land of Plenty." *Broadstreet Review*, March 7, 2017.

Holusha, John. "Gunmen Kill 2 Missionary Ctr." *The New York Times*, September 3, 2015: 1.

Hofstadter, R. (1960, March 17). Could a Protestant have beaten Hoover in 1928? *The Reporter*, p. 31.

Hoover, Amy. "Lutheran Denominational Wedding Service." The Lutheran Church, n.d.

Hosanna - Tabor Evangelical Lutheran Church And School v. Equal Employment Opportunity Commission. 565 U.S. 171 (U.S. Supreme Court, 2012).

Hughes, Allen. "Hugo Weisgall Conducts Own Works." *The New York times*, December 10, 1970: 59.

Hulse, C. (2006, July 21). By a Vote of 98-Zero, Senate Approves 25 Year Extension of Voting Rights Act. *The New York Times*, p. A1.

Hutsether, Mark. "Hate Crime Update." *Religion Dispatches*, July 27, 2008: 1.

Ieraci, L. (2016, July 3). Pope Francis Calls the Death Penalty Unacceptable. *National Catholic Reporter*, p. 1.

Jaffe, Caro, and Tracy Weitz. "Abortion Attitudes and Availability." *Contexts*, 2010: 64-65.

James, J. W. (1980). Statistics About Women's Training Schools. In *Women of Spirit* (p. 178). Philadelphia: University of Pennsylvania Press.

Jammer, Max. *Einstein and Religion: Physics and Theology*. Princeton, NJ: Princeton University Press, 2002.

Jane Roe v. Henry Wade. 410 U.S. 93 S.Ct 705 (U.S. Supreme Court, January 25, 1973).

Jenkins, Jack. "The American Media Needs to Take a Theology Class." *Think Progress*. May 13, 2014. https://thinkprogress.org/viewpoint-the-american-media-needs-to-take-a-theology-class-or-three-4b1a3aa4d6ca/ (accessed February 6, 2018).

Jenkins, Philip. *The New Anti-Catholicism: The Last Acceptable Prejudice*. New York: Oxford University Press, 2004.

Jewish Drug and Alcohol Rehab Centers. February 2, 2018. http://www.rehabcenter.net/types-of-addiction-treatment-programs/ (accessed February 2, 2018).

"Jewish Views on Homosexuality." *My Jewish Learning*. n.d. www.myjewishlearning.com (accessed 2018).

"John 1:19-29." n.d.

John Paul II, Pope (n.d.). *Ordinatio Sacerdatolis*. Retrieved May 2018, from Women for Faith and Family: http://www.wff.org

Johnson, Hall. "Notes on the Negro Spiritual." In *Readings in Black American Music*, 277. New York: W.W. Norton, 1983.

Kafsh, Abraham. *The Biblical Heritage of American Democracy*. New York: KTAV Publishing Co., 1977.

Kaleem, Jaweed. "Best Paid Pastors Make Hundreds of Thousands to Millions of Dollars, Annually." *Huffington Post*. January 19, 2012. https://www.huffingtonpost.com/2012/01/19/best-paid-pastors_n_1214043.html (accessed January 30, 2018).

Kaplan, Aryeh. *Made in Heaven: A Jewish Wedding Guide*. New York: Mozaim Publishing Co., 1983.

Katz, Jamie. *Smithsonian.com*. October 6, 2009. smithsonian.com (accessed February 2, 2018).

Keller, R. S. (1981). Lay Women in the Protestant Tradition. In R. S. Keller, *Women in Religion in America* (pp. 342-392). New York: Harper and Row.

Kiernan, K. "The Rise of Cohabitation and Child Bearing." *International Journal of Law, Policy, and the Family*, 2001: 1-21.

Kifner, John. "Death on 125th St.: The Overview; Gunmen and Seven Others Die in Blaze at Harlem Store." *The New York Times*, December 9, 1995.

King, M. L. (1963, June 12). Letter from Birmingham Jail. *Christian Century*, pp. 762-763.

Kinney, A. (2000). *Tudor England.* New York: Routledge.

Kiryas Joel v. Grumet, 512 U.S. 687 (Supreme Court of the United States 1994).

Knoester, Richard Petts and Chris. "Parents' Religious Heterogamy and Children's Well-Being." *Journal for the Scientific Study of Religion*, 2007: 373-389.

Koch, Ed. "The St. Patrick Cathedral Event." *The New York Post*, December 12, 1989.

Krout, J. A. (1940). Prohibition. In *Dictionary of American History.* New York: Charles Scribner's Sons.

Kushner, Harvey. *Encyclopedia of Terrorism.* Ann Arbor: University of Michigan Press, 2003.

Laue, J. H. (1968). Power, Conflict And Social Change. In D. a. Bowen, *Riots and Rebellions* (pp. 85-96). Santa Barbara, CA: Sage Publications.

Lawson, S. (1976). *Black Ballots.* New York: Columbia University Press.

Lee v. Weisman, 505 U.S. 577 (Supreme Court of the United States 1992).

Lemon v. Kurtzman, 403 U.S. 602 (Supreme Court of the United States 1971).

Libby, T. (2014, August 22). 5 Disturbing Stats. *Money*, p. 1.

Lichtblau, Eric. "Hate Crimes Against American Muslims Most Since Post 9/11 Era." *The New York Times*, September 18, 2016: A13.

Linde, H. (1980). First Things First: Rediscovering the Bill Of Rights. *University of Baltimore Law Review.*

Lipka, Michael. *Muslims and Islam: Key Findings in the U.S and Around the world.* Pew Research Center, 2017.

Lipka, Michael. *Muslims and Islam: Key Findings in the U.S and Around the World.* Washington, DC: Pew Research Center, 2017.

Liptak, Adam. "Supreme Court Rejects Contraceptives Mandate for Some Corporations." *The New York Times*, July 1, 2014: A1.

Little Sisters of the Poor v. Sebelius. 6 F.Supp.3d 1225 (D. Colo., 2013).

Littleton, Cynthia. "God is my TV Pilot." *Variety*, February 1999: 1.

Liu, Benjamin. "Turner v. Suffley and O'Lone v. Estate of Shabbaz." *UCLA Law Review*, 1987.

Loader, C. (2001). Puritans and Jews: Weber, Sombart and the Transvaluators of Modern Society. *The Canadian Journal of Sociology*, 635-653.

Lucretius Carus, T. (2013). *De Rerum Natura. On the Nature of Things*. Cambridge: University of Cambridge Press.

Lupfer, Jacob. "Why a Yes to Gays is Often a No to Evangelism." *The Washington Post*, June 10, 2015.

Luther, M. (n.d.). On Translating. In *Works of Martin Luther* (pp. 632-640). Weimar: Harman Boelaus.

Mahoney, Annette. "Religion in the Home in the 1980s and 1990s." *Journal of Family Psychology*, 2001: 559-596.

Mahoney, R. (1990). RU4it? *Z Magazine*."Male Circumcision." *Pediatrics*, 2012: 756.

March on Washington. (1963, August 28). *The New York Times*, p. 1.

Marks, Helen. "Perspectives on Catholic Schools." In *Handbook of Research on School Choice*, by Mark Berend. New York: Taylor and Francis, 2009.

Martin, George H. *Evolution of the Massachusetts School System*. New York: Nahu Press, 2010.

Martin, Nina. "The Growth of Catholic Hospitals, By the Numbers." *Pro Publica*, Decmeber 18, 2017: 1.

Martin, William. "The Riptide of Revival." *Christian History and Biography*, 2006: 24-29.

Marty, Michael E. *Modern American Religion: Under God, Indivisible*. Chicago: University of Chicago Press, 1999.

Masci, D. (2009). *How Income Varies Among US Religious Groups*. Pew Research Center.

Mason, W. M., and N. H. Wolfinge. "Cohort Analysis." In *International Encyclopedia of the Social and Behavioral Sciences*, by N. J. Smelser and P. B., eds. Bailes, 2189-2194. Amsterdam: Elsevier, 2001.

Mather, I. (1669). *The Mystery of Israel's Salvation*. London: John Allen.

McDermott, Jim. "Sing a New Song." *America*, May 30, 2005: 1.

McKinnon, A.M. "Elective Affinities of the Protestant Ethic." *Sociological heory*, 2010: 108-126.

—. "Reading 'Opium of the People'." *Critical Sociology*, 2005: 15-38.

Middlekauff, Robert. *Ancients and Axioms: Secondary Education in Eighteenth Century New England.* New Haven, CT: Yale University Press, 1963.

Midland Daily News. "Three killed , nine wounded in an attack on planned parenthood." November 17, 2015: 1.

Miller, E. M. (2017, January 3). Religious Makeup of the New Congress Overwhelmingly Christian. *Religion News Service,* p. 1.

Miller, Jason. "Social Media and Religion." *Huffington Post,* November 19, 2011.

Minersville School District v. Gobitis, 310 U.S. 586 (Supreme Court of the United States 1940).

Miron, J. A. (1991). Alcohol Consumption During Prohibition. *AEA Papers and Proceedings,* (p. 242).

Mohr, J. C. (1979). *Abortion in America.* New York: Oxford University Press.

Mueller v. Allen, 463 U.S. 388 (Supreme Court of the United States 1983).

Murray, R. K. (1956). A Catholic Runs for President. *The Mississippi Valley Historical Review,* 516.

National Abortion Federation. *Violence and Description Statistics.* Washington, DC: National Abortion Federation, 2015.

Neusner, Jacob. *The Blackwell Reader in Judaism.* New York: Blackwell Publishers, 2000.

"New England's First Fruits." In *The Encylopedia Britannica.* Chicago, 1976.

New York Architectural Images. n.d. http://nyc-architecture.com/UES/UES039. htm (accessed January 30, 2018).

The New York Times. "Three Leaders of a Missouri Church." August 14, 2007: 1.

Nunez, Ralph da Costa. "Homelessness." *CityLimits.org.* March 2012. https:// citylimits.org/.

Oaks, Dallin H., and Marvin S. Hill. "Carthage Conspiracy: The Trial of the Accused Assassins of Joseph Smith." *Journal of the Illinois State Historical Society,* 2004.

O'Callaghan, E. B. (1865). *Calendar of Historical Manuscripts in the Office of the Secretary of State.* Albany: Weed, Parsons & Co.

One More Terrorist Act. (1998, October 27). *The Los Angeles Times,* p. A16.

Ostilng, Richard. "The Day of Reckoning Delayed." *Time,* September 4, 1989: 30-31.

Parsons, George. "Foreign Focus: Be Careful How You Pray." *Religious Broadcasting,* 1995: 109.

Paulson, Michael. "As Vatican Rejects Divorce, Many Catholics Long for Acceptance." *The New York Times*, November 23, 2015.

Pearson, Bryan. "Holiday Spending to Exceed $1 Trillion." *Forbes*, December 21, 2016.

Persinos, John F. "Has the Christian Right Taken Over The Republican Party?" ." *Campaigns and Elections*, 1994: 20-25.

Pew Research Center. *2014 Religious Landscape Study*. Washington, DC: Pew Research Center, 2015.

—. *America's Changing Religious Landscape*. New York: Pew Research Center, 2015.

—. (2014). *Public Sees Religious Influence Waning*. Washington, DC: Pew Research Center.

—. *Religion and Education Around the World*. Washington, DC: Pew Research Center, 2016.

—. "Religious Beliefs and Practices of Jewish Americans." *Pew Forum*. October 1, 2013. http://www.pewforum.org/2013/10/01/chapter-4-religious-beliefs-and-practices/, accessed 2/6/18. (accessed February 6, 2018).

—. "Sharing Religious Faith Online." *Pew Forum*. November 2014. http://www.pewforum.org/2014/11/06/religion-and-electronic-media/ (accessed February 6, 2018).

—. *Teaching Children: Sharp Ideological Differences, Some Common Ground*. Washington, DC: Pew Research Center, 2014.

Philadelphia Bible Riots of 1844. n.d. http://unlearnedhistory.blogspot.com/2015/09/philadelphia-bible-riots-of-1844.html (accessed January 24, 2018).

Poland, History of the Jews in Russia and. *Simon M. Dubnow*. Philadelphia: Jewish Publication Society, 1910.

Pratt, N. P. (n.d.). Transitions in Judaism. In N. P. Pratt, *Women in American Religions* (p. 226). New York: James Books.

Proverbs. n.d.

"Public Law 103-141." 103rd Congress, November 16, 1993.

Pulkinnen, Levi. "Jury finds Haq Guilty In Jewish Federation Center Shooting." *Seattle Post-Intelligencer*, December 15, 2009.

Radosh, Daniel. "The Good Book Business." *The New Yorker*, December 18, 2006.

Ramji, Rubina. "Representation of Islam in American News and Film: Becoming the Other." In *Mediating Religion: Conversations in Media, Religion and Culture*, by Joylon P. Mitchell and Sophia Marriage, 65. London: T&T Clark, 2003.

Rehab.com. n.d. https://rehab. com/ (accessed February 2, 2018).

Reuther, R. R. (1987). *Sexism and God Talk.* Boston: Beacon Press.

Reynolds, Eileen. "God Bless America." *Forward,* July 17, 2013.

Richert, Scott P. "The Sacrament of Confirmation in the Catholic Church." *Thought,* May 1, 2017: 1.

Risen, J. a. (1998). *Wrath of Angels: The American Abortion War.* New York: Basic Books.

Ritter, Bruce. *Sometimes God Has a Kid's Face.* New York: Doubleday, 1987.

Robles, Frances. "Dylan Roof Had AR-15 Parts During Police Stop IN MRH." *The New York Times,* June 26, 2015: A1.

Roe v. Wade, 410 U.S. 113 (Supreme Court of the United States January 23, 1973).

Rosin, Hanna. "Televangelist Jim Bakker's Road To Redemption." *The Washington Post,* August 11, 1999: C1.

Ross, Leonard. "The Bernstein Files." *The New Yorker,* August 10, 2009.

Rossi, M. A. (1991). Priesthood, Precedent and Prejudice: On Recovering the Women Priests of Early Christianity. *Journal of Feminist Studies in Religion,* 71-94.

Rule, Sheila. "Three Synagogues to Aid City's Homeless." *The New York Times,* January 21, 1983: Region 3.

Ruta, G. F. (2013, January 24). An Amazing 1969 Account Of the Stonewall Uprising. *The Atlantic.*

Salvation Army International. n.d. http://www.salvationarmy.org.

Salvation Army USA. "Hunger Relief." n.d. http://salvationarmysouth.org/ways-we-help/hunger-relief/ (accessed February 2, 2018).

Santa Fe Independent School District v. Doe, 530 U.S. 290 (Supreme Court of the United States 2000).

Schmidt, William E. "For Jim and Tammy Bakker, Excess Wiped Out a Rapid Climb to Success." *The New York Times,* May 16, 1987.

Segal, David R., and Mady W. Segal. *America's Military Population.* Washington, DC: Population Reference Bureau, 2004.

Sessions, Kyle C. "Protestant Church Music." *Church History,* 1976: 400-401.

Shear, Michael D., and Abby Goodnough. "Trump plans to Declare Opioid Epidemic a National Emergency." *The New York Times*, August 10, 2017: A13.

Shellnutt, Kate. "Be Fruitful and Multiply: Muslim Births Will Outnumber Christian Births by 2035." *Christianity Today*, 2017: 1.

Sherkat, Darren E., and Christopher Ellison. "Recent Developments and Current Controversies in the Sociology of Religion." *Annual Review of Sociology*, 1999: 465-479.

Skill, Thomas. "The Portrayal of Religion and Spirituality on Fictional Network Television." *Review of Religious Research*, 1994.

Sledge, Robert W. "The Saddest Day: Gene Leggett and the Origins of the Incompatible Cause." *Methodist History*, 2017: 145-179.

Slomovitz, Albert I. *The Fighting Rabbis.* New York: New York University Press, 1999.

Small, Walter H. "Girls in Colonial Schools." *Education*, 1902: 534.

Smith, Nila Banton. *American Reading Instructions.* Newark, DE: International Reading Association, 1965.

Smith, Raoul N. "Interest in Language and Languages in Colonial and Federal America." *Proceedings of the American Philosophical Society*, 1979: 36-38.

Smith, Ryan. "The Cross: Symbol and Contest In 19th Century America." *Church History*, 2001: 716-717.

Smith, T. W. (1980). America's Most Important Problem - a Trend Analysis. *Public Opinion Quarterly*, 164-180.

Speyer, Leah. "Campus Watchdog; Jewish Students Single Largest Target of Systematic Suppression of Civil Rights at American Universities." *Algemeiner*, July 26, 2016.

Stark, Rodney. "Secularization, R.I.P." *Sociology of Religion*, 1999: 249-273.

Statement by Two Cardinals. (1973, January 23). *The New York Times*, p. 20.

"Statistic Brain." *Poverty Statistics.* n.d. https://www.statisticbrain.com/homelessness-stats/ (accessed February 2, 2018).

Stetzer, Ed. "What Is Church Attendance Like During Christmas?"." *Christianity Today*, December 4, 2015: 1.

Stone v. Graham, 449 U.S. 39 (Supreme Court of the United States 1980).

Stout, Daniel, and Judith Mitchell Buddenbaum. *Religion and Popular Culture.* Ames, IA: Iowa State University Press, 2001.

Stout, David. "The Case that Rocked Crown Heights." *The New York Times*, August 12, 1996: 1.

Stroup, Herbert H. *Social Welfare Pioneers*. Lanham, MD: Rowman and Littlefield, 1985.

Stumpe, Joe, and Monica Davey. "Abortion Doctor Shot to Death in Kansas Church." *The New York Times*, June 1, 2009: A1.

Sullivan, Dwight H. "The Congressional Response to Goldman v. Weinberger." *Military Law Review*, 1988: 125-152.

The Talmud. n.d.

Tammeus, B. (2014, July 23). Episcopal Church Celebrates 40 Years of Women in the Priesthood. *National Catholic Reporter*, pp. 1-15

Taylor, Ben. "What Will Living in America Be Like in 2050?" *Business 2 Community*, June 12, 2015: 1.

Teachman, J. D. "Stability Across Cohorts in Divorce Risk Factors." *Demography*, 1999: 415-420.

Teachman, Jay. "Premarital Sex: Pe-marital Co-habitation and the Risk of Marital Dissolution Among Women." *Journal of Marriage and the Family*, 2003: 444-455.

Texas Monthly, Inc. v. Bullock. 489 U.S. 1 (U.S. Supreme Court, February 21, 1989).

Thomas, Brian. *Physics, Not God, Explains the Universe?* Dallas, TX: The Institute for Creation Research, 2012.

Thomas, Judy L. "Suspect until his death supported killing abortion providers, friends say." *Kansas City Star*, June 4, 2009.

Thomas, Velma M. *No Man Can Hinder Me: The Journey From Slavery to Emancipation Through Song.* New York: Crown Publishers, 2003.

Thompson, Carolyn. "Supreme Court Playground Ruling Feeds School Voucher Debate." *Associated Press*, June 27, 2017.

Thompson, Scott. *The Pay Scale for Jewish Cantors.* n.d. http://work.chron.com/pay-scale-jewish-cantors-17855.html (accessed January 30, 2018).

Tiferes Stam Judaica. *Buying a Sefer Torah.* 2017. http://www.tiferes.com/index.php?route=information/information&information_id=8 (accessed February 19, 2018).

Tobin, Jonathan S. "Presbyterians Declare War on the Jews." *Commentary*, February 11, 2014.

Toby, J. (1954). "Role, Role Conflict and Effectiveness." *The American Sociological Review*, 164-175.

Touger, Eli. *A Child's Entry into Cheder.* n.d. http://www.chabad.org/library/article_cdo/aid/81572/jewish/Areinfirinish-A-Childs-Entry-Into-Cheder.htm (accessed January 24, 2018).

The Tower. "Why Are Student Leaders and Jewish Bruins Under Attack at UCLA." June 14, 2014.

Town of Greece v. Galloway. 134 S. Ct. 1811 (U.S. Supreme Court, May 5, 2014).

Tresolion, R. J. (1966). Congress Makes a Law: The Civil Rights Act of 1964. In *Cases in American National Government and Politics* (p. 97). Englewood Cliffs, NJ: Prentice Hall.

Twain, Mark. *The Innocents Abroad.* Morrisville, NC: Velvet Element, 2008.

U.S. Conference of Mayors. "Hunger and Homelessness Survey." 2014.

U.S. Treasury Department. *Histofy of "In God We Trust".* June 18, 2017. https://www.treasury.gov/about/education/Pages/in-god-we-trust.aspx (accessed February 15, 2018).

United States Conference of Catholic Bishops. "An Overview of Catholic Funeral Rites." *United States Conference of Catholic Bishops.* n.d. http://www.usccb.org/prayer-and-worship/bereavement-and-funerals/overview-of-catholic-funeral-rites.cfm (accessed February 6, 2018).

—. "Catechism of the Catholic Church, 2nd Edition." United States Conference of Catholic Bishops , 2016.

United States v. Secretary, Florida Department of Corrections. 14-10086 (U.S. Court of Appeals, 11th Circuit, February 27, 2015).

Vara, Richard. "Carey Says Anglican Communion is in Crisis." *The Houston Chronicle,* January 11, 2008: 1.

Wacker, Grant. "Billy Graham's America." *Church History,* 2009: 489-511.

Walters, Barbara. "The Most Fascinating People of 2006." *20/20.* New York: American Broadcasting Co., December 12, 2006.

Wansink, B. a. (2013). Are There Atheists in Foxholes? *Journal of Religion and Health,* 768-769.

Warr, Albert Bergeson & Mark. "A Crisis in the Moral Order: The Effect of Watergate on Confidence in Social Institutions." In *The Religious Dimension,* by Robert Wuthnow, 278-301. New York: The Academic Press, 1979.

Weber, Max. *The Protestant Ethic and the Spirit of Capitalism.* New York: Penguin Books, 2002.

Wecker, M. (2012, May 2). 10 High Profile People Whose Degrees were Revoked. *Newsweek.*

Weinstein, Michael L. *With God on Our Side.* New York: St. Martin's Press, 2006.

Weiser, C. (1998, January 16). Anti-abortion Violence Increased. *USA Today*, p. 7A.

Welcome to Canterbury Woods. (n.d.). Williamsville, NY.

Wertenbaker, Thomas J. *The First Americans.* New York: Macmillan, 1927.

WGN Desk. "Chicago Jewish Community Joins Efforts to Help Syrian Refugees." *WGN TV.* December 16, 2016. http://wgntv.com/2016/12/16/chicagos-jewish-community-joins-effort-to-help-syrian-refugees/ (accessed February 2, 2018).

"What We Do." *Catholic Charities of New York.* n.d. https://catholiccharitiesny.org/what-we-do (accessed February 2, 2018).

White, William W., and Alexander Lauder. "Spirituality, Science, and Addiction Counseling." *Counseling Magazine*, 2006: 56-59.

"Why Did So Many Christians Support Slavery?" *Christianity Today.* n.d. http://www.christianitytoday.com/history/issues/issue-33/why-christians-supported-slavery.html (accessed February 5, 2018).

"Why to Consider a Christian Rehab Center." *Elite Rehab Placement.* n.d. https://www.eliterehabplacement.com/christian-rehab-centers (accessed February 2, 2018).

Wile, Elise. "The Average Income of a Pastor of a Mega-Church." *The Houston Chronicle*, October 6, 2017: 1.

Williams, D. E. (1996). The Drive for Prohibition: A Transition from Social Reform to Legislative Reform. *Southern Communication Journal*, 185

Zimmerman, J. (2016, February 11). A Jewish Candidate Won a United States Primary for President for the First Time and America Yawned. *Los Angeles Times*, p. 1.

Williams, Lee M. "Religious Heterogeneity and Religiosity." *Journal for the Scientific Study of Religion*, 2001: 559-596.

Williams, Michael. *The Shadow of the Pope.* New York: Whittlesey House, 1932.

Wilson, John. *Religion in American Society: The Effective Presence.* Englewood Cliffs, NJ: Prentice-Hall, 1978.

Wilson, Micheele, and John Lynxwiler. "Abortion Clinic Violence As Terrorism." *Studies in Conflict and Terrorism*, 1988: 263-273.

Wolfe, Zachary. "Liturgy and a Tale: Revival and Sprawling as Ever." *The New York Times*, November 4, 2014.

Zborowski, Mark, and Elizabeth Herzog. *Life Is with People: The Culture of the Shtetl.* New York: Schocken Books, 1952.

Zevelof, Naomi. "Not Just Jews Eat Kosher Food in Prison." *The Forward*, April 20, 2012: 1.

Zuckerman, Philip. "How Secular Family Values Stack Up." *The Los Angeles Times*, January 14, 2015.

INDEX

Symbols

F

G

H

S

Printed in the United States
By Bookmasters